Conservati...
Natura...  W9-DAO-771

Instructor's Copy

John T. McCory

# ENVIRONMENTAL CONSERVATION

# ENVIRONMENTAL CONSERVATION

## CONSERVATION

*Second Edition*

*Raymond F. Dasmann, M.A., Ph.D.*

The Conservation Foundation
Washington, D.C.

*John Wiley & Sons, Inc.*

*New York · London · Sydney · Toronto*

Books By R. F. Dasmann

ENVIRONMENTAL CONSERVATION
WILDLIFE BIOLOGY
THE LAST HORIZON
THE DESTRUCTION OF CALIFORNIA
AFRICAN GAME RANCHING
THE PACIFIC COASTAL WILDLIFE REGION
A DIFFERENT KIND OF COUNTRY

**10  9  8**

Copyright © 1959, 1968 by John Wiley & Sons, Inc.

Library of Congress Catalog Card Number: 68-28499

SBN 471 19603 7

Printed in the United States of America

*To the memory of*

*ALDO LEOPOLD*

*whose philosophy remains a*

*permanent source of inspiration*

# Preface

Almost ten years have passed since the first edition of this book was written. During that decade much has happened in conservation. The words "conservation" or "environmental studies" are now in common usage. The need for an integrated approach to the problems of the human environment has become apparent to the various specialists in environmental management, and is being demanded from many quarters. Conservation has become popular, and even the word "ecology" appears in the daily press and is heard on commercial television. Is there cause then for rejoicing? Unfortunately, no. The reason for the acceptance of the concept of conservation lies in the rapid deterioration of the human environment.

Ten years ago the idea of including a chapter on human populations in a textbook on conservation was new. Today the population problem and the threat of famine vie for space in the newspapers with the ongoing wars in which we have become involved. The gloomy forecasts of ten years ago were too optimistic. The situation is worse than was expected.

It was possible ten years ago for a text on conservation to give minor space to the problem of pollution of water, none to pollution of air, and scant attention to the dangers from pesticides. It is no longer possible. Ten years ago it was an innovation to discuss urban problems in a conservation text. Today urban problems are the center of the struggle for conservation.

A decade ago the effort to save wild America seemed to require better management of our wild lands and wildlife. Today a major drive is needed if we are to keep remnants of the old wilderness in order to save samples of natural communities that were once widespread and little modified.

In the first edition it was hoped that people might be made more aware that conservation problems did not end at our national boundaries.

Today we know that the world we live in is one biosphere and, unless we take a global view of environmental problems, our chances for survival are slim.

The first edition was launched with hope. Today prayer is more appropriate.

RAYMOND F. DASMANN

*Washington, D.C.*
*March, 1968*

# Preface to the First Edition

This book grew out of the need for a text written from a biological standpoint, which would take the long view of conservation problems by considering the history of human populations in relation to natural resources, their present predicament, and their future outlook. I waited many years for somebody else to write this textbook. Finally, operating on the principle that "fools rush in . . . ," I undertook the job myself, with the hope that I could avoid treading on the toes of those who are better qualified in many of the fields discussed.

This textbook is written, necessarily, from the viewpoint of an ecologist with a special interest in wildlife management. It therefore expresses the opinion that in any planning for the future of man on this earth, we must also plan for the wild land and wild creatures which have been a part of his heritage and which must remain a part of his life—if such life is to have much meaning.

This book is intended as a text for a one semester course in conservation at the lower division college level, such as I have had the privilege of teaching at the University of Minnesota at Duluth and at Humboldt State College. As such, it attempts to sketch the broad background of conservation, and to allow the instructor to fill in the details from local experience.

RAYMOND F. DASMANN

*Arcata, California*
*December, 1958*

# Acknowledgments

I am indebted for the original inspiration for this book, and for many ideas, to Carl O. Sauer of the Department of Geography, University of California, in whose conservation class I sat as a student. To A. Starker Leopold, of the Museum of Vertebrate Zoology, University of California, I am particularly in debt for the stimulating ideas and philosophy on conservation which he has provided over the years, for his careful review of the manuscript in its formative stage, and for helpful suggestions for improvement.

Sincere appreciation is also expressed to the late John T. Curtis of the University of Wisconsin, Fred H. Tarp of Contra Costa College, and George Allen of Humboldt State College who reviewed the entire manuscript and provided many ideas for improvement. Thanks are also due to Gordon Wolman of the U. S. Geological Survey for his thorough review and criticism of the chapter on water conservation. The shortcomings that may remain are mine, not his. Daniel Luten of the University of California and Stanley Mulaik of the University of Utah assisted greatly in preparation of the second edition.

For the photographs I thank the U.S. Forest Service, the Soil Conservation Service, the Bureau of Reclamation, the National Park Service, and the California Division of Highways for their cooperation. I am grateful also for the photographs provided by Charles F. Yocom, Humboldt State College; Jim Yoakum, Bureau of Land Management; Thane Riney, FAO; and Jack Bernard.

In a book of this sort, it is impossible to give full credit where it is due. With this in mind, I acknowledge here the many ideas provided by my colleagues in the field of conservation with whom I have worked, or talked, and from whom I have learned much.

Finally, I owe most thanks to my wife, Elizabeth, for her assistance in every part of the work and, in particular, for the preparation of the sketches and drawings from which the illustrations were made, and to the other members of my family who contributed in various ways.

# Contents

# ENVIRONMENTAL CONSERVATION

# Introduction

Whether you are in the minority who read books or the majority who watch television, you have been hammered for years by news of recurrent crises: war and the threat of nuclear catastrophe; the population explosion and all of its ramifications, including the shadow of famine over many areas of the world; and, more persistently, evidence of the steady deterioration of the human environment, of air and water pollution, of urban congestion and decay, of battles to save the redwoods, the Everglades, the Grand Canyon, or the local swamp. Anyone who regards these problems too steadily and who concerns himself continuously with the state of the nation and of the world can readily develop a state of anxiety, angry frustration, or depressed withdrawal. Yet nobody can escape some share of responsibility; nobody can avoid the world in which he lives. Failure to act can only result in the need to live with the consequences of other people's action.

This book is an attempt to look at our environment and human problems from the viewpoint of conservation. It is an attempt to provide a factual basis on which action to improve the environment can be taken. Action without information usually leads to a worsening of the situation. This is in part responsible for today's problems.

International conflicts, population, and environmental problems are all tied together. Nations with an advanced technology have a favorable balance between human populations and natural resources, or the technological means for making resources available for their people. The trouble spots of the world, in which warfare goes on or in which the threat of war exists, are most commonly the resource-deficient areas, or those areas lacking the technology to make use of available resources. Most commonly they are the overpopulated areas, in the sense that there are more people than the existing technology and level of availability of natural resources can support. Although not capable of any threat to world peace, they are centers for dissension among more powerful nations. As world populations continue to grow and as natural resources

1

dwindle, the danger of war also grows. Any permanent solution to international problems must include provisions for meeting the natural resource needs of the nations concerned and for creating environments suitable to the people of those nations, as well as solutions to their population problems.

In nations with advanced technology, such as the United States, it is not easy to realize how bad things really are. We live with an abundance of material goods, and have taken for granted a continued supply of necessities and luxuries. Few of us are personally familiar with the constant deprivation that is the lot of a large share of the world's people. We have been interested in growth, expansion, and increasing abundance. Yet, even in the United States, we are becoming aware of the cost of continued growth and expansion. We can have more factories, but they bring more contamination of air and water; we can have more cars, but they congest our cities and our highways; we can have more freeways, but fear that more and more they will lead only to places not worth visiting. Water and air were once clean and free; now they are either costly or polluted. Land was once cheap; now we can hardly afford to buy the space needed to preserve priceless and unique natural areas or to buy breathing space for our city hordes.

We in the United States have realized that we can no longer disregard the problems of overpopulated, famine-threatened countries. No matter how great our military strength, we cannot forever defend an island of prosperity in a sea of misery. To pretend that these problems are not ours is, in the words of Paul Ehrlich,[1]* like telling a fellow passenger that his end of the boat is sinking. We are all passengers on a crowded planet. Concern for the human environment has become the concern of everyone.

There was a time, not long past, when the world was large and people were few. At that time we could and did make great blunders in our treatment of the environment without too serious consequence. If a forest were destroyed or a rangeland turned to desert, there were a thousand forests and rangelands still undamaged. Now the world is small and people are many. Serious blunders can be irrevocable. We have lost most of our margin for error.

At stake in the struggle for conservation of our environment are all of those things that add to a rich and full life for individuals. Not only is it important to guarantee food and shelter (which are basic) and mechanical devices (which seem essential) for future populations, we must also plan to provide those qualities, less easily defined in economic

* The cited references are included in a reference list at the end of the text.

terms, that enrich life: space to move in, wild lands to roam, wild scenery to admire, and wild animals to watch, study, or hunt.

The importance of our having a knowledge of the principles of conservation is simply this: how we treat our environment will determine our future. It is within our power today to take a course of action that will force us in the future to live at a mere subsistence level, if we survive at all. It is also within our power to take those steps that will help to guarantee a high quality of living and a wide range of human choice for the future. We cannot postpone our decision to take the latter course. If we wait too long it may be impossible to keep available the opportunity for choice. Already we have restricted it.

It is not the purpose here to present any easy solution to the problems of the human environment. For many we do not yet have an answer. It will be indicated that one way out of our present dilemma is by means of what is called environmental conservation, combined with self-imposed limitations on human population growth. It will be shown that certain other proposed ways can lead only to worse situations. It is the principal concern here to familiarize the reader with the problems and to indicate the necessity for taking an active interest in these problems. If each of us fails to take such an interest and fails to help in building the kind of world he wants to live in, he may find too late that the "brave new world," which someone else has created, has no place in it for him.


## DEFINITIONS

The human environment is made up of the natural resources of the earth and man's cultural modifications of them. The latter are natural resources that have been processed, changed, or arranged for the use of man. It could once be said that natural resources were those materials, areas, or living things considered useful or of value to a particular human culture. Today, however, everything on earth, from the polar ice caps to the tops of equatorial mountains and from the depths of the sea to the limits of the stratosphere, is useful or of value to man and consequently a natural resource.

It is sometimes convenient to recognize two general categories of natural resources: the renewable and the nonrenewable. However the boundaries between these classes have become mixed and interwoven as we have learned more about the nature of environments. The usefulness of the terms is therefore limited. In general, renewable resources

Fig. 1. Timber is a renewable biotic resource. Under proper management this longleaf pine forest in Mississippi can continue to produce crops of timber for future use (U.S. Forest Service photograph).

are living (or biotic) resources (Fig. 1), and nonrenewable resources are nonliving things such as minerals and fossil fuels.

There are important distinctions between biotic and nonliving resources. Biotic resources are able to reproduce or replace themselves and to increase. One can leave a breeding stock of a biotic resource and expect that with proper care it will regenerate the original supply. A nonliving resource however does not replace itself or does so at such a slow rate that it is not useful to consider it in terms of human lifetimes. A seed stock of iron ore or petroleum does not grow. Once a nonrenewable resource is consumed, it is gone. We must then find a substitute or do without.

A second important difference between the two types of resources lies in the way in which biotic resources are interrelated. If a forest is cut and burned, not only is the timber affected, but the soil can be damaged and the water relationships altered. Stream flow and under-ground water supplies may thus be influenced. Fish life in the waters and animal life on the land may be destroyed or changed markedly. Living resources in any area are intricately tied together; if you touch one you touch them all (Fig. 2). With nonliving resources it is not the same. Removing the coal from an area will not necessarily influence the minerals in other underground deposits. Nevertheless the two cate-gories of resources become closely related through man's activities. When we use coal or petroleum for fuel we spare timber, but at the same time we may pollute the air so that tree growth is retarded.

The conservation prospects for nonliving resources are always de-pressing to a degree. Good management is chiefly use for the best pur-poses, wise use with the avoidance of waste. It is possible to string out supplies for a long period of time and to use the resource only for worthwhile purposes, but if we use it at all it will eventually disap-pear. With living resources and good management, we can have a supply that will last indefinitely. In a forest managed for timber, trees can be cut each year, and yet there will always be trees in the future. With good management of agricultural soils, the land can continue to yield crops over thousands of years.

Fig. 2. When a forest burns it is not only timber that is lost, but soils and water, wildlife and fish are also affected (U.S. Forest Service photograph).

In the past, these two classes of resources have been confused. Wildlife, for example, was thought of as something bound to disappear. Conservation then meant locking the remnants in inviolable refuges. Now we know that for many forms of wildlife the best way toward preservation is through continued use, within limits set by the ability of the species to reproduce itself.

In the following pages, emphasis will be placed upon the biosphere—that part of our planet in which life exists and on which it depends. The biotic resources of the earth, the lands that support them, and the human populations dependent upon them will be emphasized. However, the human environment consists of its living and nonliving components, and because of the nature of ecological systems, it is impossible to separate the two. The nonliving resources will be given, therefore, appropriate attention. Past one-sided approaches to conservation, which have ignored the interrelationships that exist in nature, have usually ended in failure. A broad environmental approach to conservation is a necessity.

An environmental approach to conservation requires a reexamination of the meaning of the word "conservation." Conservation has had many different meanings in the past, but it now has a wider role to play in human affairs. It is defined here as the rational use of the environment to provide a high quality of living for mankind. It involves the planning for and control of man's use of his environment, with a consideration of the long-range future of the human race and with a view to providing environments suitable to the satisfaction of the widest possible range of human aspirations. It involves, therefore, the preservation or creation of diversity in environments, maintaining the greatest variety of living creatures, in order to provide suitable habitat for the varied types of people that still exist and thus to enable this human diversity to survive.

# | 1 |

# The Nature of the Environment

## ECOSYSTEMS AND COMMUNITIES

Despite his present position of dominance on earth, man is still dependent upon other living things for his sustenance. Locked up in cities, civilized man may assume that he has risen above nature, but the bread he eats comes from wheat plants formed of soil, air, and sunlight. The soil, with hosts of microorganisms to maintain its health and fertility, was itself formed by the work of generations of green plants and animals, transforming rock and sunlight energy into the organized network of materials needed for the growth of wheat plants. The meat that man demands comes also from soil materials, transformed by a great community of grassland organisms into the plant protein and carbohydrate needed to feed a steer. Beef is soil and sunlight made available to man by plant communities. Like all other animals, therefore, man is dependent upon the ecological interrelationships of living things with their physical environment.

The relationships between organisms and environment are illustrated by the concepts of biotic communities and ecosystems. A *biotic community* is an assemblage of species of plants and animals inhabiting a common area and having, therefore, effects upon one another (Fig. 3). A combination of a biotic community with its physical environment is called an *ecosystem*. *Ecology* is the study of ecosystems to determine their status and the ways in which they function. An understanding of ecology is basic to conservation.

In the broad sense the human environment is the biosphere, which has been defined already as that part of the planet in which life exists and of which it forms a part. It is the surface area of the earth, made up of the atmosphere, the oceans, the upper surfaces of the land areas of the continents and islands and the fresh waters associated with them, and the living things that inhabit this area. In the biosphere, energy from the sun is available to activate living processes; chemicals from air, water, and soil are available as building blocks for living organisms.

9

Fig. 3. A biotic community. This redwood forest in California is the home for a great variety of plants and animals, all interrelated and affecting one another (U.S. Forest Service photograph).

The biosphere can be considered as the sum of all the ecosystems of the earth and, at any one time, people exist as part of a particular ecosystem, although they may travel from one ecosystem to another. What happens to the biosphere and its ecosystems determines what will happen to people. It is impossible to separate an individual human from the biosphere of which he forms a part. The air he breathes, the water he drinks, the sunlight that warms him, and the food he eats, all tie him to his immediate physical and biological environment. Man apart from environment is an abstraction; in reality no such being could exist.

**Energy transfer.** For a biotic community to exist it must have a supply of energy to activate the life processes of the organisms that compose it. The principal source of energy for any biotic community is sunlight. However, only one group of organisms, the green plants, can make use of sunlight energy directly for the synthesis of foodstuffs. The presence of chlorophyll in the cells of plants makes possible photosynthesis, in which light energy is used in building a plant food (glucose) from simple compounds—carbon dioxide from the air and water from the soil. From glucose, with the addition of other simple chemical compounds obtained from the soil, plants can build more complex carbohydrates, proteins, fats, and vitamins. These materials, required by animals in their diets, must come from the plant world.

The dependence of animals upon plants and of plants upon sunlight brings to consideration a physical law of great importance to the understanding of any ecosystem. This, the *second law of thermodynamics*, states that in any transfer of energy from one form to another, some energy always escapes from the system, usually as heat, no transfer is 100 per cent effective. Always energy goes from a concentrated form useful to a system to a dilute form, in which it is not. Most transfers of energy in natural ecosystems are inefficient. In some instances, of the total amount of sunlight energy potentially available to green plants, only 1 per cent will be converted finally into chemical energy tied up in foods within the plants. The remaining 99 per cent escapes. Similarly, when herbivores feed on green plants and convert plant starch and protein into animal energy and protein, another high percentage of energy escapes. When carnivores feed on herbivores, there is again inefficiency in energy transfer. The limits of available energy are soon reached. Thus, in some communities, of 10,000 original calories of sunlight energy striking on green plants, only 2 calories may remain tied up in chemical energy within the body of a carnivorous animal.

The operation of the second law of thermodynamics serves to explain many of the characteristics of ecosystems. In any ecosystem the amount of green plants is limited, ultimately, by the amount of sunlight energy and the efficiency of plants in converting it to a useful form. This is a theoretical upper limit, not approached in natural ecosystems, because lesser limits are always set by shortages of required chemical elements or other factors.

In a similar way the final limit on the number of animals in an

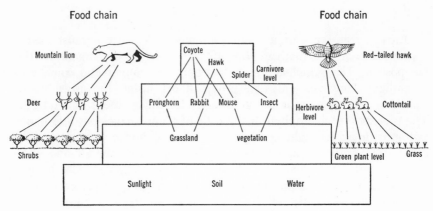

Biotic pyramid showing portion of a grassland food web

area is determined by the amount of energy available in green plants and by the efficiency of animals in converting this to a form useful for maintenance, growth, and reproduction. These relationships within an ecosystem are often illustrated in diagrammatic ways, such as the biotic pyramid, food chain, and food web (Fig. 4). In the *biotic pyramid* the greatest numbers of organisms, the greatest mass, and the greatest amount of food energy, are to be found in the lowest layer of organisms, the green plants. Partly because of the necessary inefficiency in energy transfer, numbers, mass, and energy decrease as you move up the pyramid. The pyramid is supported by the amount of sunlight energy received and the amounts of essential nutrients, minerals, water, and essential gases available in the soil or other supporting physical environment. *Food chains* are simply diagrammatic representations of the food relationships within an ecosystem. Although simple food chains may be artificially separated out and studied, most food relationships of the species in an ecosystem are more complicated. In natural systems food chains are interwoven into complex *food webs*. The number of layers in a pyramid or links in a food chain is inevitably limited through the operation of the second law of thermodynamics. Inefficiency in energy transfer keeps pyramids low and food chains short.

Man, as a carnivore, occupies the top layer of a biotic pyramid and the end link of a food chain. However, man can also exist as a herbivore and thus lower the pyramid and shorten the food chain. In those areas of the earth where human numbers are great and productive land is limited, man cannot afford the luxury of being a carnivore nor the waste of energy involved in converting plant protein to beef or mutton. In such areas he must feed on plants directly if his great numbers are to be maintained.

Of perhaps greater importance to man than the limitations imposed by the second law of thermodynamics is the role played by life in conserving energy. Sunlight energy striking a bare rock or soil surface is soon lost. Much is reflected back into the air; some heats the rock or soil temporarily but is soon radiated back into the atmosphere. The earth as a whole, before life, radiated or reflected back into space an amount of energy equal to that received from the sun. In the absence of life, energy thus became degraded, i.e., dispersed through space until it was no longer capable of doing work. When green plants appeared on earth, this loss of energy was slowed down. Sunlight energy was stored in organisms in concentrated form and transferred in food chains from one to another. With the development of complex biotic communities, a living system was developed that made maximum use of the incoming solar energy and stored a part of it for the future. Man has been dependent upon these stored reserves of energy. When he eats meat, he obtains energy that may have been stored by plants several years before. When he cuts firewood for fuel, he is obtaining energy accumulated and stored by trees for perhaps a century or more. When he burns coal or petroleum, he obtains sunlight energy stored by plant life millions of years before. Man is as yet unable to store significant quantities of energy without making use of the life processes of plants and animals. When living communities are destroyed and the land made bare, the energy on which life and man depend is again wasted and no longer is stored for future use.

**Chemical requirements.** Just as each ecosystem must have a source of energy, so must it have a source of chemical building blocks from which organisms can be constructed. In the oceans this source is seawater; on land the source is the soil and the atmosphere. Biotic pyramids rest on an energy base of sunlight, and a chemical base of soil or seawater. Both of these sources of minerals, however, are secondary, for minerals come originally from the rocks of the earth's surface or from the atmosphere above the earth.

Rocks supply minerals to the soil slowly. Rocks break apart through weathering, the action of cold, heat, wind, and precipitation gradually cracking and shattering them into small particles. They break down more quickly through the action of organisms. Plant roots, for example,

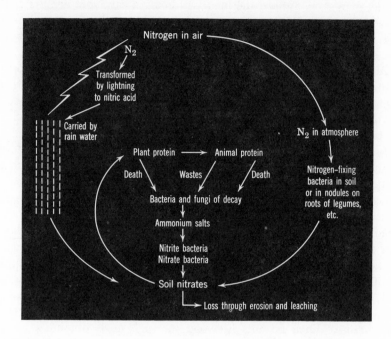

penetrate into cracks in rocks, widen them, and eventually split and separate the rock fragments. Acids released or dissolved from plant materials help the process of rock disintegration and free elements for soil formation. Organisms also help to capture elements such as nitrogen from the atmosphere and incorporate them in the soil. Nitrogen, an essential part of protein, must be present for life to exist. The cycle by which it is transferred from atmosphere to organism, to soil, and back to the atmosphere has been well studied (Fig. 5).

**Soil formation.** The evolution of soil has accompanied the evolution of life—before life there was no soil—for soil is created through the action of organisms. When life is destroyed in an area, the loss of soil follows.

In an area where rocks have long been exposed to the air we can see the stages through which soil is sometimes formed. Rock surfaces, roughened and weathered, provide a foothold for primitive and hardy land plants, the *lichens* (Fig. 6). These exert a physical and chemical effect on the rock leading to a more rapid decomposition. Small rock particles may be accumulated and added to the dead remnants of the lichen bodies. When enough mineral and organic material has accumulated, *mosses* next invade the rock surface. These crowd out the lichens, but with their more dense growth habit and more robust plant bodies they hasten the breakdown of rock and add greater amounts of organic debris to the mixture.

Eventually a layer of materials will be formed deep enough to support the more hardy types of *annual grasses* and *forbs,* and these will invade and overtop the mosses. These in turn break down the rock further and add more organic material. In a forested region they are replaced by larger *perennial grasses* and *forbs* (broad-leaved herbs); these are replaced by *shrubs* and, finally, by *trees.* Each does its part in breaking down rock and adding organic debris to it. Joining in the process are microorganisms of various kinds, bacteria and fungi, which feed on dead plant and animal remains and eventually release from them simple mineral nutrients which may be used again to support new plant growth. Also involved are the larger burrowing animals that churn and mix rock particles together and add to the complex their own waste products and dead bodies. Eventually, with the final stage of vegetation, there has been developed that complex arrangement of minerals and organic materials that is known as mature soil.

Fig. 6 and chapter opening. Primary succession on rock. Lichens have occupied the bare rock surface. Where some soil has formed, ferns are established. With more soil, shrubs and trees can take over (photograph by Soil Conservation Service, U.S. Dept. Agric.).

The process of soil formation is not always the same. Few of our soils have actually developed in place from underlying parent rock. Most, the *transported soils,* are built from materials carried by wind, water, gravity, or glacial action from other areas and are broken from rock originally by the action of heat, wind, and water. Across the northern United States, the soil materials are mostly of glacial origin, built from fragments ground from underlying rocks by the action of continental glaciers during past ice ages. These have been carried hundreds of miles and deposited where the glaciers finally melted and retreated. Over wide areas in the central United States the soils are derived from *loess,* formed from dust particles carried over long distances by wind currents. But on glacial drifts or loess deposits also the process of plant invasion, breakdown, and modification of the substrate has gone on. Where the substrate is finely divided, the lichen and moss stage may be skipped and the initial plant invasion be made by herbs, shrubs, or trees. Always, however, there is further development and change until a mature soil and a relatively stable vegetation is attained.

**Erosion.** Just as the action of living organisms is essential for the development of soil, so it is essential if the soil is to be maintained. Throughout past ages there have been two major groups of forces at work on the earth's surface. One group of forces contributes to land raising: folding up mountain ranges, elevating plateaus, forming volcanic peaks. The other group leads to the degradation of lands, the lowering of the high lands back to sea level. These forces of degradation, or erosion, consist of gravity in combination with wind, rain, and temperature, cracking apart the rocks and carrying them to lower elevations. In the long ages before life appeared, *geological erosion* went on as a slow and unchecked process. With the development of life, however, a new force was interposed. The decomposed rocks were stopped in their movement to the sea by the countless small check dams formed from plant life. Instead of washing away, rock particles remained to form soil. But once soil is formed, it becomes highly vulnerable to a much more rapid erosion than that which wears away rocks. Without a covering of green plants and a network of plant roots to hold it in place it can be lost rapidly. When plant cover is destroyed, a few decades can see the disappearance of soils that may have been thousands of years in forming. It is this kind of *accelerated soil erosion* that is of concern to the conservationist (Fig. 7).

**Biotic succession.** The role of plants in soil formation illustrates another process fundamental in any ecosystem and basic to much work

Fig. 7. Accelerated erosion. When overgrazing removed the grass cover, water running off the slope rapidly removed the soil and cut gashes in the hill slope (U.S. Forest Service photograph).

in conservation. This is the process known as biotic succession. The way in which lichens and mosses are replaced by herbs and these by shrubs and trees as soils are being formed is an example of biotic succession. Along with the replacement and change in the types of plants, goes replacement and change in the animals dependent upon each type of plant. Biotic succession can be defined as the sequence of biotic communities which tend to succeed and replace one another in a given area over a period of time. The starting point in any biotic succession is always a *pioneer community,* able to colonize and inhabit a bare surface. The end product in any succession is known as a *climax community.* This is a relatively stable community, able to maintain itself over long periods of time and to regenerate and replace itself without marked further change. It is usually the most complex type of community which a particular physical environment will support and makes the most efficient use of sun energy and soil materials. Climax communities represent storehouses of materials and energy accumulated over the long years of plant succession and soil formation.

Throughout the earth, wherever life can be supported, biotic succession goes on. Plants invade and colonize bare areas and are replaced in time by other groups of plants. Succession takes place on bare rock, sand, exposed alluvium in river bottoms, and in the water (Fig. 8).

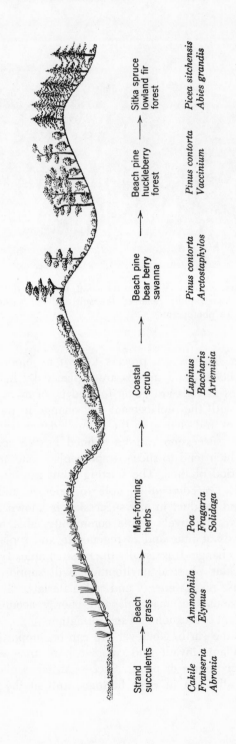

Strand
succulents → Beach
grass → Mat-forming
herbs → Coastal
scrub → Beach pine
bear berry
savanna → Beach pine
huckleberry
forest → Sitka spruce
lowland fir
forest

*Cakile*
*Franseria*
*Abronia*

*Ammophila*
*Elymus*

*Poa*
*Fragaria*
*Solidaga*

*Lupinus*
*Baccharis*
*Artemisia*

*Pinus contorta*
*Arctostaphylos*

*Pinus contorta*
*Vaccinium*

*Picea sitchensis*
*Abies grandis*

Any lake or pond, unless constantly disturbed, tends to be invaded by aquatic plants which are replaced in time by partially submerged reeds and rushes and these in time by sedges and grasses. This aquatic succession is made possible by the accumulation of soil materials washed into a lake, accumulating around the bodies of plants, and being added to by dead-plant debris. Eventually, unless the process is disturbed, each lake changes to a pond, the pond to a marsh, the marsh into meadow or forest (Fig. 9).

There are two general categories of succession. One, which has been emphasized to this point, is *primary succession*. This takes place on areas that have not previously supported life. The other, more immediately important to conservation, is *secondary succession*. This takes place on areas where the original vegetation has been destroyed or disturbed but where the soil has not been lost. This process is generally familiar (Figs. 10 and 11). A forest which has been cut down regenerates itself. The forest, if not greatly disturbed and if seed sources are available.

Fig. 9. A climax community. This forest of maple, elm, and ash in Wisconsin is a remnant of the once extensive hardwood forests of the east. An end product of plant succession (U.S. Forest Service photograph).

Fig. 10. Fire has destroyed the chaparral cover on this southern California hillside. Rainfall running off the bare slopes has cut rills as it washed the soil away (U.S. Forest Service photograph).

Fig. 11. The same area as in Fig. 10, reseeded to mustard. These annual plants will help hold the soil in place until normal successional processes lead to replacement of the chaparral cover (U.S. Forest Service photograph).

may regenerate quickly with trees replacing trees. Usually, and particularly after a fire, there are a series of intermediate stages. A weed stage follows forest clearing. Left alone this is replaced by shrubs, then by trees and, eventually, if these have not been destroyed or the environment too greatly changed by disturbance, by the species that composed the original climax forest. The process is rapid or slow, depending upon the severity of the original disturbance. In a similar way, when a rangeland has been heavily overgrazed, the original climax grassland will go through several stages, characterized by different communities of weeds and grasses, before the climax community replaces itself. Succession tends to be an orderly and predictable process. It is a heartening process for the conservationist, who knows that with care many of our badly abused lands will repair themselves (Fig. 12).

**Succession and land management.** The exploitation of biotic resources usually involves the removal and consumption of all or part of the elements that composed the climax communities of the earth. Successful conservation, or land management, often includes the manipulation of biotic succession in such a way that the climax replaces itself as quickly as possible. In this way a continued high yield of resources from an area is obtained.

The lumberman is interested in obtaining the greatest yield of high-quality timber from an area. In some places, such as the redwood forests of California, the climax forest has the greatest commercial value. Successful redwood-forest management includes a study of the way plant succession proceeds after various systems of logging and the selection of that cutting system which will lead to the most rapid regeneration of the forest. Not all high-value forests are climax, however. In the southeastern United States, the longleaf pine forests represent a subclimax stage in succession. Left alone they will be replaced by climax hardwood trees of lower commercial value. Studies of succession have indicated that the pine forests are best maintained by the use of fire, which kills the seedlings of the climax species but does not injure the fire-tolerant pine seedlings.

On rangelands where climax grasses have the greatest forage value, the range manager attempts to work out grazing systems and levels of stocking which will best perpetuate the climax. Elsewhere, successional grasses may have greater value as forage, and a different system of grazing management will be needed to suppress the climax and main-

Fig. 12. Overgrazing has broken and destroyed the grass cover in this mountain meadow, exposing bare soil or leaving a sparse cover of weeds. With protection, successional processes can restore the original meadow grasses (U.S. Forest Service photograph).

tain the succesional forms. In wildlife management it is found that many of the valuable species of game animals are not climax forms, and hence the wildlife manager may be interested in suppression of the climax through the use of fire, cutting, or some other technique which will maintain the necessary level of disturbance. Thus, it can be seen that in many types of wild-land management a knowledge of biotic succession is essential.

## LIMITING FACTORS

The human environment, whether in a natural state or in one greatly modified by man's activities, is composed of complex arrangements of matter and energy and is maintained by the interactions that occur among them. Activity within it is ceaseless as energy and materials flow through food chains. Change is also ceaseless, whether it be the relatively rapid change represented by the growth and death of individuals and populations, by the processes of biotic succession, or the slow change represented by the evolution of new races and species of organisms. In places, man accelerates the pace of change, sometimes to his own detriment; but even in the absence of people change goes on.

In the environment, life is distinguished by growth, mobility, and reproduction, among other qualities. Every species that exists tends to increase in numbers, to spread to new and suitable environments, to increase again there, and spread farther. Growth in individual size or in numbers of a population continues usually until some external factor of the environment causes it to cease, although in man and in some other species, self-imposed limitation on growth of populations may occur before external factors bring this limitation. A tree will cease to grow when water or an essential soil chemical ceases to be available in minimum quantity. A population of trees will cease to increase in numbers when the tree seeds encounter conditions that are unsuitable for their germination or for the growth of the new seedling. An animal population will cease to grow when there is no longer adequate food, water, and shelter for the sustenance of individuals, or where weather or other environmental factors result in conditions unsuitable to survival of individuals of that species. Whatever limits the growth in size of an individual or in numbers of a population is known as a *limiting factor* to that individual or population. The ecological principle of limiting factors is stated by E. P. Odum[4] as follows: "The presence and success of an organism or a group of organisms depends upon a complex of conditions. Any condition which approaches or exceeds the limits of tolerance is said to be a limiting condition or a limiting factor." This concept is one of the oldest in ecology and traces its origin to the chemist Justus Liebig in 1840. Liebig, who studied the effect of chemical foodstuffs on plant growth, first stated this concept as "growth of a plant is dependent on the amount of foodstuff which is presented to it in minimum quantity." This concept, expanded to include organisms other than plants and factors other than chemical nutrients, has been known as The Law of the Minimum.[4]

The concept of limiting factors, combined with a knowledge that the earth is limited in size and in its supplies of energy and materials, leads to the obvious, but sometimes overlooked, conclusion that growth and expansion must have an end. No species, including man, can expand its population indefinitely. Any species, including man, will be better off individually if its growth is limited through its own behavior before the time when environmental limiting factors (shortages in necessities, for example) begin to take effect.

Limiting factors can be divided into two categories: physical and biological. Physical factors that limit population growth would include factors of climate and weather, the absence of water or presence of an excess of water, the availability of essential soil minerals, the suitability of the terrain, and so on. Biological factors involve competition, predation, parasitism, disease, and other interactions between or within a species that are limiting to growth or increases. In the extreme environments of the world, the physical factors are generally limiting. These would include the very cold or very dry environments or, for land organisms, the very wet environments. Droughts, floods, unseasonable cold, or extreme cold are among the factors that limit populations in such environments. In the more optimum environments of the world (the warmer, more humid environments) biological factors more often are limiting. In such environments, complex predator-prey relationships, balances with parasites or disease organisms, and competition for light, soil minerals, or water among species with similar requirements are most frequently limiting to population growth. Thus fish populations in cold mountain lakes are most frequently limited, both in the growth of individuals and the size of populations, by water temperature and the availability of chemical nutrients. Cold temperatures inhibit biological activity and thus prevent the growth of plankton and of insect populations upon which the fish would feed. The low availability of chemical nutrients inhibits the growth of these organisms during the period when temperatures are suitable to growth. Fish populations are therefore small in numbers. On the other hand, in warm ponds fish populations may grow in size to a point of great abundance where competition among them not only prevents individuals from reaching large size but inhibits further growth of the population.

Limiting factors may further be classified into those whose operations are dependent upon the density (the number of individuals per unit of area) of the population and those that have no relation to density.[4] The *density-dependent* factors are those that increase in their intensity, that have greater effects, or that affect more individuals as the population increases in density. Thus the availability of food, grass, and other herbs may be a limiting factor to the increase in numbers of domestic cattle in a pasture. The higher the density of cattle, the less grass there is per cow and the greater number of cows suffer from food shortage. By contrast, a flood sweeping through the pasture would be a *density-independent* limiting factor. It would wipe out all the cows whether there were two or a hundred in the area.

Density-dependent factors usually hold the greatest interest to students of population because of their more general and constant operation. They are usually the factors that set absolute limits to growth, that determine the number of individuals that can be supported—the *carrying capacity* of the area. They are the factors that operate to decrease the individual well-being in a population that approaches the limits or carrying capacity of its environment. In crowded human populations in many parts of the world we see such density-dependent factors in operation.

# | 2 |

# The Major Biotic Regions

It is generally realized that there are great differences in the productivity and habitability of the various parts of the land surface of the earth. These differences are largely the result of interactions of two climatic factors, temperature and precipitation, with the geology or physiography of the earth. In the water areas of the earth another factor, light, becomes of extreme importance. A cliff face or an active volcano will not support much life no matter how favorable the climate may be. A flat plain with an abundance of available chemical nutrients will not support much life if it is too cold, too hot, or too dry. The depths of the ocean will not produce much in the way of living matter because green plants cannot grow in the absence of light.

Balances between temperature and precipitation are of major significance in determining the suitability of an area for living organisms. Temperature determines the rate at which evaporation takes place and consequently the amount of moisture which can remain in the soil available for plant growth. It also determines whether water can exist in a solid or liquid state. The Antarctic Continent and Greenland are relatively lifeless because they are too cold. The balance between temperature and precipitation in these places is such that both are almost completely covered by hundreds of feet of glacial ice. Although these areas have unusual scientific interest and considerable potential for future use, they have as yet been little used by man. At the other extreme, much of the Sahara desert is inhospitable to life because it is too hot and dry. Evaporation removes much of the rain that falls, and little falls. Only where irrigation can be made available is it possible for such desert regions to support human populations.

In between the areas of extreme climatic or physiographic factors are a great variety of natural areas, a remarkable diversity of climates, geological formations, and biological materials. These constitute man's original heritage, the diversified earth on which he evolved. Despite our accelerated dissipation of these riches, this diversity of environments

27

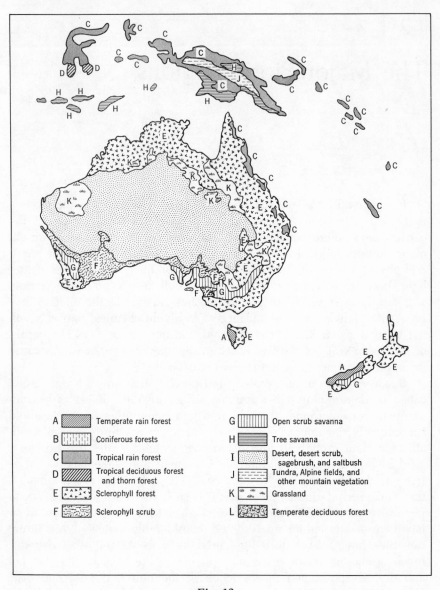

**Fig. 13.**

| | | |
|---|---|---|
| A | Temperate rain forest | |
| B | Coniferous forests | |
| C | Tropical rain forest | |
| D | Tropical deciduous forest and thorn forest | |
| E | Sclerophyll forest | |
| F | Sclerophyll scrub | |
| G | Open scrub savanna | |
| H | Tree savanna | |
| I | Desert, desert scrub, sagebrush, and saltbush | |
| J | Tundra, Alpine fields, and other mountain vegetation | |
| K | Grassland | |
| L | Temperate deciduous forest | |

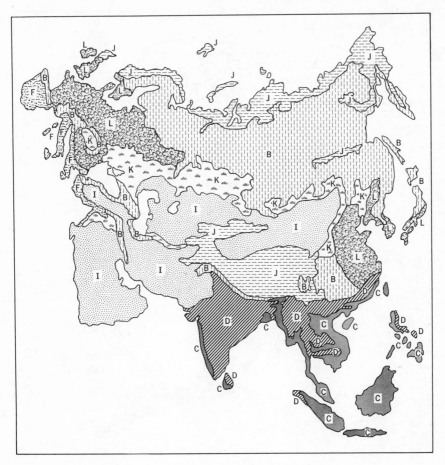

Fig. 13 (continued).

remains part of the legacy that we enjoy today and can pass on to future generations. This includes the major ecosystems or biotic regions of the earth (Fig. 13).

The climax, end product of biotic succession, and the later successional stages are strongly influenced by the climate, soils, and other physical characteristics of a region. As environments vary, so does vegetation and animal life. Hence, if the major natural climax communities of the earth are mapped, the climate and soil regions and thus the major ecosystems are also mapped. A desert in Africa is characterized by vegetation, soils, and climate that more closely resemble those of a desert in South America than they do those of an equatorial forest

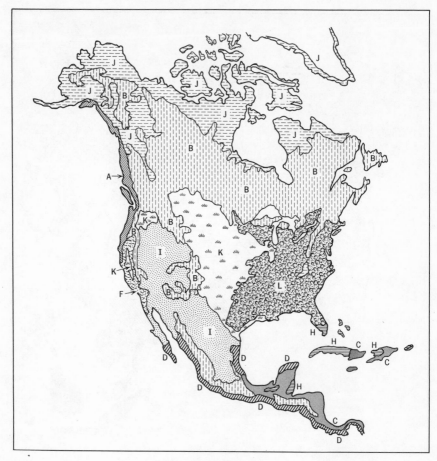

Fig. 13 (continued).

in Africa. Tropical rain forests, too, are relatively similar between Africa, Latin America, and Asia, although the species that compose them may differ. Grasslands in North America present opportunities for human exploitation, difficulties for human occupancy, and penalties for unwise land use similar to those of grasslands in Asia (Table 1).

## TUNDRA

In the far north of America is one of the more formidable biotic regions. This area, known as the Arctic barren grounds, or tundra, is one of long winters and short summers. Winters are extremely cold; summers have moderate to warm temperatures. Precipitation comes mostly as snow and is sufficiently low for the area to be characterized as an Arctic desert. It is preserved from desertlike qualities by the low temperatures and consequent low evaporation rates. Thus, despite the low precipitation, in summer the soils are waterlogged in surface layers. Below the surface of the ground the tundra has a layer of permanently frozen ground, the permafrost. Summers are not long enough for complete thawing to take place.

In such an environment organisms have difficulties. Plants are low

Fig. 13 (continued).

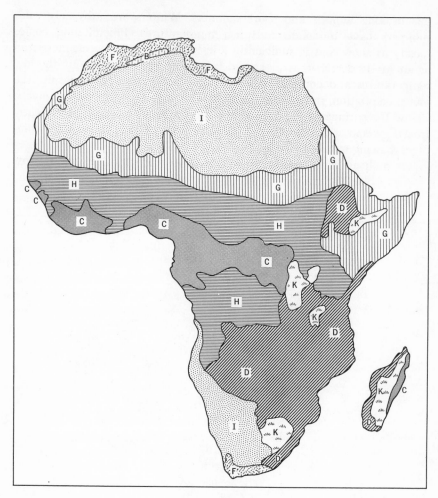

Fig. 13 (continued).

growing and thus are protected from extreme cold by the winter mantle of snow. Woody plants are dwarfed or prostrate. Most of the vegetation is grass, sedge, or lichen. All of the plants are adapted to completing their life processes in the short summers: leaves must grow quickly; flowers, fruit, and seed must be produced before the winter cold returns. Summer is a time of great activity.

Animal life is of two kinds: those active or present only in summer and those active through the year. Among the summer forms are vast numbers of migratory birds, including a high percentage of America's waterfowl. Present also are swarms of insects, which pass the winter in egg or larval state and emerge to grow, feed, and reproduce during the period of plant growth. Many mammals also emerge from hibernation or push northward in migration from the edge of the forest to join the mass of animal life feeding on the burgeoning summer vegetation. The hardy permanent residents, musk ox, caribou, Arctic fox, wolf, polar bear, lay on layers of summer fat to last them through a winter of difficult foraging.

Only a few peoples have been able to adapt themselves to the tundra. In America, the Eskimo tribes developed the cultural skills necessary for survival. Before western culture affected them they were divided into two main ecological groups: the caribou hunters, who depended upon the vast herds of caribou for food and clothing, and the coastal dwellers, who relied upon the ever-present marine life of the Arctic seas. Both groups adapted to the climate, concentrating their activities in the summer months and resisting the winter storms in weather-proof dwellings. Compared with most other biotic regions, the tundra is today little exploited or modified by man, although the effects of civilization have been felt on both animal life and vegetation. However, the prob-

**Table 1. Relationships of Vegetation, Soil, and Climate**

| Vegetation | Soil Groups | Climate |
|---|---|---|
| Tropical rain forest | Lateritic | Tropical rain forest |
| Deciduous forest | Red and yellow podsolic | Humid subtropical |
|  | Gray-brown podsolic | Humid continental |
| Temperate rain forest (Coastal forest) | Gray-brown podsolic | Marine west coast |
| Transition coniferous forest | Gray-brown podsolic | Mountain |
|  | Red and yellow podsolic | Humid continental |
| Boreal coniferous forest | Podsol | Subarctic |
| Tundra | Tundra | Tundra |
| Desert scrub | Red desert | Low-latitude desertrt |
| Sagebrush | Gray desert | Middle-latitude dese |
| Grassland | Chernozem, Chestnut, Brown, Prairie | Middle-latitude steppe |
|  |  | Humid continental |
|  |  | Humid subtropical |
|  |  | Mediterranean |
| Broad-sclerophyll forest (Chaparral) | Various | Mediterranean |

Fig. 14 and chapter opening. Alpine tundra in the high mountains of Colorado (U.S. Forest Service photograph).

lems of living in this extreme environment have so far prevented intensive use or settlement.

The tundra ecosystem of North America is repeated in a circumpolar belt across Europe and Asia and reaches southward in modified form along the higher mountain ranges (Fig. 14). It is little developed in the southern hemisphere, where large land masses do not occur within the appropriate latitudes.

## BOREAL FOREST

South from the tundra lies timberline, the northern edge of a broad belt of forest extending southward in America into the northeastern United States. This northern forest is characterized by evergreen, coniferous trees, mostly spruce and fir (Fig. 15). The region has a climate slightly warmer and with heavier precipitation than the tundra. In summer, the warmest months have enough heat to eliminate the permafrost. Without this ice barrier tree roots can penetrate more deeply, and soils can be more fully developed.

Coniferous forest vegetation helps determine the character of the soil. The leaves and litter that fall from conifers decay slowly in the cold climate and upon decaying form acid products which are carried into the soil by rain or melting snow. This mildly acid solution dissolves and leaches out of the top layer of the soil minerals which are imporant for abundant plant growth. The remaining topsoil tends to be sandy, light gray or whitish in color, and relatively infertile. The deeper layers of soil, in which some of the leached minerals are deposited, become rich in iron and aluminum compounds and darker in color. Such a soil is called a *podzol*. It is of poor quality for agricultural use.

The native animal life of this region, like that of the tundra, is seasonal in abundance. In summer, migratory birds move in to breed, and insects abound. In winter, only the few permanent residents, moose woodland caribou, lynx, fisher, wolverine, snowshoe hare, and spruce grouse among them, remain to face the period of food scarcity.

Man has settled parts of this region, but much is sparsely inhabited. The fur trapper has led the way in settlement, followed by the lumberman. Only in restricted areas where local conditions have permitted more fertile soils to develop has agriculture been successful. Most of the inhabitants are dependent in whole or in part upon the forests for their livelihood. Forest fires, often man-caused, are an important factor.

The boreal-forest ecosystem, like the tundra, forms a broad transcontinental belt in North America and Eurasia, with stringers extending along the high mountain ranges to the south (Fig. 16). Like the tundra,

Fig. 15. Boreal forest. Spruce, fir, and white pine in Maine (U.S. Forest Service photograph).

Fig. 16. Subalpine forest. This red fir forest represents a southward extension of the boreal forest along the higher mountain ranges (U.S. Forest Service photograph).

and for the same reasons, it does not occur in the continents of the southern hemisphere.

## DECIDUOUS FOREST

Farther south, in the eastern part of America, one encounters a third major ecosystem, the broad-leaved deciduous forest. In this area the predominant trees are the traditionally familiar oak, maple, hickory, beech, basswood, and other hardwood trees (Fig. 17). Unlike the northern conifers, most of these trees shed their leaves in late fall and pass the winter in a bare and dormant state.

In the deciduous forest region precipitation is relatively heavy and well distributed throughout the year. The summer rainfall and warm temperatures provide for abundant plant growth. In general, summers are warm and humid and winters cool to cold with heavy snowfall in the northern part of the region. Southward, as the area of cold winters is left behind, the vegetation gradually changes into the broad-leaved evergreen forest typical of the subtropics.

In primitive times the hardwood forests were widespread between the Atlantic and the Mississippi. However, from early times the influence of man has helped to keep portions of the forest open. Animal life was once abundant and consisted of a greater number of permanently resident species than are found further north. Characteristic of this region are the white-tailed deer, ruffed grouse, cottontail rabbit, red fox, bobwhite quail, fox squirrel, and wild turkey. All played an important role in the pioneer history of the United States.

The forest vegetation determined the soil. Temperate-zone forest litter, whether coniferous or broad leaved, tends to form mild acids on

Fig. 17. Broad-leaved deciduous forest. Maple, basswood, and elm in Wisconsin (U.S. Forest Service photograph).

decomposition. These acids, carried into the soil by the abundant rainfall, have a leaching effect. In the deciduous forest, however, because of the greater amounts of litter deposited and the more abundant mineral salts contained in the leaves, the results of leaching are less severe than in the coniferous forest. There is a constant addition of organic material and basic salts to the topsoil which help to maintain its fertility. The *gray-brown podsolic soils of* the northern part of the region, and the *red and yellow podsolic soils* of the southern part are initially fertile and readily worked when they are cleared for agriculture. Without proper care, however, they do not stand up well to continued crop production.

The deciduous forest region, more than most others, has been drastically modified by man. Originally it extended not only through the eastern United States but also through most of western Europe and northern China. However, this type of ecosystem has seen the growth and flowering of western civilization. With this growth the forests have disappeared from most areas, and the lands have been converted for agriculture.

## GRASSLANDS

In every continent a grassland region is to be found lying between the forest and the desert and with climates intermediate between the

Fig. 18. Prairie grassland. Tall grass prairie in Oklahoma, dominated by big and little bluestem, switchgrass, and Indian grass (photograph by Soil Conservation Service, U.S. Dept. Agric.).

Fig. 19. Steppe grassland in Montana (photograph by Soil Conservation Service, U.S. Dept. Agric.).

two. It is a region in which relatively low rainfall is normal. Summers are warm and in favorable years moist; winters are cool to cold with snow in the north and rain in the south. The rainfall, however, is erratic or cyclic. Wet cycles and dry cycles alternate. Droughts may last for several years, causing major changes in natural vegetation and even more severe changes where the land is used for grazing or agriculture.

The vegetation is dominated by grasses. Tall grasses predominate near the better watered forest border in the *prairie* community (Fig. 18). Shorter, sod-forming grasses dominate toward the drier desert side in a region known as *steppe* (Fig. 19). The grasses of the climax are perennial, living for several to many years. Annual grasses, which die back to seed each year, are characteristic of disturbed areas.

The climate and grassland vegetation produce grassland soils which differ markedly from forest soils. The topsoil is usually dark in color, and rich in organic matter. Minerals are not leached out of the soil because of the more limited rainfall and the abundant humus. The subsoil is usually rich in lime, whereas forest soils are normally lime deficient. On the scale of $p$H, or acidity, grassland soils are neutral or on the alkaline side, whereas the soils of forested regions are typically acid.

Animal life of the grasslands normally includes vast herds of grazing animals, the bison and pronghorn of North America and the numerous antelopes of Africa and Asia being examples. Feeding on these are large carnivores, wolves and their relatives and in Africa the big cats. A variety of mice, ground-dwelling birds, and smaller predators that feed on them are to be found. The abundance of animal life reflects the richness and fertility of the soil.

Grasslands, like the deciduous forest, have long been occupied by man—first by hunters of the great herds of big game, later by nomadic herdsmen with flocks of sheep or cattle, and finally by the farmers with their crops of cereal grains. The fertile soil has favored agriculture since the time when man developed a plow capable of turning the tough, grassland sod.

## DESERTS

The dry areas of the world vary considerable in both the amount and the dependability of the rainfall which they receive. Some authorities consider all of those regions that receive an average of 10 inches of rainfall or less per year to be deserts. This includes the extremely dry areas such as the deserts of Chile where no vegetation grows and places such as the northern Great Basin region of the United States where vegetation is relatively abundant.

In the United States there are two main desert regions, the high desert or Great Basin sagebrush region, which extends between the Rocky Mountains and the Sierra Nevada, and the low deserts, Mojave, Coloradan, and Sonoran deserts, which lie to the south of the Great Basin. In the Great Basin the vegetation is characterized by sagebrush and other low-growing shrubs, which form an open cover over the plains, and by the small conifers, junipers, and pinyon pines, which form an open woodland at higher elevations. The low-desert region is an area of desert scrub, where widely spaced creosote bushes are the most common vegetation, giving way in places to various species of cactus (Fig. 20).

In both desert regions the vegetation is drought resistant, with various adaptations to prevent or withstand water loss during the long, dry season. It is also adapted to complete its growth and reproduction during the periods when soil moisture is available.

Animal life, like plant life, is adapted to dryness. Animals avoid the heat and drought by being nocturnally active, using sheltered burrows, or remaining in cover in the hot, dry season in the vicinity of the few permanent streams and water holes. Desert rodents often have physiological adaptations that permit them to get along with a minimum of drinking water. Some receive all necessary water from their food and avoid water loss by excreting a highly concentrated urine.

The arid climate and sparse vegetation are reflected in the desert

Fig. 20. Desert. A grove of Joshua trees in the Mojave desert (U.S. Forest Service photograph).

soils. With little leaching there is a minimum loss of soil minerals. With sparse vegetation there is little addition of organic material to the soil, and therefore it may be deficient in nitrogen. Where minerals are in a proper balance and not concentrated in toxic quantities, desert soils are potentially highly fertile when water can be made available.

Deserts have played an important role in human history. The geography of western Asia and North Africa is such that many of the most fertile lands are located on river bottoms surrounded by arid deserts. Western civilization was born on the desert edge, and through history man has had important ecological effects upon the desert. Through turning his flocks of livestock out to graze on the desert vegetation or on the grasslands at the desert edge, man has changed and modified the deserts and has spread desertlike conditions into former grassland areas.

## MEDITERRANEAN

On most continents there is a relatively small area with a climate similar to that found around the Mediterranean Sea. Here there are

Fig. 21. Chaparral in southern California. This close-growing scrub vegetation is adapted to the dry mediterranean climate (U.S. Forest Service photograph).

winters with moderate rainfall but little snow and summers which are warm and dry. In North America this is the climate of much of California; elsewhere it is found in Chile, South Australia, South Africa, and in the sections of Europe, Asia, and Africa adjoining the Mediterranean Sea.

The most common type of vegetation in this region, although not always climax, is the dense brushfield dominated by medium-height, evergreen shrubs. This is known in California as *chaparral* and in Europe as *maquis* (Fig. 21). It is often interspersed with grassland, tree or shrub savanna or in more sheltered areas with broad-leaved evergreen forest. In California and the Mediterranean region, the evergreen live oaks predominate in this forest and in shrub form in the chaparral. In Australia, *Eucalyptus* forest and scrub dominates the mediterranean biotic region.

In latitude, the mediterranean ecosystem lies between the desert and deciduous forest, or, in the Americas and Australia between desert and temperate rain forest. Its location in Europe has made it the setting for much of the early development of western civilization, which spread from desert river valleys to mediterranean regions and from there to the deciduous forest.

## OTHER TEMPERATE BIOTIC REGIONS

Several other important biotic regions exist in the temperate latitudes, occupying smaller areas than those previously described. One, which can be called *transition coniferous forest*, occupies a zone in the mountains lying between the southward extensions of the boreal forest and the warmer chaparral, grassland, or desert of lower elevations (Figs. 22, 27). Pine trees of various species characterize the climax, or near climax, vegetation of this forest. Transition forest occurs latitudinally in some areas as a belt separating the boreal forest of spruce and fir from the deciduous forest. In the Lakes States and New England it occurs in this role.

On the northwestern coast of North America is an area of high rainfall, well distributed throughout the year, and mild temperatures—a climate of the marine west coast type. This favors the development of an unusually tall, dense, and luxuriant forest, the *temperate rain forest*. In North America this is dominated by redwood, Douglas fir, and other giant conifers (Fig. 23). In other continents a similar forest

Fig. 22. Transition coniferous forest. Ponderosa pine in Montana (U.S. Forest Service photograph).

Fig. 23. Temperate rain forest. Redwood forest in California (U.S. Forest Service photograph).

type is dominated by the laurel-leaved hardwood trees. Similar climates and vegetation are found in southern Chile, the South Island of New Zealand, and southeastern Australia.

## TROPICAL BIOTIC REGIONS

The most favorable climate on earth for the development of the greatest variety of organic life is to be found in the rain forest region of the tropics, and in the tropics also is to be found one of the least favorable climates for life, exemplified by the virtually rainless deserts of Peru. Tropical rain forest climates have year-round rainfall, without periods when the soil dries out, and temperatures that are always favorable to a high level of plant and animal activity. There are essentially no climatic factors limiting to plant growth. The tropical rain forests are dominated by an unusual variety of broad-leaved evergreen trees—fig and mahogany may be familiar examples—of which dozens of different species often occur in a single acre and many acres may have to be searched to find a second specimen of a particular species of tree.[13]

The trees in turn support a variety of plants that can survive without contact with the soil, known as epiphytes or perched plants. Orchids, bromeliads, lianas, ferns, mosses, and lichens are in this category. Dense, climax forest has a compact, several-layered canopy that allows little light to penetrate to the ground. The forest floor, therefore, is often relatively free of undergrowth and usually supports little in the way of large animal life. The forest canopy, however, will provide a home for a diversity of birds, insects, arboreal mammals and other animals that may exceed the great diversity of plant species.

Rain forests that have been opened up, either by natural causes or human activities, quickly grow into a dense, second-growth successional forest, the "impenetrable jungle" of tropical travelers. The prevalence of such dense, second-growth jungle in today's tropics indicates the extent of human disturbance. Similar jungles occur naturally on the edges of natural clearings, such as stream courses. Since most explorers in the lowland tropics traveled by boat, their accounts of the density of the vegetation were biased by what they saw at the edge of the rivers (Fig. 24).

Tropical rain forest soils develop under the canopy of trees, and are enriched by the continual addition of rapidly decaying leaves and litter. The high rainfall and temperatures, however, favor rapid oxidation of organic matter and leaching of minerals from the soil in areas from which the forest has been cleared. Tropical soils therefore require careful treatment and protection if they are to be maintained in agricultural use. Many of them are poorly suited to agriculture.

Temperate zone writers, in describing the tropics, often overemphasize the importance of the lowland rain forests, since these are the most spectacular and in many ways the most different of the various tropical biotic communities. However, the tropics have a greater variety of biotic communities than all other areas on earth. High on tropical mountains we encounter coniferous forests resembling those of the temperate zone, oak forests similar to those in the eastern United States, as well as purely tropical vegetation such as the puña and paramo of the higher mountains, which are unlike the vegetation of temperate lands (Fig. 27).

Fig. 24. Tropical forest in Puerto Rico (U.S. Forest Service photograph).

In those tropical areas where a wet and dry season alternate, a different vegetation replaces the rain forest in the lowlands. This, the raingreen or monsoon forest, is deciduous, the trees shedding their leaves during the dry season. In still drier regions a thorn forest or thorn scrub will replace monsoon forest. With increasing aridity this, in turn, gives way to desert. Leslie Holdridge, working from Costa Rica, has listed 37 different major biotic communities that may occur in any tropical region that displays a wide range in rainfall and altitude.[8] Each of these communities is as distinct and recognizable as the major communities of temperate regions. Compared with the temperate zone, however, the tropics have been rarely studied. They represent a major area for future research.

Until recently, man's influence on the tropics and their biota was slight. With increasing density of human populations, however, and the spread of technology, no large tropical area is any longer secure from disturbance. Without a major effort to preserve representative tropical areas, it is likely that many of the more fascinating living communities on earth will disappear before we know very much about them.

# SAVANNA

A glance at a vegetation map of the world will show that large areas in both tropical and temperate regions are covered by vegetation that has not thus far been described in this chapter—savanna. Savanna, sometimes known as parkland or woodland grass in temperate countries, is vegetation consisting of scattered trees and shrubs, or groves and thickets, in an otherwise grass-covered region (Figs. 25, 26). It is of natural occurrence along the boundary of forest and grassland where local differences in climate or soil favor an interspersion of vegetation. In such situations also there is normally a greater variety and abundance of animal life than is to be found in either forest or grassland.

Unlike forest or grassland there is no climate or soil that typifies savanna regions, although much savanna occurs within the region characterized by raingreen tropical forest or thorn forest. The great expanse of savanna over the surface of the earth is now believed to be caused largely by the activities of man and his domestic animals. Man seems to prefer interspersion of vegetation and creates it wherever he goes. Fire and grazing have been techniques used to open the forest and let the grassland enter. Grazing, irrigation, and planting are techniques for spreading woody vegetation into otherwise grassy areas.

The tropical savannas are the home of the great game herds that

Fig. 25. Savanna. Scattered oak trees interspersed with annual grasses in California (U.S. Forest Service photograph).

Fig. 26. Scrub savanna in Rhodesia, showing effects of heavy browsing by elephants.

once roamed widely in Africa and Asia and are still to be found in areas where they have been protected. The enormous variety of wild mammals in the tropics of Africa has long attracted attention. Twenty or more species of large grazing and browsing mammals from elephants to antelope may occur in a single area, each adapted to feeding on or otherwise using different species of plants, or different kinds of vegetation. In addition to these larger creatures a variety of smaller mammals, or predators, and a profusion of species of birds and other kinds of animals will occur.[4]

## AQUATIC ECOSYSTEMS

The water surfaces of the earth occupy over 70 per cent of the total world area and support a great variety of living things. However, since they are much more uniform than land areas in conditions favorable or unfavorable to life, they are not as amenable to classification. Classifications of aquatic environments are frequently based on major climatic differences, the amounts of dissolved chemicals, size and relative permanency of the body of water, and the depth of the water relative to the depth of light penetration. The greatest diversity of life is usually found on the edges or interfaces of land and water, the intertidal regions of seacoasts and estuaries, since here the widest range of physical environments will be encountered. By contrast, the open ocean is relatively homogeneous and shows much less diversity in forms of life.[11]

Classification and characteristics of aquatic environments are discussed in Chapter 10. It is worth noting at this point, however, that the range in productivity of aquatic environments is as great as that to be encountered on lands. The open oceans have sometimes been equated with the world's deserts in supporting and producing relatively little life. Cold fresh-water lakes are also relatively barren. By contrast, warm ponds and estuaries teem with life and are the aquatic counterparts of warm humid forest areas on land.

## COMPLEXITY AND SIMPLICITY

The terrestrial biotic regions of the earth show the effects of gradients that exist in climate. Tropical rainforest climates support the most complex and varied plant and animal life. However, moving out in the tropics along a gradient of decreasing rainfall or increasing evaporation, one would encounter communities that are less complex in which the numbers of species of plants and animals decrease to reach a lowest point in the tropical deserts. Similarly, moving north from the lowland rain-forest climate of the tropics along a temperature gradient, we would pass through subtropical rain forests, temperate rain forests, boreal forests, and tundra. Along this line also one passes from the most complex to the least complex biotic community, and the number of species of plants and animals would also decrease along this gradient. Thus, in the boreal forests we find the single species, white spruce, as a lone dominant in great areas of Canada and Alaska.

Within each climatic region, the climax communities will represent, usually, the most complex communities that the climate and geology of the region can support; but the climaxes themselves are more simple and less varied in regions where climatic or geological factors are strongly limiting.

Complexity appears to be accompanied by stability. Tropical forest communities are usually stable communities. They are relatively resistant to change. The numbers and arrangements of species within them vary little from month to month or year to year. By contrast, simple communities, whether of tundra or desert, are subject to regular and often violent changes in the relative abundance of species. The fluctuations of lemmings, a small Arctic rodent, are a legendary example of the instability of tundra populations. The changes in abundance of jackrabbits or mice in arid regions are well known. In the boreal forest, insect pests or diseases sometimes wipe out hundreds of square miles of trees. Locust plagues in dry regions do enormous damage. Similar outbreaks are virtually unknown in humid tropical communities, except where man has intervened.

Man seeks to simplify the complex so that he can manage it. He depends for his livelihood on foods grown in artificially created, simplified ecosystems. Such simplication, however, can be dangerous, since it sets in motion all of the factors that contribute to instability in the normally simple communities of more rigorous natural environments. In the humid tropics, the presence of a great variety of naturally occurring species guarantees competition between species, predation of one species on another, parasitic relations between species, and other complicated interspecies relationships that keep each population under control and prevent any single species population from either increasing or decreasing greatly. When these interspecific controls are removed, as when a plantation of bananas, cacao, or oil palms is established, there is little to keep the pests or parasites that feed on these agricultural crops from becoming abundant. Similarly, in drier or colder regions, simplification of natural communities also permits the natural enemies of the introduced crop plants to flourish; however, climate offers some periodic control on the abundance of these species.

Plagues and pests have harried man through history, destroying his crops and forcing him to engage in various forms of chemical or biological warfare in his own protection. Unless skilfully employed, however, such activities can make the situation worse, creating a more simple, less stable, more readily threatened system than the one that was endangered in the first place.[14] This subject will be discussed in more detail in Chapter 6.

# BIOMASS AND PRODUCTIVITY

The gradients in complexity and stability that have been described also represent gradients in the mass of living material that a particular region will support (the *biomass*), and in the amount of new living material that can be produced each year (*productivity*). Tropical rain forests support the greatest biomass or *standing crop* of living material per acre or square mile of any naturally occurring community. Extremely dry or cold areas, deserts and tundra, vie for the distinction of supporting the lowest standing crop of living material per acre.[11]

The standing crop of animal life, however, does not follow the same gradient as that of vegetation. Drier tropical savannas support a greater biomass of animal life than do the humid rain forests. Temperate zone grasslands with highly fertile soils supported, before human disturbance, a higher animal biomass than the leached soils of temperate forest areas. These differences appear related to the relative ability of the soils to produce plant proteins essential to animal nutrition. Soils in more humid areas can naturally produce a great bulk of carbohydrates, but lack the chemical balance to supply the quantity of protein per unit of area that can be supplied by the relatively unleached soils of the drier savannas or grasslands. Human populations that live away from the seacoasts in humid tropical areas have difficulty in producing their protein needs. The crop plants of the humid tropics (yams, taro, cassava, and fruits) are poor suppliers of protein.

Natural productivity varies also with the climatic and geological factors that influence complexity. The tropical rain-forest regions, with year-round growing seasons, are capable of producing more living material per acre per year than temperate forest regions where climate is seasonally limiting to plant growth. Temperate forests, however, with adequate rainfall, produce more plant material per acre than grasslands where seasonal drought restricts plant growth.

Man has long had an interest in increasing productivity of both his plant crops and of his domestic animals. To some degree he has been able to improve on natural patterns through supplying nutrients, where these were in short supply, supplying water or providing shelter against climatic factors. However, the highest yield of any land-based crop in biomass gain per acre per year is in sugar cane grown in the humid tropics. In temperate regions, forest plantations are more productive in total biomass gain than are the grainfields that have replaced natural grasslands. In the Arctic, high crop production can only take place where soils and local climate can be modified, and in the desert only the presence of irrigation, which essentially creates a different local climate, makes possible abundant crop yields.

## BIOTIC REGIONS AS HABITATS FOR MAN

In this brief description of the major biotic regions, or ecosystems, of the earth, an attempt has been made to describe the physical and

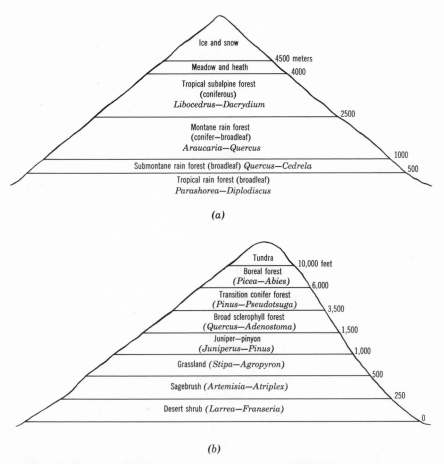

(a)

(b)

Fig. 27. Zonation of vegetation on mountain ranges. (a) Tropical mountains. (Data from Richards, 1952. Genera are typical of Malayan-New Guinea region.) (b) Temperate-zone mountains with vegetation typical of southwestern United States.

biotic setting in which man has operated throughout his history. Since man first appeared on earth, the same general biotic regions have been present, from tundra to tropical rain forest. The boundaries of these regions have shifted as climates have changed, but their general locations upon the earth have not been greatly modified in the time of man. In his development, man has first learned to adapt to the conditions of life within these biotic regions, avoiding those that were too rigorous. With increasing technology, he has learned to modify and change these regions to make them more or less favorable for his existence. Always, however, he has operated within the physical limits set by climate, soil, and vegetation. Even today's technology permits only minor modification of these physical limits. There are prospects of major modifications of climate. We already have means for modifying soils and vegetation. However, such changes are accompanied by risks unless we have an adequate understanding of their ecological consequences. When we re-place complex natural processes we must be prepared to exercise human skills if the environment is to be kept healthy and productive.

# Man's Record on the Earth

## THE UNCERTAIN PAST

**The time scale.** The length of time that man has been on earth is sometimes described as a "brief moment" in the earth's history. It depends on your viewpoint. If the age of the earth, over 3000 million years, is compared to an hour, man has been around for less than two seconds of earth time. If the years that higher forms of life have been present on earth, over 500 million, are compared to a day, man has been around for about 3 minutes of life's day. But, if we compare man's total time on earth to the duration of recorded human history, it appears that man has been around for an interminable period and that for most of it he has been doing little.

How long the species *Homo sapiens* has been active on this planet is in some doubt. It is fairly certain that the million years included in the Pleistocene or glacial epoch encompass all truly human activity. Mankind has carried out much of its physical and social evolution during a geological epoch unusual in the history of the earth. The glacial ages stand out as turbulent exceptions to the calm and stability that has prevailed during most of geological time. They are periods of unusual climate, unusual physiography, and abnormal instability of the earth's crust. During most of the eras of geology, the surface of the earth was characterized by continents of low relief, widespread inland seas, and by relatively uniform and mild climates.[2] The diversity of ecosystems present today and the consequent diversity of living organisms were not present. The significance of ice-age geography to human evolution was undoubtedly great. Its implications have yet to be explored. It is difficult, however, to think of man's history against a background of low-lying continents and uniform climate. It is equally difficult to envision the future of man in such a world.

For most of the story of man we have little record—a few fossils here and there. Written history goes back only a few thousand years.

What we call civilization, highly developed cultures that built cities and left remains in stone or brickwork, goes back about 6000 years. Before that we have various evidences in the ruins of old villages, in the cave dwellings, camp sites, and shell mounds in which the bones of man and his implements are mixed with the remains of his plant and animal associates. From such records, through comparison with the ways of existing human cultures, we can build up a theoretical picture of the past and begin to trace the probable interactions of man with his environment.

**The habitat of primitive man.** In considering the distant past it is instructive to consider man's physical nature, his limitations and requirements. For example, man was of necessity a generalized feeder, an omnivore. He lacks the fangs, claws, or speed of an effective carnivore and without weapons is poorly equipped for capturing and killing animal prey. He lacks also the dentition and digestive equipment required of effective herbivores, and thus cannot feed on blades of grass or the leaves and twigs of most trees and shrubs. He is forced to depend on those plant parts in which nutritive qualities are highly concentrated: fruits and seeds, bulbs and tubers. For animal protein, man must have acted as a scavenger, feeding on the remains of beasts that more efficient carnivores had killed, or as a minor predator, feeding on eggs and young of other animals or on the slower moving, dull-witted species that he was equipped to capture. Thus man's early culture is described as a food-gathering or collecting stage. It took a long while to advance beyond it. Throughout this period, adaptations to food-seeking alone must have restricted the human habitat to places where abundant supplies of obtainable food could be found.

Early man and his immediate ancestors were ground dwellers. Farther back in time an arboreal life had been abandoned for one on the ground. Through evolution the necessary adaptations to life in the tree-tops had disappeared. As a ground dweller, man was poorly adapted to life in heavily forested areas. In forests, fruits and seeds are produced high in the trees, and ground-dwelling animals are normally scarce. Man might venture into the forests in search of fruits which had fallen, but as a permanent home forests lack food. In known times men have shunned the forests as haunts of werewolves, hobgoblins, and ravenous beasts. Only recently have we learned to admire the primeval woods.

Man has high water requirements and lacks both the physiological and behavioral adaptations needed for life in arid areas. Thus in early times he was excluded from the deserts, except where he could enter along permanent water courses. The existing desert peoples, bushmen and aborigines, represent a long behavioral and cultural evolution of adaptations to a desert environment. On the grasslands of the earth, dominated by perennial grasses, there would be little food for early man. The plants produce little food palatable to man, and the animal life is mostly of the fast-running or burrowing types. Man was not equipped to capture either. Man also lacks the warm coat or the layers of fat required for animals that dwell in the colder places of the earth. Cold alone would have excluded him from the boreal forest, arctic tundra, and high mountains. It is only recently that he has learned to penetrate these areas.

Thus, from consideration of physical equipment alone, we have ruled out much of the earth's surface as an early habitat for man. We have left as his original home areas with tropical to subtropical climate with mixed vegetation types. It seems safe to describe early man as a creature of the "edges" or areas of vegetation interspersion where successional rather than climax vegetation dominates. Such edges are the homes of the game animals on which he relies for food or recreation today. In edge situations he could find the greatest variety of plant and animal life in available form. With the aid of his early tool, fire, he had a device for creating edges where none existed before—a device for setting back plant succession and favoring the production of useful food plants.

Some anthropologists believe that during much of the long period of time called the Paleolithic, or Old Stone Age, true men were restricted to the tropics and subtropics of Asia and Africa, or perhaps Africa alone.[10] With the glacial advances covering the northern regions, this confinement was more complete. With glacial retreats and warmer climates, man and his close relatives could move farther north, but the tropical areas remained the human center.

**Fire in the old stone age.** It is somewhat unrealistic to consider man without considering also his tools, equipment, and techniques. Man has always had the combination of hands, limbs, and eyes that would permit him to use tools, and a brain that would permit him to attempt to supplement his limited physical powers. From the earliest sites where human remains have been found, tools of one kind or another have been recovered. Associated with the remains of the prehuman ancestors of man also have been tools and evidence of the use of fire. With fire as an aid and a few simple stones and sticks to help in digging, chopping, and scraping, man could expand his occupancy beyond the area that his bodily equipment alone would permit him to occupy.

Because of recent emphasis on forest conservation, many think of fire as an enemy to be guarded against. The role of fire as a destroyer has been emphasized to the point where we forget its usefulness. For primitive man, fire meant keeping warm. It was a way of rendering otherwise unpalatable food into a tasty form. It could be used as an aid to hunting, as it is still used by primitive peoples in many lands. With fire game animals could be driven into traps or over cliffs, or the smaller forms could be caught in it, partly burned, and thus added to the larder. With the use of fire for hunting must have come the realization that fire modifies vegetation and creates successional types more favorable for human foraging than the original climax. Thus the Indians learned that fire in the brush fields created areas of sprouting brush on which deer preferred to feed and where they could be readily stalked and killed. Fire starting in grassland could sweep into the forest, causing replacement of trees by shrubs which might yield berries or nuts useful for food. In the forest also, fire used at proper seasons and intervals could replace dense woods by grassy openings, creating that interspersion of woodland and glade which man today seems still to prefer.

It is difficult to know the full extent to which primitive man used fire. More and more evidence has accumulated, however, to indicate that preagricultural men, along with their farming successors, have had major effects upon their environment through burning, both deliberate and accidental. Certain major vegetation types are now considered to be fire types and thus most probably man-created types. The tropical savanna, of which the African big game country is typical, is believed to be largely a product of repeated burning, which opened up monsoon and thorn forest and pushed back the edges of the rain forests. The process of creating savanna from forest still goes on in the tropics. The chaparral of mediterranean climates is thought to be a fire type, which would tend toward evergreen forest in the absence of burning. Some believe that most of the world's grasslands are products of man's use of fire.[30,33] Thus, it is widely accepted that certain major grassland areas were maintained by repeated burning. The former prairie peninsula which pushed eastward from Iowa to Illinois in an otherwise forested region is an example.

The probability that man from early times has been modifying environments with fire gives cause for thought when one seeks "natural" areas. The American scene when European man first arrived was one shaped by the activities of the Indians over tens of thousands of years. In the absence of all human interference, desirable vegetation of so-called natural types may sometimes disappear.

**Environmental limits and primitive man.** Even with the aid of fire and simple stone tools, primitive man was limited in his spread by the availability of habitat suited to his needs. Man in a primitive state was not adapted to a nomadic life and was therefore restricted to a limited "home range" within areas of suitable habitat. In such an area he would be dependent on the productivity of limited sources of food. Good growth years when wild plants put out abundant fruit and seed would allow a tribe to thrive and increase. Poor years when wild crops failed would bring famine. The limits set by the environment would be enforced strictly. If a tribe grew in numbers beyond what the local food supply could support, the excess must either emigrate or perish. For hundreds of thousands of years, therefore, the numbers of men were balanced against limited wild food resources, which could at best support only a sparse population.

Each new idea, each tool or cultural trait that was developed by man would make new resources available. With improved stone axes tall shrubs and small trees could be chopped down, and larger trees girdled and killed. With improved digging tools roots and tubers could be obtained more readily, and burrowing rodents perhaps captured. But ideas and changes came slowly, and for long periods it appears that little progress was made. During the time when the glaciers were making their last southward advance, ten to twenty thousand years ago, the rate of progress began to accelerate, and it has continued to pick up speed through the present time (Table 2).

During the later part of the Paleolithic period man became highly skilled at hunting and developed effective spear-throwing devices and other weapons, which enabled him to obtain food from the great herds of big game that were then present. He moved northward to the very edges of the ice sheets in his hunting pursuits and out into the grassland areas of the world. Before or during this time he extended his area to include all of the continents of the earth. Early human records in North America are of men who had attained a high degree of hunting skill. The efficient hunting techniques opened up a new food resource for man's exploitation and undoubtedly permitted a marked increase in his numbers.

Following the great expansion of the hunting cultures came a period known as the Mesolithic. The ice sheets were by then retreating northward, and forests were advancing in their wake. For unknown reasons there were marked declines in the numbers of big game animals, and many species became extinct. Man concentrated less on hunting and in its place put more emphasis on fishing and on more efficient gathering,

**Table 2. The Postglacial Time Scale***

| Date | Climatic Changes in Northern Europe | Old-World Cultural Stages | New-World Cultural Stages |
|---|---|---|---|
| 10,000 B.C. | Last glacial stage (Würm-Wisconsin ice) | Late Paleolithic hunting cultures (Cro-Magnon, etc.) | |
| 9,000 B.C. | Retreat of the glaciers (Preboreal period, cold dry) | Mesolithic fishing, hunting, collecting cultures | |
| 8,000 B.C. | | | Hunting cultures established (Folsom Man, etc.) |
| 7,000 B.C. | | ?Agricultural beginnings | |
| 6,000 B.C. | Boreal period (Warm dry) | | |
| 5,000 B.C. | Atlantic period (warm moist) | Neolithic agriculture established and spreading | |
| 4,000 B.C. | | | |
| 3,000 B.C. | | Beginnings of civilization (Egyptian—Sumerian) | |
| | | Neolithic agriculture in northern Europe | |
| 2,000 B.C. | | | American agricultural beginnings |
| | Subboreal period (colder dry) | Babylonian Empire | |
| | | Invasions: Aryans to India; Medes and Persians to S.W. Asia and Mesopotamia | |
| 1,000 B.C. | | Rise and flowering of Greek civilization | |
| B.C.–A.D. | | | Early Mexican and Mayan civilizations |
| | Sub-Atlantic period (cool moist) | Roman empire | |
| | | Invasions: Goths, Huns | Decline of Mayans |
| | | Rise of Islam | |
| 1,000 A.D. | | Norsemen to America | |
| | | Mongol and Tartar invasions | Aztecs and Incas |
| | | Voyages of discovery and colonization by Europe | |
| 2,000 A.D. | | Industrial revolution and modern period | |

* Based on data from Flint (1947), Johnson (1955), Zeuner (1950), and others.

**60**

preparation, and storage of wild plant foods. More permanent village sites developed on lake and sea shores where food resources were most abundant. In these places, with the relatively stable food supply provided by his fisheries, man acquired the leisure for thought and experimentation that made possible his greatest cultural advance, the development of agriculture.

The effects of the food-gathering and hunting stages of human culture on the environment can only be surmised. If seems likely that major changes in vegetation took place through the use of fire. Perhaps also man hastened the extinction of some animal species by his persistent hunting; however, the major cause of extinctions must be related to more general environmental changes. In all, man's early influence on the earth can be regarded as benign. Although far-reaching changes may have occurred, they were in the direction of making the earth a more suitable home for man. Destructive changes that reduce basic resources and injure the capacity of the earth to provide for man were to come with later cultural developments. For Paleolithic man, conservation problems did not exist, except the difficult one of preserving himself in a vast and often hostile and dangerous world. Nevertheless man through his use of fire had left his old position as a mere animal member of a biotic community and had become, in the words of Carl Sauer, an "ecological dominant," an organism that dominates a community and modifies the conditions of life for all other organisms within.[31]

## NEOLITHIC MAN AND AGRICULTURE

**Origins of domestication.** Perhaps the most important change in the history of man came with the domestication of plants and animals and the rise of the agricultural way of life. Some group of Mesolithic fishermen and food gatherers made the initial discoveries and opened a new period in human history. This period, because it was also associated with new and improved types of stone tools, is known as the Neolithic, or New Stone Age. Domestication of plants was perhaps a gradual development. Man's normal interest in food would lead to the focusing of his attention on the plants which seemed best to provide it. Slowly he must have learned the techniques of favoring their natural reproduction through fire or clearing. Eventually he acquired the idea of carrying them with him, preparing the ground, and planting them. It would seem a small change to make at the time, but its results affected the entire world. Through domestication man learned to channel the energy and nutrients of an ecosystem in directions of his own choosing to produce his needs.

The earliest methods of agriculture are believed by some to be those that made use of vegetative reproduction of plants—the dividing of

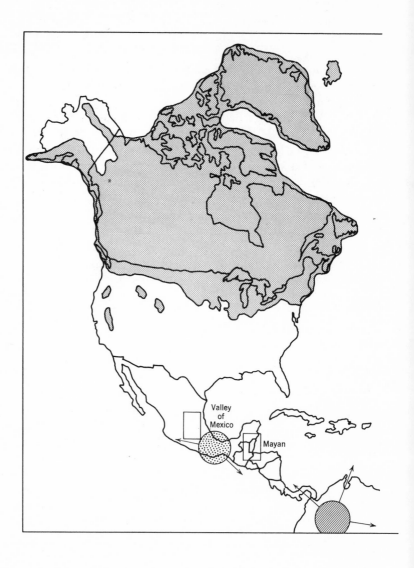

the parent plant through stem cuttings, or separation of the parts of a bulb, tuber, or rhizome, and the planting of these separate parts. The homeland of agriculture is thought to be the monsoon lands around the head of the Bay of Bengal in eastern India, Burma, and Thailand (Fig. 28). Here are to be found the wild ancestors of many cultivated

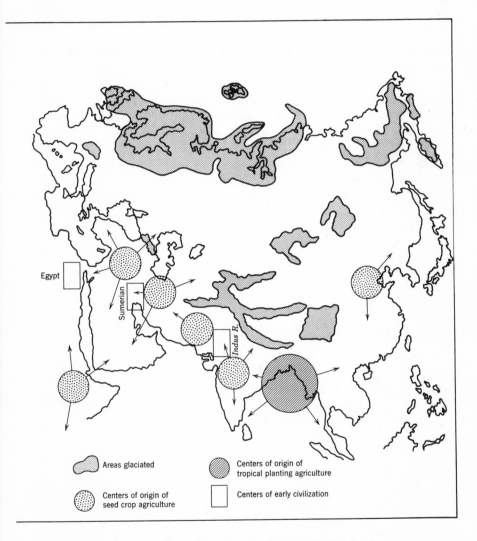

Egypt

Sumerian

*Indus R.*

Areas glaciated

Centers of origin of seed crop agriculture

Centers of origin of tropical planting agriculture

Centers of early civilization

Fig. 28. Map showing relationship of areas glaciated during the ice ages to areas in which agriculture and civilization had their beginnings [data from Flint (1947), Sauer (1952), and Wissman, *et al.* (1956)].

plants, and here too agriculture is known to have a long and stable history.[31,35,16] Perhaps the early domestic plants were related to the present-day root crops of this region, yams, taro, and the like. In this area of alternating dry and wet tropical climate the original agriculture must have centered on wooded uplands, where the soils are light and readily worked with simple hand tools. Early agricultural practice was probably similar to that still maintained in tropical forests. A forest area would be cleared through cutting or girdling of the trees; the cleared vegetation burned; and the ashes used to fertilize the soil. In these openings, cuttings, seedlings, and tubers would be planted. Following a brief period of use, yields would start to decline, and the area would be abandoned in favor of a freshly cleared and burned plot. The original clearing would then revert to native vegetation. Such a shifting, forest-clearing system of agriculture is called today *ladang* in southeast Asia and *milpa* in tropical America.[1,14] It is well adapted to tropical forest lands, as long as the pressure of human population is low and each cleared area has time to revert to forest and have its fertility restored following agricultural use.

In the southeast Asia region the early agriculturalists are also believed to be the domesticators of animals, first the dog, later the pig, and then domestic fowls. All were household or village animals, perhaps kept as much for pets as for food. None were grazing or herding animals.[31]

From its original home, the practice of planting spread throughout the tropics of the Old World and into the Pacific islands, carried by emigrants or passed from tribe to tribe. Not all adopted it; some maintained the old food-gathering ways or kept primarily to hunting or fishing. Geographical and cultural barriers prevented a complete diffusion. Australia, for example, settled by hunters and food gatherers, remained cut off from the flow of agricultural knowledge until recent centuries. There is some reason to believe, however, that the early planting practices and domestic animals spread by one route or another across the Pacific into the tropics of the Americas, for in both regions many of the customs and domesticated species are the same.[31]

**Seed crops and the western world.**[31,35] Westward from the supposed home of agriculture, in areas where the climate was too cold or dry to support the tropical root crops, the agricultural system typical of the western world had its beginnings. In this region, from western India to Ethiopia and the Mediterranean Sea, early farmers took an interest in the seed plants, particularly in the larger-seeded annual grasses.[31,35] Here again the process of domestication must have been gradual. Originally various grasses were cultivated, later through selection attention was focused on the larger-seeded, harder grains, wheat and barley, which became and remain staple food crops of the western world.

In the west, as in the east, upland wooded areas probably provided the first agricultural lands. Grassland soils were too heavy and the sod too tightly woven with a network of roots and stems to be cultivated with simple hand tools. The deep soils of the river bottoms may also have presented difficulties for early cultivation. The forest clearings in the west, in lands of mediterranean or wooded-steppe climates, probably tended to be more permanent than those in the tropics, for the soils that develop under low rainfall are little leached and therefore less quickly exhausted of fertility. The recovery of native vegetation is also more slow. Early agriculture was undoubtedly rainfall agriculture, with the planting of seed in the rainy season of early spring and the harvest in the dry, late summer or fall. The shift in emphasis in the west from vegetative planting to seed sowing brought the need for different cultivation techniques. To sow seed effectively and easily it is expedient to lay large areas bare of native vegetation; to promote rapid growth more intensive cultivation of the soil is helpful.

Western agriculture spread widely from its original center into other temperate and semiarid regions, northward into Europe, southward in Africa, and eastward across the steppe region of Asia to China (Fig. 28). In many areas an intermixture of planting and sowing developed. Thus, in southeast Asia many of the planting peoples learned to use rice, a cereal grain, although it was usually planted after the seed had sprouted rather than sown as seed on the ground. Similarly, in the Mediterranean region, some plants were reproduced by cuttings or divisions of roots and tubers. By the middle of the Neolithic, agriculture was widespread throughout the Old World.

The peoples who first cultivated the cereal grains are thought be those who first domesticated the grazing herd animals, the goat, sheep, ass, and later the cow and horse. These domestic animals, long associated with western agriculture, helped to shape its progress. With the invention of the plow, the combination of oxen and plow began to create a new agricultural pattern, the regularly plowed field, and also made possible the cultivation of the heavier soils of the river bottom lands. In the beginnings the herd animals were closely associated with the farm lands. Abandoned croplands may have provided the early grazing land. However, in western Asia with its dry, steppe grassland and shrub-covered hills there was available a broad area well suited to providing livestock with forage. As populations increased and the agricultural lands became more intensively and permanently cultivated, it became necessary to take herds farther afield for pasturing. Eventually a pastoral way of life, separate from the farm lands, developed. The new livestock herders at first may have practiced a shifting agriculture. Later, however, they came to depend upon their livestock and learned to despise the agricultural peoples. To the farm lands they eventually returned as the barbarian, nomad conquerors.

Neolithic agriculture was a subsistence agriculture. The local fields supplied local needs, with little or no export or trading. In the better agricultural lands the former shifting tribal camps gave way to a settled, permanent village life. A close relationship formed between the new peasantry and the land that permitted a high degree of land care and agricultural stability. A truly human landscape appeared for the first time on earth. Cleared fields and croplands are no part of the wild, natural scene. Man for the first time obtained, through knowledge of crops and croplands, a dependable degree of control over natural forces. There was a wholeness to this Neolithic way of living which still has a strong, nostalgic appeal to man. Each person became familiar with all of the operations and techniques needed to support himself and his family and was not dependent upon organized society to supply his needs. Admittedly life was sometimes insecure; drought, flood, or invader could sweep over and destroy the village or its lands. Perhaps it was this insecurity that contributed to the next major development in the human story.[26]

## CIVILIZATION

**The rise of western civilization.** When the Neolithic farmers began to settle in the river basins, a new way of life became possible. Here on deeper, richer soils, high crop yields could be obtained and the surpluses stored. These surpluses took away the threat of starvation and permitted time and leisure. Fewer people working on the richer soils could produce enough for all, so that some people could devote their attention to more specialized tasks. New agricultural tools were invented, and techniques of mastering the flood waters that rose each year in the river basins were improved. With more efficient agricultural tools and the new techniques of irrigation farming, still greater yields could be produced. With water available through the year, more than one crop could be obtained from the land in each year. Greater yields meant more leisure and more time for specialization. Villages grew to towns and towns to cities. A new development called civilization appeared.

The cities became the homes of specialized workers freed from the necessity of tending to the land. They brought the opportunity for the farmer to trade his surplus crops for the tools or pleasures that the city could offer. With the cities also came in time a central government, temples and palaces, armies, census takers, tax collectors, and other agencies of the state. On the land itself this resulted in a reorganization that was to have far-reaching effects. Initially it started as a funneling of surpluses into the city to be exchanged for the products of the city. But as the power of the city grew, as armies were formed and new lands conquered, there came increasing regimentation of the peasants to provide for the support of the new agencies. Large areas were reduced to the status of agricultural colonies, which sent crops, timber, and livestock to the imperial centers. The old balance, characteristic of the village way of life, between people and resources was destroyed as increasing demands were made on the farms to provide for city populations who had no contact with the land or realization of its needs. Emphasis on the farms changed from varied subsistence crops to specialized crops raised for sale and export and eventually to monoculture, the production of one kind of crop year after year on the same land. In return the farmers received a variety of material which they could not have produced on their farms. More important, however, the cities offered one thing which the old village way of life could not offer—security. Cities brought armies to defend the lands against the sudden sweep of barbarian invaders, slaves to improve and maintain irrigation works which protected against drought and flood, and temples where the priests could intercede with stronger gods than the village could offer for protection of the lands and the people. Thus, for security and a degree of material enrichment the old independent village way of life was sacrificed to the new organization of civilizaion.[26]

**Civilization and land failure.** It has long been a matter of surprise and concern to travelers in the homelands of western civilization that so many of the great cities and centers of ancient times are now desolate ruins located in desert lands incapable of providing for more than a few impoverished herdsmen (Fig. 29). It has been obvious to all who have studied the situation that the land has changed, become more desertlike, since the days of Babylon, Alexander, or imperial Rome. To document this change are some written records that describe the wealth of now impoverished lands. In other places the ruins speak for themselves; no city could be supported now where the ancient cities flourished. To account for this change in the land the idea of climatic change has been advanced.

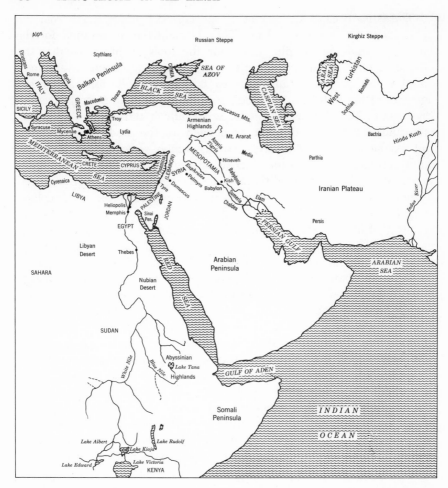

Fig. 29. Location of ancient civilizations in the Mediterranean and Western Asian regions (from various sources).

For a time it was believed widely that the glacial periods in northern Europe and Asia were accompanied by widespread pluvial periods in the now arid lands of the Asian-African desert belt. Ellsworth Huntington[18] and others have advanced the theory that the decline of civilization in parts of Asia and Africa was associated with a gradual dessication of these regions, the result of a change from a pluvial to a warmer, drier climate. That climatic changes have certainly occurred, are still taking place, and have their effects upon man's use of the land can no longer be disputed.[2,32] However the picture is by no means as simple

Fig. 30. Upper photograph: Mediterranean woodland in California. Lower photograph: Mediterranean chaparral in California. Vegetation similar to this once covered the now barren slopes of the Mediterranean lands of Asia and Africa (U.S. Forest Service photographs).

as once was supposed. The bulk of the data now indicate that there have been a great number of climatic changes in the areas of the ancient civilizations but there has been no one-way trend toward warmer, drier climates since early historical times. Man, and not the climate, must be held accountable for the encroachment of desert upon the formerly fertile lands of the old empires (Fig. 30).

The Nile River and the Tigris-Euphrates rivers provide a contrast which throws light on the question of land deterioration in the region where western civilization began. The agricultural lands of Egypt, irrigated by the flood waters of the Nile, have been farmed for at least 6000 years and yet remain productive. Egypt is still a densely populated center of civilization. By comparison the lands of Mesopotamia now support only a fraction of their former population. Yet these lands were the first home of civilization and since Sumerian times have supported a series of great empires. A look at the headwaters of the two river systems provides part of the answer to the differences between these regions. The headwaters of the Nile lie in the swamps of Uganda and the high mountains of Ethiopia (Fig. 29). Until recent times these headwaters were remote from the main stream of western history. Native populations and livestock numbers were kept low by the pressure of an adverse environment. The Nile has had its annual flood throughout history, fed by the monsoon rains from the Indian Ocean. It has carried a load of silt and humus which when deposited each year upon the farming lands of Egypt has added to their fertility. However, until recent times the silt load of the Nile has been relatively light and manageable.[7]

The headwaters of the Tigris and the Euphrates lie in the highlands of Armenia, in areas that in the past have supported high populations of people and higher numbers of sheep and goats. They have been in the path of wave after wave of migrations of nomads from the plains of Asia. They have been subjected, therefore, to all of the pressures which hillside farming and overgrazing by livestock can bring to bear. They have been deforested to provide timbers for the growing cities or to provide new grazing land for flocks and herds. The erosion that has resulted has caused an ever-increasing silt load to be carried by the Tigris and Euphrates. In Sumerian times the indications are that the silt load was manageable. Subsequent empires have had an increasingly difficult task in controlling it. Armies of laborers and slaves have been kept busy keeping the irrigation canals free of silt. The silt has filled in the Persian Gulf to a distance of 180 miles out from where the rivers emptied in Sumerian times[9] (Fig. 31). As long as strong empires centered in the lands between the two rivers the canals were kept open. The final breakdown came with the Mongol and Tartar invasions in the thirteenth and fourteenth centuries A.D. These nomadic horsemen from Asia were interested in destroying permanently the powerful Arab states which had opposed them. They destroyed the irrigation canals and killed or carried off the inhabitants of the region. Until recently, the task of coping with silt and rebuilding the canal system was too much for the peoples who remained in the area. The silt-laden flood waters carried soil, without interruption, from the highlands to the sea.[9]

In the country of Lebanon is other evidence of what has happened to these lands. Here the Phoenicians founded their maritime empire and built the greatest navy of their day from the timber that grew on their mountains. On these mountains grew the famous cedars of Lebanon that helped to shape the Egyptian cities and were used in the temple of Solomon. Cutting of the timber started the trouble. Regeneration of the forest was prevented when the cleared lands were heavily grazed by goats and sheep. Only in a few protected spots do cedar groves remain, and forests of any kind are no longer extensive. Many formerly forested hills are now incredibly barren and almost devoid of soil (Fig. 32). From their appearance it would be thought that the climate was now too dry to support trees. Yet, where soil remains, in the vicinity of the ancient groves, the cedars continue to reproduce and grow.[23]

**Effects of Mediterranean land-use practices.** Much has been written of land destruction in Mediterranean countries which cannot be reviewed here. Because the damage has been so spectacular it is well to review

Fig. 31 and chapter opening. Ruins of the city of Kish, once a capital of the Sumerian civilization. These ruins were excavated from silt and sand, erosion debris which covered the once populous city. The barren lands of this area now support only a fraction of the former number of people (photograph by Soil Conservation Service, U.S. Dept. Agric.).

Fig. 32. Lebanon hill country. Vegetation was destroyed and erosion removed the soil from most of these hills. Only where terraces were built does enough soil remain to support agriculture (photograph by Soil Conservation Service, U.S. Dept. Agric.).

the causes. At the heart of the difficulty is the nature of the environment. These are lands of mediterranean scrub and forest, grassland, and desert, characterized by low rainfall, warm summer temperatures, and long dry seasons when desert winds move all but the best-protected soil. Vegetation growth and land recovery following the clearing of vegetation is slow. The soils are relatively rich in nutrients and therefore encourage permanent rather than shifting agriculture. To such an environment came a cereal-grain agriculture which laid bare the land for part of the year to the blowing winds and at best covered it with crops which offered much less protection to the soil than the native vegetation. To make matters worse, the farmers of this region developed a system that was intended to conserve soil moisture but that exposed the land to serious erosion. The system involved leaving an area of cropland fallow for one year out of two. During this fallow period the soil was closely cultivated but not sown to crops. Rain falling on this land in winter soaked in, and in the dry season the finely cultivated layer on top broke up the channels through which water would have evaporated from the soil and eliminated weeds which would have drawn on the soil moisture. Water loss from the deeper layers of the soil during the dry season was therefore slowed down, and extra moisture preserved in the soil. This made possible a better growth of crops in the following year when the land was again sown. Although serving some purpose in conserving soil moisture, this "dust mulch" on top of the soil led to serious loss of soil when dry winds swept across its surface or when late rains caused heavy runoff from the fields. In general, then, the agricultural system developed in this region did not effectively prevent soil erosion. Where sloping hill lands were farmed without special precaution, soil loss would be rapid (Fig. 33).

Fig. 33. Terraced slopes in Syria. Where terraces have not been neglected this hill country has supported agriculture over thousands of years (photograph by Soil Conservation Service, U.S. Dept. Agric.).

A second cause of land deterioration was the activities of the grazing animals. Extensive rangelands favored their spread and encouraged pastoralism as a way of life. Unfortunately the herdsmen did not learn that an area of rangeland can stand only a limited amount of grazing pressure. Continued heavy grazing by herd animals, particularly where concentrated in large numbers year after year, led to disappearance of the plant cover and the exposure of the bare and trampled ground. Erosion followed.

Demands for more grazing land, the need for wood for fuel, and the desire for timber for ships and cities led to the cutting of the forests, the third cause of land deterioration. Regrowth of the cutover lands was prevented by heavy browsing of sprouts and seedlings by livestock and by continued cutting for fuel wood. Again the soil was left bare, and without protection it washed or blew away. Deserts spread into former scrub, forest, and steppe areas, and within the original deserts the sparse vegetation gave way to bare rock or moving dunes (Fig. 34).

It should be pointed out, however, that all was not destruction and damage in these homelands of civilization. Man learned from his mistakes and began to develop systems that would correct them. The Phoenicians can be remembered for their poor management of forest and range, but they should also be remembered as people who, among their

Fig. 34. Ruins of a Syrian city that was inhabited in Roman times. The eroded hills in this area can support only a few hundred people in place of the previous thousands (photograph by Soil Conservation Service, U.S. Dept. Agric.).

Fig. 35. Terraced vineyards in southern France (photograph by Soil Conservation Service, U.S. Dept. Agric.).

many contributions, developed the techniques of terracing hillside farm lands to prevent soil loss. Terraced farm lands in southern France, still in production today, are thought to date back to Phoenician times[23] (Fig. 35). The Greeks, although known for poor management of flocks and forest, contributed the ideas of manuring and crop rotation to agricultural practice. The Romans, with great engineering ability, developed irrigation practices to a marked degree and made many contributions to scientific management of farming lands.[17] All of these ideas and techniques later flowed northward into Europe to form the foundation for sound land management.

## CHANGES IN TROPICAL LANDS

**The tropical environment.** Before following western agriculture into Europe and the Americas another look is needed at the area where agriculture had its beginnings, the tropics. In southeast Asia the nature of the tropical environment and the agricultural practices that developed combined to give form to a remarkably stable type of land use.

In tropical forests the deep-rooted trees go far into the earth for their nutrients. Minerals are thus brought into the tree structures and as leaves fall or trees decay are added to the surface soil. Here the warm temperatures favor rapid decay and incorporation of the organic material into the soil, where it is picked up by surface roots and returned to the vegetation. Thus soil nutrients are kept in continual circulation within the complex forest food chains.

When tropical forests are cleared and the fallen vegetation is burned, nutrients locked up in the plants are returned to the soil. Here they become exposed to two destructive forces: high temperatures which favor rapid oxidation of the organic matter and heavy rainfall which washes away the mineral salts. Thus tropical forest lands cleared for agriculture have a short life if sown to shallow-rooted crops. The remaining soil nutrients are quickly depleted, yields decline, and the land must be abandoned. Fortunately, if the area is not too badly depleted, the natural cover of deeper-rooted trees and shrubs quickly invades this abandoned land and restores the old channels for returning nutrients from deeper layers to the surface soil.

**Shifting and permanent tropical agriculture.** To the tropical environment the farming practices of southeast Asia were well adapted. Clearing of the forest was seldom complete, and cover was left to screen the soils. A variety of root crops, shrubs, and trees were planted which in turn provided additional soil cover. Usually the crops had different ripening periods so that there was no distinct harvest season followed by exposure of bare ground. Cultivation of the soil with hand tools left no long furrows of upturned soil exposed to sun and rain. Abandonment and return to forest in the ladang system prevented permanent damage. The absence of herding and grazing animals in most areas prevented the pressure on watershed vegetation with the consequent erosion and flooding that has destroyed farm lands elsewhere. So long as populations were low in relation to the available land area, the amount of damage done through land use was negligible. However, with expanding population pressure, the continued existence of climax rain forest is threatened by the too rapid spread of forest clearing.

In many parts of the tropics shifting ladang agriculture has given way to more permanent types. These have been chiefly of two kinds: the permanent village garden and the irrigated field. In the vicinity of many of the villages the practice developed of keeping certain areas in permanent cultivation, a practice which gave a food supply close to home when travel to more distant forest clearings was restricted. Such village gardens were carefully tended. Emphasis on a variety of crops has kept cover on the ground. Exhaustion of fertility has been prevented by the regular addition of manure from village animals and people, combined with crop remains and other plant debris. Constant care given to such gardens has kept them permanently productive despite the handicaps of tropical climate.[1,14]

The greatest yields in tropical lands, and the basis for the crop surplus that has permitted the rise of cities, have come with the farming of the deep soils of valleys and delta areas. This was made possible by the development of the hydraulic skills that permitted control of rivers and runoff waters and their use in irrigation. On these rich lands the same care and attention that made possible the permanent village garden has been given to the soil. Over thousands of years such soils have remained productive.[1,14]

Land failure in the tropics has resulted from several types of pressure. The ladang or milpa system breaks down when populations grow too rapidly. Then the land does not receive the rest and regeneration it needs. It is farmed too long and returned to again before there is time for soil damage and fertility to be repaired. Soil depletion results. This is thought to be the reason for the collapse of the Mayan civilization in the American tropics which was supported by milpa agriculture. Extensive deforestation, resulting from demands for wood for fuel or construction, also takes place in the tropics where civilizations give rise to dense populations. This is thought to be a cause for the collapse of the ancient civilization of Ceylon. Here an extensive system of irrigation reservoirs and canals was destroyed by floods and silt washed from the deforested mountains.[7] Some of the most far-reaching land damage in eastern Asia has taken place in China and India where many bad features of both western and eastern agricultural systems were inherited and combined.[23]

# EUROPE AND THE NEW WORLD

**Western Europe and agricultural stability.** At the time when the early river-basin civilizations were beginning to appear in Mediterranean lands, the first Neolithic farming peoples were becoming established in western Europe. They brought with them the cereal-grain culture of western Asia and the domestic livestock associated with it. In Europe, however, they encountered a far different environment from that of the homeland of seed-crop agriculture. Europe was largely covered with dense, broad-leaved forest, except for clearings made by its earlier inhabitants and some naturally open areas. The climate was humid with rainfall moderately high and well distributed throughout the year. The soils were of the deciduous-forest variety, initially fertile and easy to work. The combination of soils, climate, and vegetation produced a durable environmental complex, much less subject to damage than those of the drier regions.

The usual pattern of primitive agriculture was followed in Europe. Forests were cleared, the plant debris burned, and seeds sown in the ash-enriched soil. Initially land clearing and abandonment probably went on at a nearly equal rate, with the abandoned clearings serving for a time as grazing land. Gradually, as populations grew a more stable pattern of agriculture emerged on the better soils. With forest vegetation predominant and no extensive areas of hill range to invite flocks and herdsmen, there was initially little opportunity for the development of pastoralism apart from agriculture. Thus from early times livestock were kept close to the farm lands, and the growing of feed for the stock became as important a part of farming as the growing of food for man. The presence of livestock close to the farm meant the regular addition of manure to the soil, and with this the organic content of the soil was replenished. On lands regularly pastured a grazing-resistant group of plant species developed which was able to support a high degree of livestock pressure without soil damage. As farming progressed northward in cooler regions, the wheat and barley of Mediterranean lands were replaced to a large extent by oats and rye, better adapted to the cooler climate. These were as often raised for hay crops as for grain.[8,11]

Agriculture changed little in Europe until Roman times. With Roman conquest or influence many of the farming practices developed by the higher cultures of the Mediterranean region spread to the croplands of western Europe. They proved better adapted to the new area than to their lands of origin.

While agricultural practices were developing, the heavy forests served as a barrier against too rapid extension of farming lands. As time passed and more efficient means of clearing forest land were discovered, a relatively sophisticated and conservative type of agriculture was applied to the new land. Crop rotation, alternating cereal grain, root or leaf crop, clover or grass pasture on the same area in successive years, was widely practiced and served to maintain the soil. There developed also the practices of using plant and animal manures and of liming to reduce acidity, and other fertilizing practices which helped to maintain soil nutrients. With time came the rise of a well-established European peasantry, deeply attached to the land and attentive to its needs. The result was an unusual pattern in world land-use history. Not only was erosion and loss of soil fertility widely prevented, but to a large extent the land was actually improved through use. A stable agriculture, adapted to soil and climate, was achieved.[8,11]

With the industrial revolution came the spread of European power and influence throughout the world. Western Europe became a great industrial center, importing raw materials from other lands. The great increase in European population that followed was not, therefore, supported entirely by the products of European soils. Had this been necessary it is doubtful that the land could have been so well maintained.

**Spanish colonies in America.** One of the regions on which Europe was to draw extensively for raw materials was the new world of the Americas. In pre-Columbian America a variety of cultural stages were to be found. In the Andes region of Peru and Colombia, the Incans had developed an advanced system of irrigation agriculture. An elaborate system of terracing conserved soil where mountain slopes were farmed. In the Valley of Mexico and elsewhere in Central and South America, civilizations had also arisen. Where these civilizations had resulted in heavy pressure on the land, there was to be found a record of agricultural failure and erosion, associated with the decline of the peoples who had caused it. In most of the Americas, however, civilization had not appeared. Many Indian tribes were still in a good-gathering stage of culture; some had become efficient hunters and fishermen; others had developed fairly effective agricultural practices. For most areas, Indian land-use practices were conservative; vegetation was modified, but soil preserved.

Into the Americans came two main streams of European culture: from the Mediterranean and from western Europe. The Spanish colonizers came from a land with a long history of disregard for conservation. Spain had been unusually plagued by overgrazing. An organization of Spanish sheep raisers, the Mesta, through special concession from the crown, had for many years overrun the country. Forests had been ruthlessly cut and burned to provide additional grazing land; vast herds of sheep had moved across the plateaus and hills to create desertlike conditions in wide areas.[28] To the American mainland, Spanish livestock came with Cortez and spread from Mexico northward to the United States in the sixteenth century. The horse, escaped from domestic herds, ran wild into the plains and prairies of North America, where the Indians soon learned its use. Spanish livestock spread into the dry grasslands along the desert margins where they became an agent operating to extend the desert borders. In the late eighteenth century, Spanish missions were established in California, and sheep, cattle, goats, and horses began to occupy the ranges of that state.

Where Spanish livestock traveled, they brought with them a plant complex from the Mediterranean region, a variety of annual weeds and grasses. In areas of favorable climate, such as California, these exotic annuals took hold and spread widely. Aided by uncontrolled livestock numbers, drought, and overgrazing, the new annual grasses and weeds so completely occupied the grassland ranges of this region that it has been difficult to determine the nature of the original vegetation.

Spain, however, was not interested in finding a new homeland for her people but in obtaining gold, silver, and other products of value from her new colonies. Spanish colonization was restricted to local areas of favorable climate and to mining centers. Over much of Latin America, the mountainous country and the vast tropical forest, the Indians concontinued to live in ways little modified from pre-Columbian times. Thus, Latin America in places today presents a pattern of land use strange to North American eyes, a combination of westernized population centers, around many of which the lands have been severely damaged because of the almost complete lack of conservation practices, and remote hinterlands supporting a sparse population or primitive peoples. The hinterlands, however, are becoming less remote and the area affected by dense populations is increasing.

**Western Europe and North America.** North of the Spanish colonies, settlers from western Europe poured into the United States and Canada in ever-growing numbers. Seeking a homeland, not a colony, their influence on the land was to be far reaching and permanent. Before the advancing tide of Europeans the Indians retreated and shrank in numbers, eventually to be confined to reservations in the less desirable lands. With a forgotten history of land use and abuse behind them the American settlers in a short space of time repeated every mistake that man has made since the first Neolithic farmer sank a digging stick into the ground. Land destruction that had taken millennia in the lands of Asia was matched in two short centuries in America.

Through the southern states went waves of settlers, clearing and burning the forests to plant corn and tobacco or, later, cotton. Their crops made great demands on the soil and offered it little protection Combined with careless husbandry, cotton and tobacco in particular were to leave a permanent mark on the American South. The soil was lost through erosion or impoverished through loss of fertility. This was to be reflected later in the impoverishment and malnutrition from which the people suffered. Only recently is the damage being repaired.

Farther north the early settlers accepted corn from the Indians but failed to take with it their methods of soil conservation. In the hands of westward-moving pioneers, corn planted in forest clearings led also to erosion and soil exhaustion. Fortunately, however, much of the north was settled by western Europeans skilled in farming. These people brought with them the mixed grain, clover, hog, and dairy-cattle husbandry from their homeland and found it well adapted to the similar soils and climate of the American north. With them a measure of permanent land care was provided.

Before the settler's axe much of the hardwood forest of the eastern United States disappeared (Fig. 36). North of the hardwood belt, the white pine forests of New England and the Lake States provided the resource base on which the American lumber industry was formed. Chopping their way across the top of the nation, the white pine loggers, with the destructive fires that followed in their wake, created a desola-

Fig. 36. Broad-leaved deciduous forest. Settlers from western Europe found the vegetation and soils in eastern America similar to what they had known at home (U.S. Forest Service photograph).

tion so impressive that the American public at last realized that resources even in a new continent are not inexhaustible. With that realization, at the end of the nineteenth century, the conservation movement in America had its beginnings. The process of slowly putting back together the land that had been so quickly taken apart was under way.


RECAPITULATION

In this brief summary of man's record on earth we have considered how man has sought to come to terms with his environment. He has looked for ways to obtain food, shelter, and other necessities for himself and his offspring and along with these to have a little leisure for creative work or simply for play. At times he has found them.

At first man was forced to adapt to his natural environment much as any other animal would, subject to the same strict controls. Later, with fire and simple tools he obtained a degree of mastery and could form for himself more suitable living areas. In these early days his influence was seldom destructive, but with each new advance came new problems and dangers.

When environments were first shaped with agricultural tools and man could depend for subsistence upon his farming skills, he obtained a high degree of control over nature and could harness cycles of energy and nutrient flow and put them to work producing the materials he required. If, however, through failure to adapt his techniques to the necessities of the environment he damaged or destroyed his lands, he perished. Fortunately he was most often preserved by his own ineffectiveness in bringing great changes. An early tropical farmer, clearing forest with fire and stone axes, could not create the bare exposed soil that would have invited disaster. By the time more efficient tools made this possible, he had learned certain lessons of living with tropical soils and had adapted his farming methods to them. At the worst, where he has too efficient for his own good and lands were damaged, the failure was local; adjoining peoples could learn by the mistake.

With civilization and its consequent specialization came the opportunity with new invention and discovery leading to greater control over the environment. The development of transportation and food-storage facilities made possible the support of local populations over bad years, when local lands had lost their productiveness. Thus, the pharaohs stored food in the fat years against the coming of the lean years, and the peoples were preserved. But a people protected by civilization against the hazards of nature could persistently misuse the land, despite droughts, floods, and other signs of danger that would cause an isolated group to perish or flee. More complete land destruction thus became a possibility. With the control of natural forces through the organization of civilization came the possibility of great enrichment but also of complete failure. Mesopotamia remained prosperous so long as its people were powerful enough to protect and maintain the irrigation system but failed completely when the canals were destroyed.

Even with civilization the amount of change or damage was limited so long as the land was exploited by hand tools or the power of domestic animals. A man clearing forest or brush land with a hand axe or cultivating with horse and plow has time to consider his activities and redress his mistakes. In the Old World, man had time to learn to live with his environment, study its weather cycles, and the peculiarities of its soils. He even learned in many areas the techniques of controlling his own numbers, so that he did not increase beyond the limits for which the land could provide. Where, for one reason or another, he failed to learn the lessons of the land, he disappeared, and only the desolate wastes remained. In much of the Old World, however, we find a pattern of land use that shows how man has fitted in with the natural framework of his habitat by learning to avoid its dangers and compensate for its lacks with cultural improvements. In such areas are often to be found remarkably charming human landscapes of farms and villages, pastures and woodlands, which blend with the natural scene as though a permanent part of it.

With the rise of industrial civilization came the greatest dangers. Equipped with the harnessed power of rivers, coal, petroleum, and the atom, armed with machines capable of doing the work of an army of men and horses, industrialized man is able to shape any environment into a landscape of his own choosing and channel its materials into an industrial network which can create for him a high degree of security and material enrichment. But, with these new powers and techniques has disappeared the opportunity for long periods of adjustment to nature through small errors, small failures, and new beginnings.

The settlement of the Americas and the other new lands was part of the new industrial achievement. American raw materials and crops went first to feed the growing industrial machine in Europe. Later, industry centered in America, and demands for raw material intensified. Throughout the world spread western influence, civilization, technology, and agricultural ways. With this spread there returned an old conservation problem, not serious since the Old Stonge Age, the problem of conserving man himself. Unique human cultures and the peoples that formed them disappeared or were incorporated by the engulfing flow of western industrial civilization.

When western man moved into the forests and fields of the new world and reinvaded the settled landscapes of the old, his new powers should have been tempered with sober judgment learned over centuries of experience with the land. That they were not has been evidenced by the far-reaching destruction of both nature and human culture. Too frequently observed is the new industrial landscape, often raw and ugly, at odds with the environment and at war with nature. Until industrial man, armed with powers greater than his ancestors could imagine, makes use of the wisdom which his ancestors so painfully acquired, he remains in peril. Like the gods of old, he can make the earth into a paradise if he so chooses, or he can destroy it.

# | 4 |

# The Conservation of Environments

In this book the traditional separation of conservation into its various fields has been, to a degree, respected. To develop an understanding of the problems of timber management, for example, it is useful to regard it separately. But it must be emphasized that this separation is artificial, that the management of forest for timber production cannot be carried out in isolation from the management of the same forests for wildlife, water, soil, range forage, natural areas, and recreation, and can only be conducted rationally with a view toward population distribution and growth in the nation and the world. What is done to one category of biotic resources influences them all. The demand for one particular use of an environment influences all other potential uses.

The approach to conservation, therefore, that holds the most hope for the future is an ecological approach, that takes into account the ecology of man. Each natural area, be it defined as a watershed, a vegetation and soil community, or in other terms, represents an ecosystem, a physical and biotic environment, with certain potentialities and certain problems. The objective of management should be to develop that area, or to protect it, in order to provide the greatest yield in improved *quality of living* for mankind. To consider a natural area merely as a source of range forage, wood products, wildlife crops, or a site for urban housing, is to emphasize only the quantitative aspects of environmental management. Such an emphasis has led to serious conflicts in the past and has failed to provide the quality of living that man requires.

An environmental approach to conservation implies that each broad natural region be regarded as an organic whole and developed to provide an optimum habitat for man. Looking at the spectrum of land and land-use patterns, ranging between highly industrialized cities at one extreme and empty wilderness at the other, we must seek to develop each area to express its fullest potentialities. Cities should no longer be ugly work centers, in which the economically unfortunate are forced to live a closed

and barren life and from which the more fortunate flee at every opportunity. Cities can be developed not only to provide the qualities of urban
living which are implied in the word "civilization" but also to combine
the lost values of rural beauty and natural scene. By proper planning,
cities can become places of charm and appeal to the human spirit in
which the dweller will consider himself fortunate. This may mean, ultimately, for most cities a complete reshaping, a tearing down and rebuilding to combine scenic beauty, recreational space, and other aesthetic
values, with the more functional necessities of working, marketing, eating, and sleeping. Although economically unfeasible in the short view,
such a large-scale re-creation of cities is now under way and is a necessary long-term task toward which much wealth and energy in the future
must be directed. In some of the better residential districts of today
and in the elusive charm of many Old World cities, which were forced
through the ages to adapt to the natural landscape, we can see patterns
that could emerge throughout the whole of urban space in the future.

Fig. 37. In place of the unplanned sprawl of city and factory into fertile farm
lands. . . .

Fig. 38. . . . we can have attractive rural landscapes merging gradually with the city (photographs by Soil Conservation Service, U.S. Dept. Agric.).

The cities and towns of the future can be developed in close relationship with the surrounding rural areas. Farm and city have long been separated by the devastated land of the "urban fringe." Farm hands have been cut off from city dwellers by fences and "no trespassing" signs in a somewhat vain attempt to defend them against the inconsiderate and the vandal. In a pattern of environmental conservation, farm land and town land may flow together. Good agricultural soils would continue to grow better crops, but building sites, homes, gardens, parks, and recreational areas could flow from the city outward into the hilly ground, the stream side, the now weedy and barren waste areas that are a part of most farming regions. Rural junk heaps and wastelands can, with proper effort, be transformed, planted, and shaped into landscapes of rural beauty or attractive home sites. By an integration of farm, town or city, and recreational land, each rural region can come to contain the features needed for a full, satisfying way of living. The farmer need no longer flee from his "crop factory" to the mountains to seek the natural landscape he has destroyed at home nor to the city to seek the cultural values, which have thus far not penetrated to the farming lands. The type of rural scene that is here portrayed can be found in some of the older, settled farm lands of Europe and Asia, and even in parts of North America, where farmstead, cropland, and village appear as integral parts of a natural scene. However, for the future we can go beyond this, for such Old World farming areas, while preserving rural beauty, often lack the opportunities for intellectual and cultural stimulation and remain places from which the young flee to the cities in search of a more meaningful, adventurous life. To accomplish this, however, we shall need to take a hard look at our social and economic policies toward land. If all land is to be valued only according to the price it will bring on the market, cities will continue to sprawl and farm lands will be overrun in unplanned urban-industrial expansion.

Farther from the city, in the forest lands and rangelands, we now find the greatest extremes of natural beauty and man-shaped ugliness. In western North American in particular, the towns and dwelling places in forest and range seem completely apart from, and at war with, their surroundings. Few scenes are more ugly than a recently logged-over hillside, with its eroding tractor trails, its piles of broken logs, slash, and debris, unless they are the logging towns themselves. In such areas the intensive land use of the type associated with city and farm land will probably not lie in the future pattern. However with growing land

Fig. 39. With planning for total environment devastated farm lands can be recreated. . . .

Fig. 40. . . . into rural scenes like this one in Vermont (photographs by Soil Conservation Service, U.S. Dept. Agric.).

and resource values the economic incentive has appeared for a more intensive husbandry of forestland and rangeland. The more careful forestry characteristic of northern Europe will with time become part of the North American scene. More consideration of rangeland productivity also will be forced by economics, if not by conscience.

The environmental approach to forest land and rangeland must consider all the values and potentials of these areas. They must be regarded, in the future, not just as sources of wood and forage, but as part of living space for all of the people, urban as well as those who work locally. As watersheds they must be maintained to produce maximum amounts of clear and useful water. Soils need be kept at a high productive level. Forests must provide a variety of wood products of value, and ranges an abundance of forage. Forest- and range-management systems must be planned to maintain vegetation which will support a great variety of wild animal species, and these species in turn should be managed to maintain a balance with the forage supply and to provide abundant recreation for the hunter or outdoor enthusiast. This means that timber-harvesting methods must be adapted to leave a habitat suited to a great variety of animal life rather than one suited, as most are at present, to the production of great numbers of forest-damaging pests. Research toward this goal has scarcely begun. Studies of the food habits of and the competition between domestic and wild animals will point the way toward optimum utilization of rangeland by both livestock and wild game. Thus, these range and forest areas can become part of a human environment, meeting the wide range of human wants and needs.

Still farther from city life, the area of wilderness and primitive scenes will become of even greater importance as forest lands and rangelands are modified by management. Wilderness stands as a unit of measurement against which we estimate progress or loss in our deformation of natural landscapes in managed areas. It stands as a reservoir and refuge for those wild plants and animals difficult to fit into the managed landscape. It stands as sanctuary for people seeking to keep contact with primitive values. We require great tracts of wilderness land of all biotic types, from desert and high mountain to the lands that are now, or will be, occupied by farm, managed forest, or managed range. Although in percentage these wilderness areas need never amount to more than a small part of the total land area, their value in the future will far exceed their extent. The present system of wilderness areas and national parks is a strong beginning but not adequate for future needs.

With proper attention to city, farm, forest, and range, the wilderness and natural area will be preserved against the present onslaught of

Fig. 41. Uncontrolled mining development devastated this mountainside in California . . . .

Fig. 42. . . . Reforestation has started the process of putting the environment back into functioning order (U.S. Forest Service photographs).

recreation-seeking hordes. If most recreational needs are met closer to home, those who visit the wilderness will come prepared to seek the values which can be found only in primitive areas. Under these circumstances national parks would no longer need to provide the mass recreation which is best supplied by lands closer to the cities. Through an environmental approach to conservation, encompassing all lands, the wild lands can remain wild.

A regional approach to conservation of environments would involve the development in each region of a core area representative of the unchanged biota of the region—a wilderness or a natural reserve. Surrounding such an undisturbed core and buffering it from the more intensively used lands would be wild areas used for low-intensity recreation, or a combination of recreation with those forms of land use that depend upon the continued production of wild-land resources, timber, livestock forage, and wildlife among them. Next would be the lands used intensively for farming, intensive pasture management, or intensive wood production. Finally would come those lands used primarily as location sites for housing, industry, or other urban-industrial purposes, and in these urbanized areas would also be located much of the land used for intensive, mass recreation.

Such an arrangement is schematic at best and would normally be dictated by topography, soils, and other ecological factors, along with social and economic factors. In some regions farming would be absent, in others there would be no rangeland or timberland, in others no major urbanized center. All regions, however, require natural area systems, whether of wilderness quality or of smaller size. All regions should provide recreation space for people. Any overall system of local, regional, state, or national land-use planning should consider this entire spectrum of land-use intensity.

Unfortunately, in most areas, we cannot simply impose an overall land-use pattern, but must work with existing patterns. In southern Florida, for example, we might fifty years ago have imposed a pattern that would have allowed for the rational development of metropolitan areas, recreation centers, agriculture, and forestry while still preserving the wilderness values of the Everglades. But development took place mostly with short-range, economic factors as a guide and a minimum attention to the physical and biological realities of the environment. In the 1960's the Everglades, the farm lands, and the urban areas alike compete for limited water supplies, and the Everglades usually lose out in the competition.[9] In the 1960's priceless natural areas were sacrificed to add more of the same kind of housing developments. It is still not

Fig. 43 and chapter opening. Development of recreation areas close to centers of population, like this one in northern California . . . (Calif. Division of Highways photograph).

Fig. 44. . . . can save remote mountain lands like these in Colorado for those who seek primitive values (U.S. Forest Service photograph).

too late to control further development so that those who live in southern Florida in the future may benefit from the presence of some remnants of the once vast wonderland of wild nature that once existed there. But such an approach is incompatible with continued, unlimited population growth and economic expansion.

Thus, environmental conservation represents a goal toward which we must work, not something that can be achieved tomorrow by appeal to self-interest. For it to be attained at all will require a basic change of attitude on the part of many people. It will require, as Aldo Leopold has described in his *Sand County Almanac*,[5] an *extension of ethics* from people to the land, and with this the development of an *ecological conscience*. People, in particular the landowner or land manager, must feel a deep sense of personal responsibility toward the land. In discussing the past failures of conservation, Leopold has stated:[5]

To sum up: we asked the farmer to do what he conveniently could to save his soil, and he has done just that, and only that. The farmer who clears the woods off a 75 per cent slope, turns his cows into the clearing, and dumps its rainfall, rocks, and soil into the community creek, is still (if otherwise decent) a respected member of society. If he puts lime on his fields and plants his crops on contour, he is still entitled to all the privileges and emoluments of his Soil Conservation District. The District is a beautiful piece of social machinery, but it is coughing along on two cylinders because we have been too timid, and too anxious for quick success, to tell the farmer the true magnitude of his obligations. Obligations have no meaning without conscious, and the problem we face is the extension of the social conscience from people to land.

No important change in ethics was ever accomplished without an internal change in our intellectual emphasis, loyalies, affections, and convictions. The proof that conservation has not yet touched these foundations of conduct lies in the fact that philosophy and religion have not yet heard of it. In our attempt to make conservation easy, we have made it trivial.

This change in ethics can come only through education, not conservation education in the old sense, which too often has emphasized only the economically profitable aspects of resource management, but a new type of education based firmly upon a knowledge of human needs and land ecology. A knowledge of psychology and the social sciences, physical science and engineering, and biology are all an integral part of the requisite educational pattern. The education must reach not just the experts and specialists in conservation but must filter through to everyone who is responsible for the land. Through this type of education can come the "sense of pride in the husbandry of wild plants and animals" and the "sense of shame in the proprietorship of a sick landscape" which Leopold has called for and which is essential to environmental conservation.

The environmental approach to conservation seems difficult; however, there are many hopeful beginnings. In the "multiple-use" ideal for management of the national forests there is expressed the same goal. Admittedly there is a long way to go before we can claim that the national forests are managed in keeping with this ideal, but a start has been made. The approach to regional development exemplified by the remaking of the Tennessee River Valley by the T.V.A. is another attempt at achieving the same ideal.[6] The goals for the soil conservation districts and watershed projects of the Soil Conservation Service lie in the same direction, particularly as exemplified by the writings of Edward Graham.[3] City planners throughout America are attempting to reshape urban areas in keeping with the aims of environmental conservation.[7,8] The national park system and wilderness system represent attempts to preserve the natural core areas of America's landscapes. All of these efforts have been handicapped to some extent through being handled too much by specialists in one field or another. Specialization in conservation fields has been essential to progress but, for an environmental approach, it will be necessary to broaden the knowledge and widen the view of the resource specialist and to see to it that each environment is studied and planned from many viewpoints before major changes are made.

Fig. 45. Preservation of areas like this must start by paying attention to the quality of living within the distant cities (U.S. Forest Service photograph).

We can no longer afford to leave any area in the hands of experts trained to see only one or a few sides of an environmental problem.

Were this not the "age of the atom" when each day we are drastically changing the face of the earth and the ways of life for man, it would appear that the goals of environmental conservation were unobtainable. However, at a time when we spend billions for exploring outer space, it should not be beyond our means to provide the highest quality of living for man, here on earth.

# | 5 |

# Agriculture and Soil

Through the ages the relationship of man to the soil has been of first importance to his survival. We have seen that where soil is lost, civilization often goes with it. Today, soil is as essential for the production of food, shelter, fiber, and fuel as it was in the Neolithic. Loss of agricultural soils through erosion has been and remains a major conservation problem. Loss of soil fertility is almost equally serious. To maintain future production and to provide for growing populations, we will need all of the scientific knowledge that we can bring to bear upon the job of soil conservation. To understand the nature of the job to be done, it is necessary here to look carefully at the characteristics of soil.

## SOIL CHARACTERISTICS

Soils develop in widely varying climatic regions under many different kinds of plant cover and from various parent materials. Consequently there are many distinct kinds of soils, each with its own capabilities and each presenting peculiar problems to the man who would make use of it. One of the tasks which a resource manager must face is that of learning the ways in which soils differ and from this determining how best to keep them productive. Differences in the parent material, climate, or vegetation influence the physical characteristics of the soil, the soil chemistry, and the organic composition of the soil. All of these things, and more, must be studied.

**Texture and structure.** The size and arrangement of the various particles of which soils are composed are among the most important properties of soil in that they influence most other soil characteristics. Soil texture is the term that refers to the size of the soil particles. The broad

**99**

classes of texture range between coarse gravel at one extreme and fine clay at the other (Table 3). A soil consisting of both coarse particles such as gravel and sand, and fine particles such as silt and clay is called a loam. Most agricultural soils are in this category. Soils may be named according to their textures, such as a sandy-clay loam or a gravelly-silt loam.

The textural classes to be found in a soil contribute to its structure, a term describing the way in which soil particles are grouped together into larger combinations such as lumps and clods. Soil structure is dependent upon the amount of clay and organic matter present. Clay, in the colloidal size range, has the capacity to adsorb water on the surface of its particles and to link together these particles to form aggregates. This quality of clay is familiar to the potter, who moistens dry clay and from it forms a mixture which will hold together in whatever shape he molds it. Organic colloids in the soils have properties similar to those of clay, with a high ability to take on water and to link other particles together. Soils that are a mixture of clay, organic colloids, and larger particles develop an aggregated structure in which the coarse particles are joined with the fine into crumbs or aggregates of varying sizes and shapes. Soils deficient in clay or organic colloids are structureless—pure sand is an example. Soils too rich in clay and lacking in larger particles may form heavy clay pans almost impenetrable to water or plant roots.

The structure of a soil is of importance in that it determines many other soil characteristics including permeability to water, water-holding capacity, aeration, the ease with which the soil can be worked with farming tools, the ability to stand continued cultivation, the ability to supply nutrients of plants, and finally the resistance to erosion.

**Table 3. Soil-texture Classes**

| Texture Class | Size Range of Particles, Diameter in mm. |
|---------------|------------------------------------------|
| Gravel | Over 1.00 mm. |
| Sand | 0.05 to 1.00 |
| Silt | 0.002 to 0.05 |
| Clay | Less than 0.002 mm. |

Modified from Oosting (1956) after U.S. Dept. Agric., Soil Conservation Service.

**Soil water.** The water-holding capacity of a soil determines its value for agriculture. Permanently dry soils are lifeless. Permanently water-logged soils can support only special types of aquatic plants. Light, structureless sands and gravels are easily penetrated by water. The air spaces between these larger soil particles provide convenient channels through which water can sink deep into the soil. Such soils, however, have little ability to hold water near the surface and thus to make it available to plant roots. Sand dunes, even in rainy climates, can be colonized only by drought-resistant plants or others with ability to obtain water from deep in the ground. At the other extreme, heavy clay soils which lack pores or channels are difficult for water to penetrate. Once water soaks in, however, it is slow to leave, and such soils remain moist after others have dried. Unfortunately for plants, much water that enters clay soils is held tightly to the clay particles by chemical forces. It is therefore unavailable to plant roots. Such tightly bound water in the soil is called *hygroscopic* water.

The soil best able to hold water and supply it to plants is one that combines the qualities of pure sand or gravel and heavy clay. Such a combination is found in soils with a well-developed granular structure. Between the aggregates or crumbs of soil are channels and air spaces. Within and between the aggregates are spaces where water can be held, whereas excess water can readily drain through. The presence of numerous capillary-sized soil channels in well-aggregated soils permits water to rise from deep in the soil through capillary action when the surface water is used or evaporated. It is this *capillary* water which is of greatest value for plant growth rather than the so-called *gravita-tional* water which drains off through the larger channels. In general soils rich in organic matter hold more water than soils low in organic matter, both because of the capacity of humus for absorbing and holding water and because of the ability of organic matter to improve the general soil structure.

An example of the way in which structure and therefore permeability to water is affected by cultivation has been provided by work at the Seabrook Farms in New Jersey.[38] The Seabrook Farms were faced with the problem of disposing of large quantities of waste water from the processing and freezing of vegetables. The water was too highly polluted with dirt and organic matter to be discharged directly into nearby streams. An effort was made, therefore, to dispose of it by spraying it on the agricultural lands, where it would serve the dual purpose of irrigation and fertilization. It was found, however, that the plowed lands could not absorb the quantities of water involved. With soil structure broken down by farming, the soil pores quickly became sealed and clogged, and water ceased to penetrate. The water was then sprayed on an area of previously uncultivated forest land. These forest soils, with structure undisturbed by plowing, were able to absorb 5 inches of water per 10-hour period, compared to no more than 1 inch on the cultivated lands. The equivalent of 600 inches of rainfall a year was sprayed on these forest soils and was absorbed. In response to this excess of water, the vegetation in the forested areas flourished.

**Aeration.** In addition to their ability to take on and hold water, soils with a well-developed structure are usually well aerated. Plant roots engaged in respiration require a steady supply of oxygen and give off carbon dioxide. Heavy clay soils may lack sufficient air spaces to provide this oxygen; light sandy soils may be well aerated but fail to hold water. The well-aggregated soil represents the best medium condition between these two extremes, holding air in the larger pores and channels through which water quickly drains.

**Erosion resistance.** Soils with poorly developed structure readily wash or blow away through the action of water and wind. Under natural cover they are more or less protected from erosion. Under agricultural use, however, they become exposed. Well-aggregated soils are erosion resistant, both because they can readily absorb water and thus eliminate much surface runoff and because the coherence of their particles resists much surface blowing by wind.

**Stratification.** Most soils are stratified, meaning that they lie in more or less distinct layers. Different types of soil vary in the appearance and characteristics of these layers or in other words in their *soil profiles*. A profile is the cross section of a soil revealed when a trench is cut down into the ground. In mature soils, developed in place from underlying rock, the profile will show four major layers known as *soil horizons*.

At the base of the soil lies the *D* horizon, which consists of unmodified rock or parent material. Next above that is the *C* horizon, a layer of partly weathered and broken down parent rock. Above the *C* horizon are the two layers which make up the true soil: the *B* horizon or subsoil, and the *A* horizon or topsoil. Not all soils will show these characteristics clearly. In alluvial soils there may be little evidence of distinct horizons. In soils which are still in early processes of development the separate layers may not yet be apparent.

The topsoil is the organic, living portion of the soil. Here the litter deposited on the soil surface or added from plant roots is broken down by the action of countless soil organisms and in the form of humus becomes mixed with the mineral particles of the soil. The topsoil is also a zone of leaching from which rain water percolating through from the surface dissolves out and removes the soluble minerals. The subsoil is a mineral layer, without organic material, in which minerals leached from the topsoil may be deposited. For farm crops and also for most native plant growth, the topsoil is by far the most important layer. It is here that plants obtain much of their nutrients. It is here that the materials essential to life are present in the most readily available form.

**Soil biota.** It has been emphasized earlier that soil is more than just a combination of finely divided rock particles but has living components equal in importance to the inorganic materials. Some idea of the great number and variety of organisms in the soil is provided in the following table.[39]

| | |
|---|---|
| Missouri corn land | 648,000 nematodes per acre in top 6 inches. |
| Manured soil | 72,000 amoebae per gram in top inch. |
| | 62,000 algae per gram in top inch. |
| Saturated soil | 25,280,000 bacteria per gram of topsoil. |
| Manured and fertilized soil | 111,000 fungi per gram of topsoil. |
| | 2,920,000 actinomycetes per gram of topsoil. |

The total weight of microorganisms in the soil is remarkably high. The weight of bacteria alone has been estimated at 1 ton per acre or higher.[22]

The importance of soil microorganisms can perhaps best be illustrated by an example of what happens where they are scarce or inactive. In the cold, undrained lakes and ponds of northern regions, bacterial and fungal action is inhibited both by the temperature and the acidity of the water. Decomposition of plant remains is therefore largely prevented, and the debris of dead vegetation accumulates on the lake or pond bottom. The end result is a bog with deep deposits of peat, a compacted mass of plant remains. Such areas are poorly suited to most forms of life and support only the most acid-tolerant plants.

Undoubtedly the major role played by microorganisms is in the breakdown and decay of dead organic matter and the consequent return of its chemical constituents to the soil for reuse by other organisms. Without such decay, minerals would be tied up in organic debris and soils would stagnate. The production of either native vegetation or cultivated crops would decline and eventually cease. Such minerals as nitrates, phosphates, and potassium are normally scarce in soils and are to a large extent tied up in plant and animal bodies. Return of these elements to the soil through decomposition is essential if plant growth is to continue. Microorganisms of the nitrogen-fixing variety live both free in the soil and in nodules attached to the roots of various plants such as the legumes. As noted before, these play an essential role in restoring soil nitrates. Soil microorganisms also produce growth-stimulating substances, the plant hormones, which may be essential for maintaining vigorous plant growth.[25]

One of the important reasons for adding organic fertilizers such as manure to soils is the stimulation these provide to the growth and proliferation of soil microorganisms. Chemical fertilizer alone may not be sufficient.[39]

In addition to microorganisms, the larger biotic components of the soil are also important. The role of earthworms in churning, mixing, and processing the soil is well known. In addition to earthworms however, a variety of other organisms play an important mechanical role in building and maintaining soil structure and also take part in the interchange and circulation of soil nutrients.

**Soil fertility.** The fertility of a soil refers to its ability to provide essential chemical nutrients for plant growth (Fig. 46). The mere presence of these chemicals is not adequate to make the soil fertile. They must be present in an available form, which means in solution, or capable of going into solution in the presence of water, organic acids, or other soil solvents. These essential nutrients include those required in large quantities by plants, the macronutrients such as nitrates, phosphates, calcium, potassium, magnesium, etc., and also those required in minute quantities, the micronutrients or trace elements such as copper, cobalt, zinc, and manganese. These trace elements may actually be poisonous to plants if present in excess amounts but in trace amounts are essential for nutrition.

The fertility of a soil is influenced by its structure and its living components. Soils with sufficient clay and organic matter can hold more essential nutrients in a form available to plants than can soils that are light and sandy. As noted above, an abundant flora and fauna of soil microorganisms is also important for maintaining fertility.

Under natural, undisturbed conditions, there is a constant turnover of nutrients in any natural area. Minerals go from soil to wild plants to wild animals, are returned to the soil through animal wastes or when the animal dies, are liberated by soil bacteria and fungi, and made available for use again. Nothing is lost except the small amount taken by the slow processes of geological erosion or by plant or animal emigrants to other areas. When man first entered the picture, he did little to change this circulation. What was removed from the soil was returned in the form of manure or eventually by the death of man or his domestic animals. However, with the advent of civilization, trade, and commerce, crop plants or livestock were not used locally but shipped away to population centers. With the development of sewage systems and various burial customs, little was returned to the soil. Thus a steady drain of nutrients from the soil began, which was accelerated still further when erosion washed the soil itself to the sea. In some areas, soil fertility was exhausted. In other areas, crops continued to be grown, but the ability of these crops to provide adequate nutrition to man or animal was impaired. As a result, dietary deficiencies (shortages of vitamins, essential minerals, or proteins) developed and caused decline in human health and efficiency. It has been pointed out that the protein quality of wheat grown on the rich farm lands of Kansas declined over the 11-year period between 1940 and 1951.[1] In some counties the decline was as high as 8 per cent, from a high of 18 to 19 per cent protein in 1940. The buyer paid more for his 1951 wheat than he paid in 1940, but the food value was less

Fig. 46. Effects of soil fertility on the yield of corn in Arkansas. The corn on the left is grown in soil enriched through the planting of lespedeza, a nitrogenfixing crop (photograph by Soil Conservation Service, U.S. Dept. Agric.).

Fig. 47. Effects of malnutrition. Cattle on deteriorated range in New Mexico (photograph by Soil Conservation Service, U.S. Dept. Agric.).

Greater skill in soil management, the use of fertilizers in properly balanced combinations, and the direct addition of vitamins and other supplements to food have now corrected dietary deficiencies to a large degree. All of these inputs to the agricultural process are of course reflected in the higher price of farm produce. Some observers have pointed out that what was once simple peasant fare, good nutritious food produced directly from fertile soils by careful husbandry, is now a luxury reserved for the fortunate few.

## SOIL DEVELOPMENT AND CLASSIFICATION

The soil characteristics which have been described thus far are used in classifying soils into different types and groups. Major soil differences, related to climate and vegetation, result from the operation of three different processes of soil development, each of which is characteristic of a major natural region. In cold, rainy climates under coniferous forest cover, soils undergo a process called *podsolization*. Coniferous forests add little organic material to the soil. The leaves and litter that fall remain on the surface and only slowly decay to form humic acids. Rainfall, percolating through this litter, becomes acidic. With high rainfall, water can penetrate deep into the soil. This acidic water is able to leach most of the soil nutrients out of the topsoil, so that the A horizon comes to consist of little but sand. Some minerals, mostly iron and aluminum salts, are redeposited in the subsoil which becomes dark colored and heavy with clay (Fig. 48). Many important minerals are carried deeper or washed away. In an extreme form, podsolization occurs under deep coniferous forest. Most forest soils, however, in temperate climates are podsolized to a degree. Where broad-leaved deciduous forest predominates the process is arrested to some extent. Deciduous forest litter contains basic salts and minerals which become incorporated with the topsoil as the litter decays. Such soils are therefore less acidic and more fertile than true podsols. They form the groups known as brown or gray-brown podsolic soils. Nearly all of the soils in the forested region of

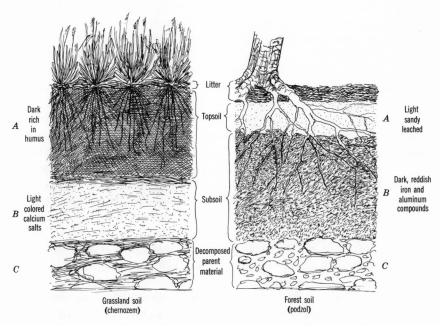

Fig. 48. A comparison of the profiles of forest and grassland soil.

North American can be lumped together on the basis of being more or less podsolized. These soils are called *pedalfers.*

In drier climates, under grassland vegetation, a process called *calcification* takes place. Rainfall, percolating through grass litter does not become charged with acid. Because of the relatively low precipitation, complete leaching of materials out of the soil does not normally occur. Lime and other carbonates are dissolved out of the topsoil but are redeposited in a calcified layer in the subsoil. Grasses add great amounts of organic matter to the topsoil and thus serve to replace essential nutrients and keep it dark and rich in humus. Calcification is best developed in grassland areas with moderate rainfall. Here the topsoil is deep and the calcified layer well below the surface. In desert areas, with very low rainfall, some calcification occurs, but in general there is little leaching of soil materials. The topsoil remains rich in lime and basic salts, but, because of the sparse vegetation, it is low in organic matter and nitrogen. Grass land, dry scrub, and desert soils, all more or less calcified, are lumped into a major group called the *pedocals.*

In the tropics where rainfall is heavy and temperatures high, both leaching and baking of the soils removes most nutrients. In extreme cases, even much of the sand is removed from the topsoil. The remaining soil in the A horizon is composed mostly of iron and aluminum salts, which under extreme conditions form a tough, hard skin called laterite. The process of soil development is therefore known as laterization. In its extreme form, such laterization is not common, but most soils in tropical or subtropical forests are more or less laterized. In the United States, the red and yellow soils of the southern states have undergone both podsolization and laterization to a mild degree. The details of all three of these processes are compared in Table 4.

Lesser differences in climate and vegetation within each major climatic area lead to further modifications of soils. In addition to climate and vegetation, the underlying rock exerts an influence. Thus, soils forming from limestone resist podsolization and may for long periods remain neutral in reaction and highly fertile, even in cool, high-rainfall areas where forest vegetation predominates. Soils forming from acid, igneous rocks such as granite are low in basic salts, are likely to remain sandy, and are slow to show calcification despite climate or vegetation. Podzols may develop even in the tropics from quartz sands.[31] Man-caused influences in vegetation also exert an influence. The prairie soils, for example, lie in a forested area with a forest climate. Maintained in grassland, probably by man-caused fires, these soils have developed characteristics intermediate between forest and grassland soils and lack a calcium layer. The operation of all of the factors influencing soil development gives

**Table 4. Comparison of Soil Development Processes**

| Process | Calcification | Podsolization | Laterization |
|---|---|---|---|
| Precipitation | Low | High | Very high |
| Temperature | Moderate to high | Low | High |
| Vegetation | Grassland | Boreal forest | Tropical forest |
| Soil reaction | Basic to neutral | Acid | Acid |
| Top soil: | | | |
| Color | Dark brown | Light grey | Red |
| Texture | Loam, friable | Sandy | Clay, loam |
| Principal minerals | Various | Silica | Iron, aluminum |
| Humus content | High | Low | Low |
| Fertility | High | Low | Low |
| Subsoil: | | | |
| Color | Whitish | Red | Red |
| Texture | Loam, friable | Heavy clay | Heavy clay |
| Principal minerals | Calcium | Iron, aluminum | Iron, aluminum |
| Typical zonal soil group | Chernozem | Podsol | Lateritic red |

rise to the many zonal soil groups illustrated in the map (Fig. 49). Each of these groups, in turn, is further subdivided into soil series and soil types. For the land manager, a knowledge of soil types and characteristics in his region is essential.

## SOILS AND AGRICULTURE

The amount of land on earth with soils suited to agricultural use is difficult to estimate. Land surveys have not yet been carried out in many countries. Many areas are still cultivated by a shifting, tropical agriculture. One estimate is that there are between 2½ and 3 billion acres of land currently under cultivation and perhaps there is a total of 4½ billion acres in all suitable for agriculture use.[5] This means that there is slightly less than 1 acre under cultivation at the present time for each person on earth. For the United States, figures are more reliable. Of the total land area of nearly 3,676,000 square miles or 2,273

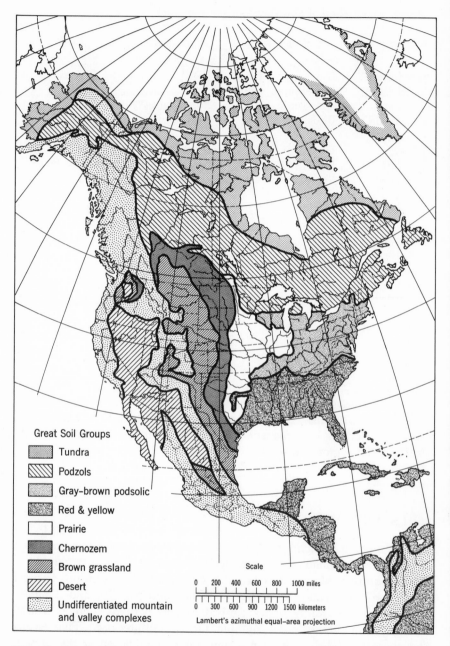

Great Soil Groups

- ▨ Tundra
- ▨ Podzols
- ▨ Gray-brown podsolic
- ▨ Red & yellow
- ☐ Prairie
- ▨ Chernozem
- ▨ Brown grassland
- ▨ Desert
- ▨ Undifferentiated mountain and valley complexes

Scale

0    200   400   600   800   1000 miles

0    300   600   900   1200  1500 kilometers

Lambert's azimuthal equal-area projection

Fig. 49. Distribution of the zonal soil groups of North America [adapted from Finch and Trewartha (1942), Elements of geography, physical and cultural, McGraw-Hill, New York, after C. E. Kellogg, Yearbook of U.S. Dept. Agric., 1938].

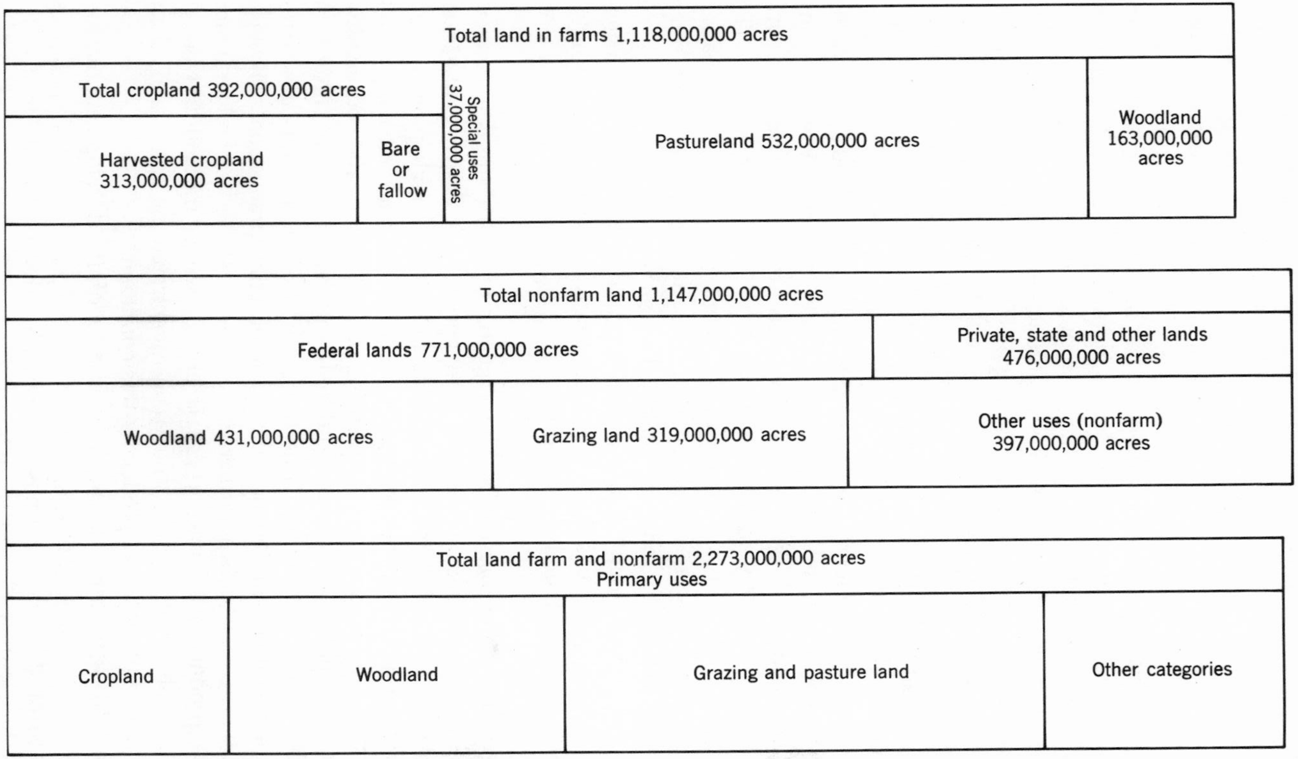

Total land in farms 1,118,000,000 acres

Total cropland 392,000,000 acres

Harvested cropland 313,000,000 acres

Special uses 37,000,000 acres

Bare or fallow

Pastureland 532,000,000 acres

Woodland 163,000,000 acres

Total nonfarm land 1,147,000,000 acres

Federal lands 771,000,000 acres

Woodland 431,000,000 acres

Grazing land 319,000,000 acres

Private, state and other lands 476,000,000 acres

Other uses (nonfarm) 397,000,000 acres

Total land farm and nonfarm 2,273,000,000 acres
Primary uses

Cropland

Woodland

Grazing and pasture land

Other categories

Fig. 50. Land use in the United States, 1964.

111

million acres, somewhat less than 300 million acres or about 13 per cent of the total were in harvested cropland in 1966. This is a marked decrease from past years. In 1956, 477 million acres were classified as cropland, of which 344 million acres actually produced harvested crops. The acreage of crop land per person has been decreasing in the United States, not just because the population has been increasing, but because all food needs can now be met from a smaller acreage. The story of United States agriculture over the past two decades has been a major success story in conservation. Food production per acre has been increased enormously, and it has been possible to retire marginal lands from cultivation. The reasons for this will be discussed below.

A comparison of the distribution of soil groups with that of cropland indicates that agriculture is still largely restricted to certain soil groups. The prairie, chernozem, and brown grassland soils are the great centers of cereal-grain production and yield the bulk of the world's food. Some of the tropical and subtropical lateritic soils, particularly in Asia, are intensively cultivated, but most of these soils are not in permanent agriculture, although they may be cultivated by the ladang system. The gray-brown forest soils are intensively used but mostly for a combination of crop and pasture land. Podsols are usually not cultivated but in some places support a dairy industry combined with the growing of specialized cold-climate crops adapted to acid soil conditions. Except where irrigation is possible, the desert soils are not cultivated, nor are the tundra soils of the far north under cultivation.

**Agriculture and forest soils.** The objective of agriculture is to convert the nutrient materials of the soil into agricultural crops. Cultivation of the soil is intended to facilitate this process. Through plowing and harrowing the farmer breaks up the soil surface and the larger soil chunks, making it easier for the planting of seed and for the germinating seedlings to obtain water, air, and nutrients. In his initial cultivation also he removes competing natural vegetation or weeds and thus channels soil materials in the one direction of crop production. Through generations of experience, farmers have found that the best soil structure for the production of most crops is one in which the soil is worked into relatively small crumbs and easily penetrated by water and plant roots. Cultivation aims at producing this condition.

Western agriculture in the long history of its development in the brown forest soils of Europe, became characterized by those practices suited to produce the best possible agricultural structure in forest soils. It will be recalled that these soils are characterized by a layer of leaf litter and debris, a relatively leached topsoil, and a darker-colored subsoil

Fig. 51. An agricultural landscape in Wisconsin (photograph by Soil Conservation Service, U.S. Dept. Agric.).

in which the materials leached from the topsoil are deposited. Shallow cultivation does little for these soils. Deep plowing however tends to mix together the litter and humus, the light topsoil, and the deep mineral- and clay-rich subsoil. The resulting mixture is a stable, less erodible soil complex, with a better structure than the original forest topsoil.[23] Addition of lime, which reduces acidity, and manure, which adds nitrogen and organic compounds, further improves the structure. With care and with the standard European practices of crop rotation, cultivation can continue to improve these soils. Without this care and particularly under a system of farming based on the continued production, year after year, of a single cash crop, the structure of the soil breaks down, the soil nutrients leach out, crop yields decline, and eventually the soil becomes exhausted. If the soil lies on sloping ground, rainfall removes much of it by erosion once the structure is destroyed. When the eastern United States was settled, the European immigrants who were capable farmers continued their well-suited agricultural practices on the new lands. Where the settlers were poor farmers or interested only in production of cash crops for quick profit, the forest soils were depleted.

**Agriculture and grassland soils.** When the wave of settlement reached the grassland belt of soils, an entirely different set of conditions were encountered. The grassland soils naturally possessed the structure which cultivation over the years produced in forest soils.[23] In their natural state they were resistant to erosion and slow to lose fertility. Because of this, many of the practices used on forest soils were gradually dropped. The new soils of the West gave continued high yields, year after year, of corn or wheat without crop rotation. Liming and fertilization seemed unnecessary. So long as farm animals were used to pull the agricultural machinery, a certain amount of crop rotation took place to provide hay for the farm livestock, and manure was added to the soil. However, with the advent of farm machinery even these elementary soil-preserving practices were abandoned. Monoculture, emphasizing high-value, high-yield grain crops in the northern plains and cotton in the southern plains, became the rule.

Despite their depth, excellent structure, and fertility, the grassland soils were not inexhaustible. Under natural conditions they were continually restored by additions of vast quantities of organic material from grass roots and stems and the droppings and remains of grassland animals, and they were maintained in structure by the mechanical action of grass roots and the burrowing of animals. Under continuous cultivation all of the factors which originally contributed toward building the soil were removed. Gradually soil structure has broken down and with it the capacity of the soil to absorb and hold water. Dry spells, which under natural conditions did little damage, became severe when the soils failed to take on and hold the rain that did fall. Yields began to decline as natural sources of nitrogen, organic materials, and mineral nutrients were removed. Farming in this region reached its lowest ebb during the decade of the 1930's.

**The dust bowl.** In the better watered grassland soils of the East, the damage has not been so severe as that which accompanied the westward move of agriculture. In the brown soils of the arid Great Plains the most serious difficulties arose. The Great Plains region has been subjected throughout history to periodic droughts.[36] The dry, hot areas of the southern Great Plains in particular have been plagued by long spells of below-average rainfall. Under their natural cover of short, sod-forming grasses, the droughts did little lasting damage. In the 1880's, however, the first wave of settlers moved into the southern Great Plains during a period of relatively high rainfall and lush growth. In 1890 a severe drought hit the plains and persisted for the better part of the decade. Many of the early settlers gave up and moved on to better farming lands elsewhere. In the late 1890's the rains returned, and the area again looked green and productive. A new wave of settlers arrived, plowed the plains, and planted the rich, brown soil to wheat.

In 1910 there was another dry spell and more damage. On the farm lands with bare soil exposed and soil structure broken down by cultivation, dust began to blow. An extensive area was damaged, and again many farmers gave up and moved on. In 1914 there was a great demand for wheat as the grain belt of Europe was ravaged by war. With high wheat prices, previously abandoned land looked like a good investment. Returning rains further improved the outlook. All of the land now judged suitable for agriculture was plowed, and in addition an estimated 6 million acres that should not have been plowed were put into wheat production. High rainfall and good times remained in the southern Great Plains until 1931.

In 1931 the nation was in the grip of a severe economic depression.

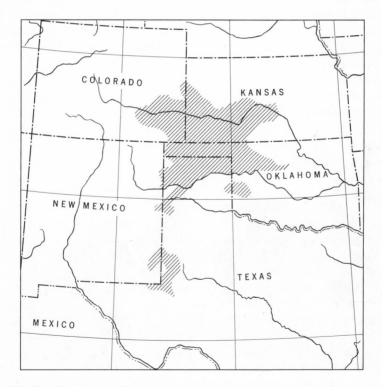

Fig. 52. The dust bowl, showing area of serious wind erosion (from map by Soil Conservation Service, U.S. Dept. Agric.).

In 1931, also, drought returned to the plains. Accentuated by previous damage to soil structure, the new drought surpassed all previous ones in severity. In the fall of 1933 began the series of dust storms which gave to the region a new name, the Dust Bowl (Fig. 52). Dust blew across the continent, darkened the skies, reddened the sunsets, and made the plains region almost uninhabitable in spots for man or livestock (Fig. 54). Millions of acres of farms were damaged, with an estimated loss of topsoil ranging between 2 and 12 inches in places. Drifting dunes moved over farms, burying roads, fences, and even dwellings (Fig. 53). A mass exodus of farmers, ruined by drought and unable to find work, streamed from Oklahoma, Kansas, Texas, and adjoining areas and moved west to California or east into city bread lines. It was a period of misery and privation difficult to match in American history.

Drought, dust, and despair did what countless written and spoken words by soil scientists had failed to accomplish—it brought the nation to an awareness of the need for soil conservation. In 1935, in Washington, the Soil Conservation Service was created. The federal government and state legislatures soon passed enabling legislation that permitted the forming of soil-conservation districts. On these districts the Soil Conservation Service provided the aid and technical knowledge which farmers needed to put sound land-use principles into effect. In the Dust Bowl the process was begun of putting land back into grass where the plow should never have been used. On soil types better suited to farming, the use of conservation techniques was started.

Fig. 53. A dust storm in Colorado (photograph by Soil Conservation Service, U.S. Dept. Agric.).

Fig. 54. Wind-blown sand covering farm lands in Kansas (photograph by Soil Conservation Service, U.S. Dept. Agric.).

In the 1940's the rains came again. Through efforts on the part of farmers and with the help of state and federal governments, many farms were restored to productivity. For a time it looked as though the Dust Bowl was a thing of the past, as though we had finally learned the lesson of conservation. But the 1940's also brought world war. In 1941 the German Wehrmacht swept across the rich, wheat lands of the Ukraine and brought the retaliatory measures of "scorched earth" and "lend lease." Grain from America went overseas to feed the allied armies and peoples, and grain prices in America went up. Economics and patriotism were mixed in the drive that sent the plow biting deep into millions of new acres of plains grassland. The armies were fed, the Nazi war machine was broken, and the war-starved peoples of Europe were supplied. But in 1950 drought returned.

The drought of the 1950's set a new record in severity. Again the dust storms arose from eroded farms and overgrazed ranges. Crops failed, and farmers gave up trying. An emergency was proclaimed, and federal aid funds were poured into the area. That the conditions of the 1930's did not return was due in part to the generally high level of national prosperity. Farmers could afford to support their homes by working in factories in nearby cities. The land-ownership pattern had also changed. The family-sized farms that failed in the 1930's have been incorporated to an increasing extent into larger units. Fewer people were on the land to stand the brunt of the drought. In 1957 a second consequence of land misuse was felt throughout the Southwest. The rains returned but not as gentle, life-restoring showers. Torrential downpours fell on the dust-blown eroded lands of the southern plains. Rivers swelled to flood proportions and poured over towns and cities, carrying with them the soil from once productive grassland ranges.

The Soil Conservation Service estimated in 1955 that at least 14 million acres in the Great Plains currently under cultivation should be returned to grass. It was pointed out that more than three-fourths of the plains cropland could be kept in crops but only if soil- and water-conservation measures were used.[23]

The Dust Bowl is an object lesson on the effects of erosion. We have had many such lessons, from the dongas of South Africa to the gullies of South Carolina. We have had scientific studies of erosion on many soils and in many areas. The results of two such studies, in California and Missouri, tell their own story and show what happens when prairie is changed to cornland or left fallow, or when land is unprotected by conservation farming practices (Tables 5, 6). Erosion remains a major problem, from the wind erosion that brings the dust storm or the spectacular gully erosion, to the less noticeable sheet erosion which each year removes a thin film of topsoil from farms until finally all of the topsoil has gone and the farmer is left pouring fertilizers and dollars into barren subsoil.

**Table 5.  Cropping Systems and Soil Erosion**

| Cropping System or Cultural Treatment | Average Annual Loss of Soil per Acre (tons) | Percentage of Total Rainfall Running off the Land |
|---|---|---|
| Bare, cultivated, no crop | 41.0 | 30 |
| Continuous corn | 19.7 | 29 |
| Continuous wheat | 10.1 | 23 |
| Rotation: corn, wheat, clover | 2.7 | 14 |
| Continuous bluegrass | 0.3 | 12 |

Average of 14-years measurements of runoff and erosion at Missouri Experiment Station, Columbia. (Soil type: Shelby loam; length of slope: 90.75 feet; degree of slope; 3.68 per cent.) From *Cropping systems in relation to erosion control*, by M. F. Miller, Missouri Agric. Exp. Sta. Bul. 366, 1936. (Adapted from Jacks & White, 1939, p. 111.)

**Table 6. Effect of Cover and Conservation Treatment on Erosion Loss from a Heavy 3-day Rain Storm**

| Average Depth of Erosion (Inches) | Erosion Protection Provided | | | | No Erosion Protection Provided | | | |
|---|---|---|---|---|---|---|---|---|
| | Cover Crop | Basin List-ing | Ter-races | Native Cover (Grass Brush) | Grain | Volun-teer Cover | Bare | Cultivated (Fallow, Orchard, Vineyard) |
| | Percentage of area in each type of treatment that was eroded to the indicated depths, from survey of 5 areas | | | | | | | |
| No erosion | 88 | 69 | 12 | 53 | 30 | 37 | 4 | 0 |
| $\frac{1}{8}$ to $\frac{3}{8}$ | 11 | 31 | 84 | 37 | 58 | 37 | 62 | 45 |
| $\frac{3}{4}$ to $1\frac{1}{2}$ | 1 | 0 | 4 | 8 | 12 | 21 | 15 | 42 |
| 3 | 0 | 0 | 0 | 2 | 0 | 5 | 19 | 13 |
| Area in acres | 32,515 | 788 | 5,614 | 41,160 | 12,119 | 15,376 | 18,495 | 15,705 |

Adapted from Bamesberger, 1939, SCS publication, p. 7.

## SOIL CONSERVATION

The most important step in soil conservation is first to hold the soil in place. If the soil remains, its other qualities can be improved. If it has washed or blown away, nothing more can be done. There are many ways of preventing erosion which can be summed up in one term, intelligent land use. In detail, they can be broken down into two major categories: mechanical or engineernig methods, and biological methods.

**Engineering methods.** Of the engineering techniques, the first and most basic is to adapt cultivation to the contours of the land. The square field and the straight-plowed furrow have a place only on flat land. Unfortunately, our land-subdivision system has favored the square or rectangular field, and our past plowing practices have favored the straight furrow for economy of effort (Fig. 55). It is now generally realized, if not always practiced, that when sloping ground must be cultivated cultivation should follow the contour of the land. *Contour plowing* is a first step toward keeping soil from washing downhill. When the furrows follow the contour of a slope, each furrow acts as a check dam and reservoir to prevent water from following its normal course downhill (Fig. 57). Excess runoff can be accommodated in grassed-over waterways or natural drainage channels.

Where slopes are greater and the danger of soil loss higher, contour cultivation needs to be supplemented by *terracing*. The flat terraces of the Far East or the old Incan lands are not suited to the farm machinery of today. In their place a broad-based contour terrace has been developed which permits contour cultivation (Fig. 58). Behind the terrace a channel forms, which should usually be maintained in sod. This leads excess water into diversion ditches or channels which permit adequate drainage.

If erosion in the form of sheet erosion, wind erosion, or rill erosion (the incipient beginnings of gullies) is present, contour treatment of the land will help to halt it. Where gullies have cut into the land however, they must be reclaimed. In the absence of reclamation, gullies work up hill, biting deeper into otherwise well-managed farm land. Mechanical methods of gully control involving damming are a first step. Usually, biological methods of revegetation must also be applied (Fig.

Fig. 55. Erosion following downhill plowing in Oregon (photograph by Soil Conservation Service, U.S. Dept. Agric.).

Fig. 56. Severe gullying of loess soil in Mississippi. Thirty-five years before this picture was taken this area was a cotton field (photograph by Soil Conservation Service, U.S. Dept. Agric.).

59). In some instances old gullies have been dammed and converted into farm ponds.

**Biological methods.** Biological methods of erosion control are those making primary use of organisms rather than of tools and mechanical equipment. These methods are an attempt to provide through the manipulation of domesticated plants the same degree of soil protection formerly provided by natural vegetation. One biological method of erosion control on sloping ground is *strip cropping,* the alternation of grain or other crops which give little soil protection with strips of close-grown leaf crops or grass sod, which give more adequate protection (Fig. 60). Where grass or legume strips are alternated with crops, the soil structure, organic content, and nitrogen content may also be improved. Strip cropping is often combined with contour cultivation, or where necessary, terracing.

Fig. 57. Contour cultivation (photographs by Soil Conservation Service, U.S. Dept. Agric.).

Where wind erosion has proved serious, shelter belts are useful. Such shelter belts consist of plantings of shrubs and trees in wind-breaking barriers along the windward edges of croplands (Fig. 61). During the conservation-conscious days of the late 1930's, shelter belts were widely planted across the plains states to break the wind velocity.

Fig. 58 and chapter opening. Terraced land in Iowa (photograph by Soil Conservation Service, U.S. Dept. Agric.).

Fig. 59. Gully reclamation. This gully in Illinois shown in the upper photograph was planted to trees. After 3 years it appeared as shown in the lower photograph (photographs by Soil Conservation Service, U.S. Dept. Agric.).

One of the most important factors to consider in preventing water erosion is the destructive force of rain drops. Rain falling on bare soil breaks up structure and bounces soil particles high in the air. These are caught by water running over the ground and are carried down hill. Without the impact of rain drops on the soil, runoff removes surface

Fig. 60. Strip cropping in Iowa (photograph by Soil Conservation Service, U.S. Dept. Agric.).

Fig. 61. Shelter belt in North Dakota (photograph by Soil Conservation Service, U.S. Dept. Agric.).

124

particles only. With rain drops new particles are continually being broken loose and added to the soil carried away. Natural vegetation and ground litter break the force of rain and prevent its impact on the bare soil. Many crop plants, however, do not provide this protection. One method, therefore, of preventing erosion is to keep crop litter and crop residues on the surface of the ground instead of turning them under in plowing. Special subsurface tillers have been developed which break up and loosen the soil without turning under the litter. Where this is not sufficient, the direct addition of mulches or plant remains to cover the soil surface may provide the necessary protection.

Crop rotation, where it involves the alternation of soil-conserving crops, such as legumes or grass, with other crops also serves as an effective measure of erosion control, both through giving more complete protection during the period when the grasses or legumes are present and through improving the soil structure. Manuring and the use of other organic wastes also help in preventing erosion through improvement of soil structure.

**Maintaining soil fertility.** The final step in soil conservation to be discussed is the maintenance of soil fertility. A decrease in soil fertility may be masked by increased crop yields brought about by improved varieties of crop plants. A high yield per acre may mean a much greater output of carbohydrates per acre but can disguise a reduced output of proteins, vitamins, and essential minerals. Measured in terms of energy units (calories) produced the increased yields are comforting. But man does not live by calories alone and is selling himself short if increased yields do not mean increased nutrition.

Many studies have now been carried out to show the effects of soil fertility on wild and experimental animals. Crops grown on more fertile soil, although similar in appearance, give higher growth rates, stronger bones, and increased reproductive rates when fed to animals than those from less fertile soils. A greater number of animals per acre and a greater average body weight per individual can be supported on fertile soils.[27] Experiments show that a lack of nutritional balance, such as a decrease in calcium relative to potassium or calcium relative to phosphorus, can have serious effects upon animal nutrition, even where total plant growth is not affected (Fig. 47). The absence of a single trace element such as cobalt once rendered large areas of range in Australia useless for livestock production. Addition of minute amounts of this element through a top-dressing of fertilizer has brought this range into livestock production.

Vitamin, mineral, and protein deficiences where severe enough to take the form of human deficiency diseases are easily recognized. Where they simply add to a general, slow decline in health and vitality, they are less apparent. It is nevertheless a sufficiently serious matter for every citizen, no matter how far he may be removed from the land, to concern himself with the conservation practices which produced the food that he buys.

Many of the techniques described above are also of value in maintaining soil fertility. Techniques which maintain soil structure also prevent the excessive leaching of soil nutrients. Crop rotation, the planting of legumes and grass, and the addition of animal manures and plant remains to the soil are valuable techniques. The balanced use of chemical fertilizers, based on careful study of soil chemistry and soil needs, can help to compensate for the drain from agricultural crops. In extreme cases, complete rest from crop production under some type of soil-restoring cover may be necessary.

The techniques of conservation farming cannot be described adequately in a textbook of environmental conservation. Each piece of land is different and has its own peculiar problems. For most farmers, however, technical advice and knowledge is readily available through the offices of the Soil Conservation Service or the county farm advisors maintained by the state land-grant colleges and universities. Ignorance is now rarely an adequate excuse for the misuse of land.

## LAND CLASSIFICATION AND USE

The first step toward sound land use and soil conservation is land classification. Throughout the world marginal-land farmers have attempted to squeeze a living from lands not suited to crop production and have ruined the lands in the process. Elsewhere in areas otherwise suited to farming, the agricultural machinery is too often run over acres that were best put to some other use. Such areas are poor producers and can serve as focal points for damage that will spread later to the better lands. With proper classification of lands, such misuse can be avoided.

In an effort to see that land is treated according to its capabilities, the Soil Conservation Service has worked out a detailed land-classification system.[19,20,41] This takes into account the soil types, slope and drainage of the land, the erodibility and rockiness of the soil, and all other factors that influence the capability of the land. Although the complete system is elaborate, its principal features are shown in modified form in Table 7. In soil-conservation districts, the Soil Conservation Service is

# Table 7. Land-capability Classification

| Land Class | Land-capability and Use Precautions | Primary Uses | Secondary Uses |
|---|---|---|---|
| | **Group I. Lands Suitable for Cultivation** | | |
| I. | Excellent land, flat, well drained. Suited to agriculture with no special precautions other than good farming practice. | Agriculture | Recreation Wildlife Pasture |
| II. | Good land with minor limitations such as slight slope, sandy soils, or poor drainage. Suited to agriculture with precautions such as contour farming, strip cropping, drainage, etc. | Agriculture Pasture | Recreation Wildlife |
| III. | Moderately good land with important limitations caused by soil, slope, or drainage. Requires long rotation with soil-building crops, contouring or terracing, strip cropping or drainage, etc. | Agriculture Pasture Watershed | Recreation Wildlife Urban-industrial |
| IV. | Fair land with severe limitations caused by soil, slope or drainage. Suited only to occasional or limited cultivation. | Pasture Tree crops Agriculture Urban-industrial | Recreation Wildlife Watershed |
| | **Group II. Lands Not Suitable for Cultivation** | | |
| V. | Land suited to forestry or grazing without special precautions other than normal good management. | Forestry Range Watershed | Recreation Wildlife |
| VI. | Suited to forestry or grazing with minor limitations caused by danger from erosion, shallow soils, etc. Requires careful management. | Forestry Range Watershed Urban-industrial | Recreation Wildlife |
| VII. | Suited to grazing or forestry with major limitations caused by slope, low rainfall, soil, etc. Use must be limited, and extreme care taken. | Watershed Recreation Wildlife Forestry Range Urban-industrial | |
| VIII. | Unsuited to grazing or forestry because of absence of soil, steep slopes, extreme dryness or wetness. | Recreation Wildlife Watershed Urban-industrial | |

Modified from land-classification system of U.S. Soil Conservation Service, Department of Agriculture. (From Wohletz and Dolder, 1952.)

*Note:* The Use columns in particular depart from the usual SCS form.

Fig. 62. Land classified according to capabilities (photograph by Soil Conservation Service, U.S. Dept. Agric.).

prepared to work out a land classification and use plan for each farmer who requests it (Fig. 62). Outside of the soil-conservation districts, other agencies such as the Agricultural Extension Services are usually willing to perform a similar service or to provide the information on which such a system can be based. With a classification worked out, the farmer not only can put his best lands to work but also knows what conservation measures are required to maintain all of his lands in top condition.

**Land zoning and environmental conservation.** A second step in conservation planning follows after land classification and becomes a community responsibility. This step is land zoning, supported by adequate legislation, to prevent the misuse of land. Although this involves additional restriction upon individual choice and freedom in a day when restrictions are already too burdensome, it is a necessary step where populations are dense and increasing. Anyone familiar with the population expansion in the state of California or in the urbanized area of the East Coast following World War II has seen the consequences that follow on lack of zoning and planning. There is a normal tendency for cities to expand along lines of least resistance into lands, level and clear of heavy vegetation, on which housing or industrial construction can be carried out at minimum cost. Such lands, unfortunately, are usually also the high-value farm lands. City lots can always compete in price, if not in real value, with agricultural use of the same land. City taxes, extended to farm land, can force the most resistant farmer out of business. Industries, airports, and superhighways are all equally effective at forcing the farmer off his land. Into the orange groves of the Los Angeles basin and the cherry orchards of the Santa Clara Valley, suburban housing has moved like a crop-destroying blight. Fruit growing and crop production is forced into marginal areas of less suitable soil. That the houses might more attractively and fittingly be built upon lands that are poorly suited to agriculture is a form of common sense difficult to hear when "money talks." Some states have taken steps to protect farm lands from urbanization and forest lands from misguided farming efforts by laws that encourage the assessment of land according to its use rather than its value if sold for real estate development, that give other forms of tax relief to farmers who choose to keep their lands in productive agriculture, and that encourage counties to zone according to land capability.[35] In most instances, however, local zoning has not held up against severe economic pressure, and it is difficult to keep a man farming the land when by selling to a developer he could make more than he might expect in ten or more years of farming effort. Whether better effects would be achieved were the state governments to take zoning power from local communities is debatable. To date, direct land purchase by the state or local government, purchase of development rights, or purchase with leaseback to a lessee who will use the land for the desired purpose have been the principal methods that have proved effective in controlling land use. Much, therefore, remains to be done to guarantee that lands will be used in accordance with the best planning principles. In England, where the situation has been particularly severe, a National Town and Country Planning Act was adopted after World War II. This gave the national government restrictive control over land use, and was the instrument used in accomplishing the establishment of a green belt around London and of new towns located beyond the green belt. However, even this has not been entirely effective and Great Britain still suffers from urban-industrial encroachment into agricultural lands and other open space. There seems no final answer except a willingness of the citizen to submit to stronger regulation and control over the use of land, even where this means financial sacrifice.

Fig. 63. A balanced rural landscape in Pennsylvania (photograph by Soil Conservation Service, U.S. Dept. Agric.).

A final step toward the planning of conservation on agricultural and other lands must be the realization that we can no longer afford single-purpose use of extensive areas. Croplands of good quality must be reserved primarily for crop production. Such farming use of these primary agricultural lands necessarily rules out for much of the year most other land uses. However, even the best farming region has lands that are not suited to crop production, for example, roadways, streamsides, rock outcrops, and steep slopes. If the entire landscape is to be considered in an environmental approach to conservation, these waste areas need attention and development also. Properly cared for they can provide recreation space, retreats for wildlife, sources of timber and range forage, or simply add to rural beauty. Uncared for they become garbage dumps or sources of disruption of the whole land complex. If rural living is to remain a part of the American scene, its quality must be considered (Fig. 63). The elements that once lent a wholeness to rural life, firmly established in our national background and culture, must be retained or regained. Rural factories grinding out cash crops at the expense of human values may feed an excess of people but cannot provide the qualities that make life worthwhile.

## THE WORLD FOOD PROBLEM

The story of agriculture in the United States during the 1960's has been marked with much success. Many lands that were damaged by misuse in the past has been to a large degree restored. Other lands that should not have been in agricultural use because of low capability have been retired from farm production. Dense pine forests have sprung up on the abused and abandoned farm lands of the southeastern United States, repairing the damage done by agriculture and adding to the national supplies of timber and pulpwood. Pastures grow on formerly damaged farm lands in the West and Middle West and support thriving herds of cattle. Agricultural yields from the existing farms not only provide, in general, adequate food for Americans but produce a surplus that has been used to help stave off hunger in other parts of the world. No expert would doubt that yields can be further increased. But the same success is not found in other parts of the world. Over most of the world there is an agricultural and food crisis.

Even in the United States the food picture is not entirely clear if viewed from the standpoint of world needs. In a world that is chronically short of protein, the United States was, in the middle-1960's, the largest importer of fish. Meat is imported from Mexico, Argentina, New Zealand, Australia, and Canada. Luxury and specialty crops such as coffee, tea, sugar, bananas and other tropical fruits, cacao, and copra are brought in from many lands. Acreages in food-deficient areas that could perhaps be used to produce food for local consumption are instead yielding luxury crops for export to the technologically developed countries, because this means more economic profit for the landowner and builds a favorable exchange balance for the country involved. Furthermore, if the entire food surplus in the United States, when it was at its peak, was used to feed the hungry people of the world, it would represent at best only a few months supply. There is no basis, therefore, for complacency.[5]

The enormous gains in production from farmlands in the United States have been accomplished by the careful application of chemical fertilizers, by the use of herbicides to destroy competing weeds, by the use of pesticides to destroy insects or other organisms that attack crops and, in particular, by the application of genetics, the breeding and selection of superior strains of crop plants such as the high-yielding hybrid corns and wheats. Gains per acre have been more than matched by gains per man-hour of farm labor. Farm machinery now does much of the work formerly accomplished by the farmer, his hired hands, and migratory workers. Farm populations have declined steadily, from 32 million in 1935 to 13 million in 1963, during a period when total population has increased rapidly. But these gains have depended on the existence of a highly industrialized technology.

The human energy that used to be poured into farm work is now replaced and exceeded by the fossil-fuel energy, the diesel oil, and gasoline burned by the farm machinery and by power from hydroelectric, steam, or nuclear plants transmitted to the farms. The chemical industries produce the fertilizer, herbicides, and pesticides. Highly skilled agricultural scientists determine new techniques for managing farm soils for maximum production, or breed the superior genetic strains of crop plants. Such skills and facilities, such industry and sources of power are not available in most of the underdeveloped nations of the world.

During World War II it became apparent to all who were looking ahead to postwar years that a major effort would be needed to restore order to the chaos that had been created around the world by the destruction and dislocation brought by the war. The famine in Bengal in 1943, during which millions died, was a portent of the type of problem that would face many parts of the world unless great improvements were made in the food and agricultural status of most nations. Consequently, in Quebec in October 1945, the nations of the new United Nations joined together to form the Food and Agricultural Organization of the United Nations (FAO). The purpose of FAO was spelled out at its first conference by Lester B. Pearson of Canada, "FAO will bring the findings of science to the workers in food and agriculture, forestry and fisheries everywhere. . . . It will assemble, digest, and interpret information to serve as a basis for the formulation of policy, national and international. It can suggest action, but only through the activities of governments themselves can the objectives be finally won."[44] FAO, among its other objectives, sought to increase world food supplies at a rate exceeding the growth of population, with a view to restoring the balance between food and population, initially to what it had been in 1939 before World War II, but hopefully to move on from there to end shortages of food and other agricultural and forest products everywhere.

In 1955, after ten years of effort, FAO and its member nations had some success and some major failures.[15] In 1939, some 49 per cent of the world received less than 2200 calories of energy daily from their food supply, an amount believed to be the minimum needed by a person doing active work. By 1955, according to figures published by the Political and Economic Planning group in Great Britain, 66 per cent of the world population received less than 2200 calories per day. Still, some success was achieved during the first decade of FAO and the publications of FAO in 1955 sounded hopeful:

"What is almost within human grasp is nothing less than the abolition of primary poverty in the last strongholds of poverty, the bringing of the low-income peoples, not to equality of income with the wealthiest peoples, but to within hailing distance, so that there is no longer a wide social and material gap between them."[44]

In 1965, after 20 years of effort, a pattern had clearly emerged. In the technologically advanced countries, which were initially well off in food supply, it proved to be relatively easy to increase food supplies more rapidly than population. In most of the world, where the food situation was most critical, it proved to be difficult, if not impossible, to increase food supplies at a rate equal to population growth. Despite enormous efforts, the amount of food produced lagged behind the increase in population. All of Africa, all of Asia outside of the USSR, and most of Latin America had an average consumption of less than 2200 calories per person per day. The Director-General of FAO in a 1966 reported stated:[16]

"The outlook is alarming. In some of the most heavily populated areas the outbreak of serious famines within the next five to ten years cannot be excluded. And if food output everywhere just kept pace with population growth at the present level of consumption, by the end of this century the number of people who would be subject to hunger and malnutrition would be double what it is today."

In 1967, famine stalked India and hit hard in Bihar Province. There was no way of predicting how far it would spread or how serious it would become. Much of the tropical world had reached or was approaching a crisis. This occurred in a world where the scientific knowledge and technological skills available to the more advanced peoples could, if everywhere applied, produce adequate food for the existing population.

The nature of the problem can be illustrated by comparisons between Japan, a nation with an advanced technology, but one heavily hit by World War II, and India, a country that has not succeeded in establishing an advanced technological society.

In 1960, Japan had a per capita food consumption of 2360 calories per day, adequate to meet its needs. India averaged 2060 calories, a continuing daily food deficiency. In Japan the average population growth in the decade 1950–1960 had been 1.2 per cent and declining. In India, population had grown at 2 per cent per year. The annual increase in real per capita income had been 7.6 per cent in Japan during 1950–1960; in India, only 1.7 per cent. Japan in 1960 had an average agricultural output per hectare of arable land of $961 compared to $91 for India. The agricultural output per farm worker in Japan was $402, in India $114. In 1967 the Japanese were experiencing prosperity; India faced famine.[12,24]

The reasons for the contrast between the two countries were apparent. The illiteracy rate in Japan in 1960 was 2 per cent; in India 76 per cent of the people could not read or write. Japan used an average of 303.7 kilograms of chemical fertilizer per hectare of agricultural land; India used 2.3. Nearly 64 per cent of Japan's population was urban compared to 18 per cent in India. Japan, still dependent upon hand labor in farming, had 1.55 tractors per 1,000 hectares of arable land in 1961–1962; India, however, had only 0.21. In 1960, Japan used nearly 150 thousand metric tons of pesticides, fungicides, and herbicides in agriculture; India used only slightly more than 10,000. One hundred per cent of the crop area in Japan was sown to improved varieties of cereal grains. Figures were not available for India, but nearby Pakistan sowed only from 5 to 8 per cent of the total grain cropland to improved grain varieties.[12,24]

There is no need to labor the contrasts further. Japan was a country with a highly educated peasantry, a high level of industrial technology, and a willingness to apply its products to the land. It was also a country with a birth rate well under control. India was low in education and technology and high in birth rate. Unless the birth rate in India is brought under control, a miracle will be required to bring any long-range solution to the food problem. On the land itself the situation in India is not even static, but deteriorating. Erosion continues, deserts spread, and soil fertility declines over extensive areas.

There are agricultural success stories in many parts of the world outside of the technologically advanced nations. Thus the Rockefeller Foundation sponsored an agricultural improvement program in Mexico that made use of improved varieties of corn and wheat. In 1941, Mexico was producing only 50 per cent of the wheat that its people consumed. By 1960, despite an increase in population of 60 per cent, Mexico was self-sufficient in wheat production. In the Sudan the annual crop output gained an average of 8 per cent between 1948 and 1963. However, for each success there are many failures. Jordan, between 1948 and

1963, showed an average annual decline in crop output of 1.9 per cent per year. Tunisia also registered an average annual decline.[12]

In the late 1960's it has been generally recognized that no nation can afford to remain as an economic dependent. Either alone or as part of a regional grouping of countries, it must achieve self-sufficiency in agricultural production. To achieve this there must be not only marked gains in crop production but corresponding declines in the rates at which people are produced. This latter topic will be discussed further in Chapter 14.

## THE PESTICIDE PROBLEM

An important contributor to the gain in world food production has been the introduction on the land of new types of agricultural chemicals, the various pesticides or biocides. The first of these, DDT, was developed during World War II and proved highly effective in controlling populations of lice, fleas, and other disease-carrying insects. The initial impact of these chemicals on both public health and agriculture was so encouraging that they were adopted and widely used with little investigation of their side effects. The use of DDT virtually eliminated malaria in some parts of the world. The use of this and other insecticides knocked back populations of crop-destroying insects and brought marked gains in crop yields. But unfortunately, biotic communities are complex and not amenable to simple solutions to their problems.

Insect pests initially can be controlled by application of a pesticide such as DDT at a level that will not be harmful to birds and mammals. Control, however, is not eradication, and some insects always survive. Frequently, these will be the individuals most resistant to the pesticide. If this resistance is inheritable, a DDT-resistant population of malaria mosquitoes, fruit flies, or other insects may well breed up following several applications of the chemical. It then becomes necessary to increase the dosage or find a more lethal chemical. Eventually, control efforts may lead to applications of poisons at levels that are toxic to birds, mammals, or to man himself. Insects breed rapidly and produce large numbers of offspring. It takes relatively little time to develop pesticide-resistant populations. The slower breeding vertebrates are not so fortunate. But this is only part of the problem.

In 1962, Rachel Carson attracted national attention to pesticides with the publication of her book, *Silent Spring*.[7] In her words the consequences of our continued careless use of pesticides might result one year in the arrival of a springtime in which "There was a strange stillness. The birds, for example—where had they gone? Many people spoke of them, puzzled and disturbed. . . . On the mornings that had once throbbed with the dawn chorus of robins, catbirds, doves, jays, wrens, and scores of other bird voices there was no sound; only silence lay over the fields and woods and marsh." *Silent Spring* has been accused of scientific inaccuracy, but Miss Carson's emotional approach accomplished what a thousand scientific papers could not do—awakened the people to an awareness of the hidden dangers of pesticides. Later, more sober accounts, but equally valid indictments, were to appear. These have been well presented in Robert Rudd's book, *Pesticides and the Living Landscape.*[32]

The pesticides that have been effectively and widely used in recent decades are organic in nature. One group, the chlorinated hydrocarbons, includes DDT, DDD, dieldrin, chlordane, and endrin among others. The other group, the organophosphates, includes malathion, parathion, and TEPP. Of the two, the first group has presented the most problems. DDT, for example, persists on soil and vegetation long after it has applied. Repeated dosages may therefore be consumed by animals. It is also a broad-spectrum pesticide, meaning that it effects many kinds of animals other than the particular insect for which it was intended. It is a cumulative poison; animals store it in their fatty tissues and may build up high concentrations in their internal organs even though the initial field concentration was at a level not toxic to most species. The organophosphates, although highly poisonous, are generally not cumulative nor do they as a rule persist on the ground.

As a method for control of pests, the most widely employed pesticides have this disadvantage: since they affect the entire community and not just the pest species, they kill off the predators and parasites that normally feed on the insect as well as the pest itself. They thus simplify the biotic community and generate instability. Lacking effective enemies, the pest species can increase more rapidly and to higher levels, before the populations of its former predators and parasites can recover sufficiently to again exercise some control. The control chemicals thus tend to create a continuing demand for more or better control chemicals. The agriculturalist who seeks to protect his crops is likely to make this demand. If other methods were available, he might turn to them, but chemical control seems simple, cheap and, initially at least, effective.

An example of the kind of problem that has developed has been presented by Rudd.[32] In the 1930's a reddish fire ant was accidentally introduced into Alabama and, thereafter, spread widely throughout the southern states. These ants built earth mounds that interfered with crop cultivation, they were capable of delivering a stinging bite, and they reportedly did some damage to crops and livestock. In 1957 the United States Department of Agriculture took action against them in cooperation with the states involved. A major program of control started using the chlorinated hydrocarbons, dieldrin and heptachlor. During 1957–1958 over two and a half million acres were aerially sprayed with these chemicals. As a result, "Fish, wildlife, livestock, and poultry suffered losses; the destruction of wildlife bordering on catastrophic." Outbreaks of other insect pests, presumably stimulated by the destruction of their natural enemies, took place. Fifteen million dollars were spent on the control program. The fire ant remained in the South.[32]

At Clear Lake, California, the use of DDD to control a gnat population caused a reduction to near elimination in the population of the western grebe, a diving bird for which the lake was famous. Subsequent studies revealed that the grebes concentrated the chemicals in their tissues to a level 80,000 times as great as the amount originally applied to the lake.[32] Elsewhere, control programs against spruce budworms and gypsy moths, insects that do serious damage to forests, caused significant wildlife losses from DDT poisoning. Dieldrin and aldrin, used against Japanese beetles, caused wildlife mortality. Elsewhere in the world, in Japan for example, losses of wildlife to a point of near extinction for some species have been reported.[43] In Ecuador, massive fish kills followed the spraying of banana plantations with a fungicide. In Malaya, the use of insecticides in oil palm plantations stimulated much more serious outbreaks of the bagworm pest than those that occurred before the pesticide was used.[9] In the tropics generally, where biological controls are normally more operative, the potential hazards from continued use of pesticides are known to be high, but have yet to be fully assessed.

Undoubtedly, much more can be done toward expanding and assisting controls that already exist in nature. Biological control has had great success in some areas against some species. A bacterium has been used successfully against the Japanese beetle. Introduced predators have controlled scale insects in California citrus groves and alfalfa fields. There are many other examples, but we cannot pretend that all of the answers lie in this direction.[32]

Not all use of agricultural pesticides causes damage. Chemicals that are not cumulative or persistent, chemicals that are specifically directed to the insect to be controlled, can be used to solve local problems and alleviate damage. The answer to the pesticide problem is not to abandon pesticides. Part of the answer lies in encouraging biological diversity and promoting those species that act to control pests. Part of the answer lies in finding new chemicals. Thus in 1967 a chemical TCPA was found effective against the Dutch elm disease when injected into the tree. It was apparently harmless to animal life and thus a major advance from the former use of DDT for this purpose.[18] Part of the answer, however, remains in the careful, balanced used of pesticides.

Unfortunately, pesticides, like other pollutants, can have effects in areas remote from their point of release. DDT residues are found in animals all over the world including antarctic seals and penguins.[37] Runoff from midwestern farm lands has added significant amounts of pesticide to the already polluted waters of Lake Erie. Runoff from Florida's farm lands carries pesticide-laden water into the wilderness of Everglades National Park. Pesticide problems are not localized; they are global. Consequently, the President's Science Advisory Committee in 1963 recommended a careful monitoring of the environment to keep a check on the level of pesticide residues, a phasing out of the use of persistent toxic chemicals with a view to their eventual elimination, and continued research toward the development of selective, nonpersistent chemicals and toward improvement of nonchemical control methods.[29] Some progress toward the elimination of pesticide hazards has been made, but they remain a major conservation problem.

# | 6 |

# Civilization and Water

Water has the peculiar quality of being an inexhaustible natural resource which is nevertheless in short supply. In the broad sense there is not and in the foreseeable future will not be a water shortage. Water in the oceans, the atmosphere, and falling upon the land is more than adequate to meet all human needs now and in times to come. However, water of usable quantity and quality, present in the right place at the right time, is not inexhaustible. It is a renewable resource, but one for which in many areas of the world the demand is far greater than the supply. Water shortages are becoming increasingly a problem of western civilization. In earlier times man first looked to the water supply before he attempted to settle in an area. Modern man too often settles in a desert and demands that water be brought to him, or he settles in a flood plain and demands that water be kept away.

The rise of civilization came with the ability to manage the floods and irrigation waters of the river basins of the Old World. Western industrial civilization, more than any preceding it, demands water. Industries engage in processing raw materials require vast quantities of water for their functioning, and could not grow or be maintained without the ability to obtain these quantities from streams or underground water sources. Cities could not have reached their present size without drawing water from distant hills and mountains, the watersheds from which rainfall drains into the lakes and rivers. If our ability to manage water falls short, the entire framework of civilized life is threatened.

## THE LOS ANGELES STORY

An example of the unbalanced distribution of population and water supply characteristic of the western world is provided by the coastal plain of southern California. Here in an area one-eighth the size of

141

Fig. 64. Flood damage in Hollywood, California, 1938 (U.S. Forest Service photograph).

California lives more than half the population of the state. Los Angeles alone is the second largest city in the United States. The warm, dry mediterranean climate, with its prospects for outdoor living throughout the year, the miles of bathing beaches and recreational grounds, and the employment offered by industry have attracted people from afar. Early in the twentieth century the motion-picture industry moved to the Los Angeles area, attracted by the clear air and the climate conditions favorable for year-round open-air photography. The air is no longer clear, but the industry remains. Aircraft and other industries, since attracted to the region, have provided employment for the people and have in turn attracted more people.

The same climate which brings people to southern California does not bring water. The rainfall may be between 10 and 20 inches annually, on the average, over most of the coastal plain and only reaches a more adequate 30 to 40 inches in restricted areas of the higher coastal mountains. The rainfall is erratic, dry cycles alternating with wet, and much of the annual rainfall may come in a few gully-washing storms (Fig. 64). The area receives less than 1.5 per cent of the state's total water. By contrast the sparsely peopled northwest coast of California receives more than 38 per cent of the total rainfall.[15]

Water problems are not new in southern California and cannot be related entirely to misuse of the land. Since the Spanish first arrived in 1769, there have been an estimated 25 major floods, alternating with long periods of drought and crop failure.[24] In the late nineteenth century an effort was made to bring the local water supply under reasonable control through the construction of dams and aqueducts and through the placing of timber and brush-covered mountains in federal forest reserves for protection of the watershed cover. Underground water supplies were tapped by drilling numerous deep wells.

By the early 1900's it was realized that local water supplies were inadequate for the growing population. Los Angeles City began to reach out for water, first to the Sierra Nevada in the north. After much controversy with the local residents, Los Angeles obtained control of the Owens River watershed, draining the east slope of the Sierra 250 miles away. A great aqueduct carried the first water from this region to Los Angeles in 1913. With further population growth, this supply proved

Fig. 65. Parker Dam and reservoir on Colorado River. A source of water for Southern California (U.S. Bureau of Reclamation photograph).

Fig. 66. Hoover dam on the Colorado River. One of the first and the highest of the multiple-purpose dams (U.S. Bureau of Reclamation photograph).

inadequate, and the city reached farther north to tap the Mono Lake watershed in the period between 1934 and 1940. Realizing that even this supply would be insufficient, Los Angeles next looked to the waters draining from the western slopes of the Rocky Mountains into the great Colorado River. In 1933 work was begun to impound the Colorado at Parker Dam (Fig. 65), 155 miles south of the giant Hoover Dam, (Fig. 66), and to carry this water across the desert 242 miles to Lake Matthews in southern California.[24]

Other southern California cities and communities, faced with similar problems, have engaged in equally heroic efforts. In all, an estimated sum of over 7000 million dollars has been spent in an attempt to solve

California's water problems. Yet they are not solved. With ever-growing populations, Southern California has had to look still farther afield. In 1951 a project was approved to bring water from Feather River in the northern Sierra Nevada through some 567 miles of conduits to the south. As part of the California state water plan the Feather, the Trinity, and other northern rivers are being tapped to provide water for urban populations and irrigation farming in the drier southern regions of the state. However, the end is not in sight as yet, and plans exist for channeling water from the Columbia River southward.

In many places throughout the United States, although nowhere on such a colossal scale, similar water problems have developed. Good farming soils, good industrial sites, and centers for trade or commerce often fail to coincide with dependable year-round water supplies. Populations grow and water demands increase. The alternative to bringing water over great distances to these areas could lie in locating industry and encouraging people to settle in areas where water is abundant, while limiting growth in areas where it is scarce. This approach, however, has not been seriously tried in the United States.

## THE HYDROLOGIC CYCLE

Water-conservation problems are unusually complex and are too often approached with simple solutions which are ineffective or even disastrous. The conservation of water requires the best efforts of those concerned with the conservation of all biotic resources and also draws on the specialized knowledge of hydrologists, geologists, and engineers to an extent that few other renewable resources require. To begin to understand the nature of the problems it is necessary to examine the hydrologic cycle (Fig. 67), the cycle through which water moves from ocean to atmosphere to land and back to the oceans, and to consider the many and complex uses to which it may be put along the way.

The source of most of the rain that falls on the land ultimately is the ocean. Air masses lying long over the seas pick up large quantities of water through evaporation. When they move inward over the continents, much of this water falls out as precipitation. The movement of air masses, which to a large extent controls climate and weather, is and probably will remain a natural phenomenon over which man has little or no control. The timing and distribution of rainfall may be affected in the future by human activities as techniques for inducing precipitation are improved; however, it is likely that dry climates will

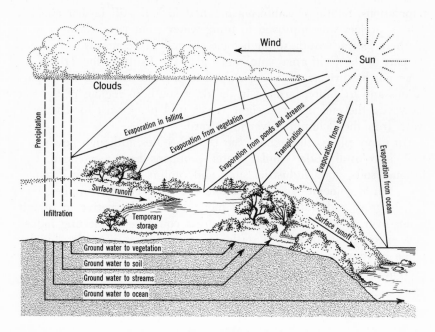

**Fig. 67. The hydrologic cycle.**

remain dry and that man will remain unable to squeeze water from a dry air mass. Indeed, the ecological consequences of any massive attempt at weather control are so enormous and potentially dangerous that the writer hopes that we will move slowly in this direction and only after the most rigorous research. We cannot afford the kinds of blunders that we have already made in the use of atomic energy or in the careless application of pesticides to the land.

When water first reaches the ground in mountain areas in the form of rain, snow, sleet, hail, or surface condensation, it becomes useful to man. Falling on areas covered with natural vegetation it provides the soil water from which forests and range grasses must grow. Combined in vegetation it provides timber or forage for livestock or wildlife. The excess, running off the surface or sinking in the ground to reappear in springs or as base flow in streams, again becomes useful, providing drinking water for livestock and game and habitats for fish and aquatic life. Meanwhile much is returned to the air by evaporation from vegetation, soil, streams, lakes, or rivers, and by transportation from the vegetation of the area, and this is returned once more to the ground in further precipitation in other areas. Another portion has gone deep into the ground and has moved downhill slowly through underground strata of porous rock or sediments not yet consolidated into rock. This ground water may later reappear as base flow into streams, lakes, or ponds, maintaining the flow or level of these bodies of water during the dry season when surface runoff is no longer available. Ground water may also travel further to lie under the valleys, perhaps to keep their soils saturated and give rise to meadow or marsh or perhaps to lie deeper and provide soil water in the dry seasons or feed the deeper-rooted plants. The depth to which it is necessary to go to find saturated ground is known as the depth to the *water table*. Water tables in the lowlands are maintained by water seeping into the ground in the hills and mountains. Still other quantities of ground water may remain for long periods in underground storage, until tapped by wells.

Water falling on farm land follows a similar course. Sinking into the soil it provides the water from which crops are made. In the process much is transpired or evaporated back into the air. If the amount of rainfall is great and the ground porous, some water sinks through to add to underground supplies. Some will run off to add to stream flow and eventually reach the ocean.

In the larger rivers and streams water can supply transportation for man and his products. It also provides for additional fisheries, and, everywhere that it lies in quantity, water provides recreation. Man has always been attracted to stream or lakeside for rest and pleasure. He may seek only the scenery and beauty that the water provides; he may seek the joys of fishing; or perhaps swimming, boating, and related sports will attract him.

With the growth of civilization the course of waters has been changed from the simple original pattern. Water running from the mountains in streams is impounded behind dams. From here it may be lead into irrigation canals to provide water for dry but otherwise fertile lands on which crops can be grown. It may be diverted into aqueducts and carried to meet the needs of towns and cities, or it may be used to provide electric power.

Water that reaches population centers is put to greatest use. It must first meet the living needs of the people, to provide drinking, cooking, and washing water. It is used to suppress city fires, to wash down streets, and to water lawns and gardens. It provides an efficient means of disposing of waste products, from sewage to the vast quantities of waste created by industry. It must be used in industrial production, the processing of foods, the milling of timber, and the manufacture of countless products used by civilized man.

Excess water must also be coped with. Dams and levees are constructed to reduce floods. Drainage ditches and canals are built to remove excess waters from otherwise adequate farming lands.

Most who deplore the demands made by civilization upon water supplies are still not willing to forego the benefits that civilization has brought. Yet the problems have become severe. Each portion of the hydrologic cycle and each use that we make of the water present us with new dilemmas.

## WATER NEEDS AND PROBLEMS

**Urban water supplies.** Water that reaches a city should be clean and pure. Water that leaves a city is often dangerously contaminated. The provision of adequate supplies can be difficult; and disposal of wastes sometimes more so. The extent to which a city must go to meet its water needs has been exemplified by Los Angeles. Other problems that are encountered are pointed up by the experience of another Cali-

Fig. 68. Gibraltar reservoir in the Santa Barbara area. The steep chaparral-covered slopes erode readily when fire or disturbance removes the vegetation (U.S. Forest Service photograph).

fornia city, Santa Barbara. Santa Barbara is built on a narrow, coastal plain backed up by high, chaparral-covered mountains. From early days it has had difficulty in obtaining water. In 1920, Gibraltar dam was built on the Santa Ynez River in the mountains behind the city, and water from the reservoir was carried through the mountains in a tunnel 4 miles long (Fig. 68). Shortly after the dam was built it became obvious that the reservoir was filling with silt and losing its storage capacity. To stop silting, two additional dams, Mono and Caliente, were built upstream (Fig. 69). Within two years their reservoirs were completely filled with silt and debris. In 1946–1947 siltation had reduced the capacity of Gibraltar reservoir to one-half, and it was necessary to build the dam higher. In 1948 a severe water shortage hit the city and caused great restrictions and inconvenience. To obtain additional supplies a new and larger dam, Cachuma dam, has now been completed on the Santa Ynez River below Gibraltar dam.[24] The expense of all of this construction has been considerable, and yet no permanent solution has been achieved if population and industrial growth are to continue.

The Santa Barbara problem is one shared by many arid regions. The watershed cover in the mountains is highly inflammable. Despite extreme efforts at protection, including the closing of the entire watershed to public use during the dry season, fires start and sweep over vast acreage. Burned over slopes erode badly, and the resulting debris fills reservoirs (Fig. 70).

Thus the provision of adequate water to a city involves the careful management of vegetation in sometimes distant mountains. Such watershed management must include the prevention of erosion with consequent siltation and also the provision of maximum quantities of usable water. Natural vegetation, while maintaining soil, preventing erosion, and regulating runoff from watersheds, can also be a source of much water loss through water transpired from leaf surfaces. Some transpiration is an unavoidable cost of the protection and other values which vegetation provides. However, there is much difference in the amounts of water transpired by different types of vegetation. Replacement of one type by another could be one way to increase water yields from a watershed without loss of benefits provided by well-covered hillsides. Where the natural vegetation, like chaparral, is highly inflammable, the danger of fire and resulting erosion loss could be minimized where it could be replaced by a less inflammable type. The danger in such management, however, comes when one set of values such as high water yield is placed above all others such as timber, forage, wildlife, and recreation values which may contribute to an enrichment of the lives of people in the area concerned.

Fig. 69. Mono reservoir in Santa Barbara area. This dam was built to stop silt from flowing into Gibraltar reservoir. In the upper photograph, taken in 1938, the area behind the dam has been completely silted in. In the lower photograph, in 1949, vegetation has invaded the silted area, and the former reservoir site now supports an open woodland (U.S. Forest Service photographs).

Fig. 70. Before a brush fire burned the area in the mountains enclosed by dotted line in the upper photograph, this single storm drain handled the runoff in this orchard. Following the fire, in 1941, runoff from a light rain filled the orchard with the debris shown in the lowei photograph (U.S. Forest Service photographs).

In the humid eastern United States it was once thought that any serious water crisis would be unlikely. In the early 1960's, however, New York and other eastern seaboard cities faced water shortages that only partially could be blamed on a series of below-average rainfall years. Mostly the water problem was the result of blundering in the management of water to a degree that seemed to reflect a serious inability to plan for the future. At the worst of the drought, the Hudson River continued to flow past New York City, much as before. Its water, however, was too dangerously and heavily polluted to be considered for the city water supply, since the means for purifying it had not been installed, and the possibility of bringing any quick control to pollution was remote. New York used over a billion gallons of water per day but, since it had long been believed that water would remain abundant, there was no control over individual use. New Yorkers paid a flat rate for water and the amount used was not metered. Furthermore, the aqueducts and mains that supplied water to the city were found initially to be wasting water through numerous leaks.[20,29]

South from New York in the nation's capital, the drought forced Washingtonians to take a hard look at the Potomac. It was found to be seriously polluted and flowing at a dangerously low level. It was unsafe for swimming and could be made safe for urban use only after expensive purification. A major campaign to clean up the Potomac was initiated by the federal government with a view to having a river fit for recreational use. Even Rock Creek, flowing through the capital's famous Rock Creek Park, was so polluted from seepage from septic tanks and other sources that it was unsafe for children to wade in. In the late 1960's, water pollution control had become a major national issue to which Congress and the Administration were devoting major attention. It was realized that an expenditure of forty billion dollars over a ten-year period might be required to bring the nation's rivers back to, not their original purity, but a reasonably clean condition.

**Waste disposal.** Disposal of sewage is a problem that has confronted mankind ever since populations started to concentrate in towns and cities. The removal of human wastes by water transportation has been a major advance in sanitation achieved only in the technologically advanced countries. One needs only to recall the precautions against eating unwashed fruits or vegetables or against drinking unboiled water encountered by travelers from the western world to most other areas of the globe to realize the significance of this advance. Amoebic dysentery and a variety of other gastrointestinal diseases are a widespread cause of death or debilitation in many countries, largely because of poor sanitation practices. On the other side of the ledger, soil fertility and structure have been maintained over the centuries in these same countries by the return of organic material, including human wastes, to the soil.

In the western nations the problem of waste disposal in large cities became acute when obnoxious accumulations of waste developed and epidemics spread. Removal of sewage through water dilution and transportation tended initially to reduce greatly the health hazards. Dangers of infection were reduced by the dilution and dispersal of disease-causing organisms in water. However, with increasing populations it became apparent that water facilities would prove inadequate. Rivers became highly contaminated, and ocean beaches were lined with sewage where currents failed to carry sewer discharges offshore.

Apart from the health hazard, disposal of sewage in watercourses presents other problems. Organic wastes decompose in water and in the process use large quantities of oxygen. Where high concentrations of organic wastes occur, oxygen may be exhausted and aquatic life destroyed. Water disposal of sewage also removes a potentially valuable substance, which if properly treated would provide a fertilizer to help restore depleted soils. To meet these difficulties many cities have now installed sewage-disposal plants. In these plants the solid organic matter is separated from the liquid through various washing, skimming, and settling processes. The solids, when processed, disinfected, and dried, become valuable as fertilizer. The liquid effluent, however, must in most cases still be disposed of by water transportation and therefore remains a source of pollution. To avoid this, some cities are now using sewage effluent for industrial processes. The city of Baltimore, for example, makes use of sewage effluent water by piping it to the steel mills of Bethlehem Steel Company. Here it is used in large quantities in the manufacturing and processing of steel. By this method, the normally high demand for fresh water for the steel mills is reduced, and pollution is alleviated.[54]

Disposal of wastes from canning and food-processing industries presents difficulties similar to those of sewage disposal in that high concentrations of organic matter are carried in the waste waters. Lumber mills and other industries also have water-borne wastes which are highly charged with organic materials and can cause serious stream pollution. One effective means of disposing of these wastes was described in the previous chapter when the Seabrook Farms problem was discussed. Similar disposal has been used at State College, Pennsylvania, and St. Charles City in Maryland.[48] Such land disposal, however, is seldom possible in large urban areas. Ways of concentrating and removing waste products and finding uses for them must be found.

Mills, mines, chemical industries, tanneries, and other industrial concerns often have waste waters containing highly toxic or objectionable chemicals which can render large streams unfit for any further use. Some pulp mills, which have exceedingly toxic wastes, have devised recirculating systems whereby the waste water is processed, the chemicals reclaimed for further use, and the water rendered pure enough for reuse. Such systems, although expensive to install, cut down on the freshwater requirements of the mill and make it possible to operate where water supplies are limited. Similar processes can now be considered completely essential for all polluting industries.

Much progress has been made in waste disposal. As a result of public pressure, education, and research directed toward finding ways of avoiding water pollution, industries have become conscious of the dangers and more cooperative about finding ways to avoid them. However, much remains to be done, and with increasing populations new problems will develop. The development of nuclear energy as a new power source and a weapon of war has brought a new source of pollution—radioactive contamination of air and water—far more dangerous and lasting than any other type of pollutant. Scientific opinion is as yet divided about both the extent of the danger and the ways to avoid it (see Chapter 13). In America as in other new lands, man has considered fresh air and clean water to be part of his heritage. With his new industrialized way of life, however, he is finding both difficult to maintain.

During the late 1960's it was obvious to most Americans that all previous efforts toward solution of water pollution had been inadequate. Thus Lake Erie, a lake that absorbs the wastes from the factories of Detroit, Toledo, Cleveland, Erie, and Buffalo, the sewage from a still larger range of communities, the runoff, laden with pesticides and excess fertilizer from a vast area of farmland, has lost its normal aquatic life, has become choked with some of the more obnoxious kinds of algae, has become unsuited to recreational use, and in many respects is dying.[23] Niagara Falls, over which Lake Erie drains, has become the nation's most spectacular sewer outfall. Despite all the brave words of earlier decades, most factories still have not installed recirculating or waste-reclaiming systems, most communities still have inadequate sewage-disposal systems, and siltation of water from accelerated erosion still goes on at disturbingly high rates.

Congressional and administrative action by the federal government has been taken. Water pollution control was moved in 1966 from the Department of Health, Education, and Welfare to the Department of the Interior. A bill was passed in 1965, the Clean Rivers Act, which required all states to develop water standards, subject to federal review and modification, in order to restore the nation's rivers and streams. In 1966, Congress appropriated 3.6 billion dollars for the development of waste treatment facilities. Yet it was obvious that these measures were only a beginning. Industries must spend more money, communities must spend more money, regions and states must spend more money if the job is to be done. This means that the average citizen must pay more for the clean water he once considered to be free. The alternative would be a situation that would become increasingly intolerable.

**Water power.** That running water could be put to work was discovered early. Stream flow was used first to turn simple water wheels which turned stones to grind grain or which dumped water into flumes to be carried elsewhere. Later, with the discovery of electricity, the rivers were further harnessed. Simple water wheels were replaced by rapidly spinning turbines, generating electric power to do work a hundred miles away.

The need for water power, in addition to the needs for municipal water supplies, irrigation waters, and flood control, has spurred on the building of dams. Furthermore the sale of electric power from federally constructed water projects to private power companies or to municipalities has helped to pay, in part, the costs of dam construction. Water has an advantage over the fossil fuels (coal, petroleum, and natural gas) as a source of power in that it is a renewable resource. It has the disadvantage that the possibilities for its development are limited. Compared to the total energy requirements of the United States, the amount of power provided by hydroelectric installations is small, approximately 5 per cent of the total.[5] Future development of hydroelectric sites will not greatly increase the percentage contribution of water power to total energy needs. Locally, however, water power is highly important, and without it many industries could not have been developed in their present location, and many communities might lack electricity.

The sale of water power, however, has provided an economic justification for the construction of projects that might otherwise appear less feasible. In 1966, for example, the Bureau of Reclamation proposed that two dams, Marble Canyon and Bridge Canyon, be constructed in the Grand Canyon.[37] These would have detracted not only from the wild quality of one of the nation's most important scenic resources, but would have backed water into the area of Grand Canyon protected by the National Park Service. The sole justification for these dams was the production and sale of hydroelectric power for income to be balanced against the cost of other facilities, designed to bring irrigation water to central Arizona. Fortunately, an outcry from conservation organizations caused the Department of the Interior in 1967 to withdraw its plans for these dams.

Perhaps one of the greatest "boondoggles" proposed under the justification of hydropower production has been the Rampart Dam on the Yukon River in Alaska.[45] This immense structure, to be built at a cost of over a billion dollars in the Yukon wilderness, would have flooded 8 million acres of land and have done almost incalculable damage to fish and wild life resources. It would have generated an excess of power beyond any foreseeable needs within Alaska. Fortunately a study sponsored by the National Resources Council and conducted under the leadership of Stephen Spurr of the University of Michigan, revealed the high costs and doubtful benefits of this project before plans for it had become too far advanced. It was shown that Alaska's power needs could be met by smaller dams closer to its centers of population.[44]

On a worldwide basis, the future development of hydroelectric power sources would provide only a fraction of anticipated power needs, because many lands lack the combination of elevated lands and fast-flowing rivers needed for hydroelectric development. Yet for many countries and areas, which have not yet developed their waterpower potential and are poorly endowed with coal and petroleum, such development would bring great gains in living standards. In the future, however, the cost of providing power from water will have to be matched against a new competitor, power from atomic energy. The costs of power from atomic plants are steadily being reduced through research and development of new techniques. In time it may well supplant most other power sources. However, with atomic power plants comes new dangers of pollution, and these we have not fully faced (Chapter 14).

**Irrigation.** Throughout the drier parts of the world there is a great demand for water to be used in irrigation of farming lands. To provide such water highly expensive dams and water-diversion projects have been built and are being built in many places. In general, areas with less than 20 inches of rainfall annually can be farmed only at a risk of crop failure unless irrigation water is available. There are complicating factors, such as temperature and evaporation rates and the regularity and dependability of the rainfall, which make farming successful in some areas with less than 20 inches of rain, but these are exceptions. The soils in the drier lands, because of the low rainfall, are relatively unleached and therefore rich in surface minerals. Where water can be made available in quantities sufficient for washing out excessive accumulations of salts, even the soils in dry, desert lands can become highly productive (Fig. 71).

Fig. 71. Irrigated land growing date palms in what was once a desert. Coachella Valley, California (U.S. Bureau of Reclamation photograph).

One of the most successful irrigation projects in the United States is the Imperial Valley of southern California. Here, some 500,000 acres were brought into cultivation through the private and doubtfully legal construction of the all-American canal from the Colorado River which provided the necessary water. Here, because of the warm climate, crops can be grown in seasons when they are unavailable elsewhere in cooler areas, and subtropical crops such as dates and citrus fruits can be produced in quantity.[24] Other areas throughout the southwestern United States have also been brought into production. Their value to the nation is high.

In 1960 the total area of irrigated farm land in the United States amounted to 33 million acres (Fig. 72). Of this, over 30 million acres were in the seventeen western states. The remainder consisted largely of lands supplementally irrigated to increase crop yields where the rainfall was otherwise adequate. The U.S. Bureau of Reclamation has estimated that an additional 12 million acres in the West can be brought

Fig. 72. The Friant-Kern irrigation canal of the Central Valley Project, California (U.S. Bureau of Reclamation photograph).

under irrigation. This would make a total of slightly over 42 million irrigated acres in the West, compared to nearly 190 million acres being dry-farmed. Although, under present conditions of crop surpluses in America, it hardly seems worthwhile to add to our agricultural acreage, this new land may be needed in the future. The expected increases in population over the next few decades could require a further expansion in agriculture if needs are to be met at present standards. Yet it must be faced that the cost of irrigating new land is extremely high and that water used for this purpose is no longer available for other uses. Gains in new agricultural acreage must then be met by losses in other areas toward which our national effort might equally well be directed. It is one of the anomalies of present-day America that we pay money, through various federal programs, to take land out of agricultural production and, at the same time, pay through the financing of reclamation and irrigation projects to bring new land into production.

**Excess water.** The spread of man over the face of the earth has been accompanied since early times by his attempts to settle in areas where an excess of water was a problem. Low-lying seacoast lands, marshlands, and alluvial plains have attracted him as potential agricultural or urban sites. In each such area he has sought ways to dispose of the surplus water. One of his most heroic efforts in this direction has been the reclamation of land from the sea in the lowlands of the Netherlands and Belgium. Here an elaborate system of dykes, drains, and pumps has been put to work to reclaim over a million acres of land for urban and agricultural use from the Zuider Zee.[13,34]

In the United States reclamation of marsh lands has long seemed a good way to bring new areas into agricultural use. Drainage of marshes has in some instances succeeded in providing first-class farming land. In other instances unfavorable consequences of marsh drainage have become obvious. Marshes, through providing areas of storage and later slow release of excess water, can be of great value in regulating stream flow and preventing floods, in increasing the quantity of ground water and keeping water tables high, and in providing a habitat for vast numbers of waterfowl and other wildlife. Drainage not only has brought wildlife destruction but also has contributed to increased floods and lowered water tables. In many cases the damage has overbalanced the gains.

Fig. 73. Flood damage. Oregon. Overflow of the Willamette River washed 1 foot of topsoil from this orchard, leaving tree roots exposed (photographs by Soil Conservation Service, U.S. Dept. Agric.).

One of the worst examples of a conflict between drainage projects and other environmental values has been in southern Florida. Here irreplaceable natural areas are being sacrificed to bring additional land into housing or agriculture by drainage and impoundment of water.[19] However, over much of the eastern seaboard the same process may be observed. The Great Dismal Swamp in Virginia is about to vanish before the developer, the Great Swamp in New Jersey, one of the few wild areas in the New York City region, is in danger of being reclaimed for a jetport.

Where man has settled in the flood plains of rivers he has run the risk of being drowned out. In ancient Egypt man learned to live with the Nile flood waters, allowing them to rise each year, deposit their thin layer of silt, and retreat once more to the river channel.[11] In America we have seldom adopted this reasonable way of living with nature but have instead sought to control and confine the rivers. Such control has brought gains in increased crop yields, has permitted the building of cities and residences on the flood plains, and in general has permitted more intensive land utilization, but at a cost.

Along the lower Mississippi and other major river systems one method of controlling floods has been to build levees which keep the river in a restricted channel. The normal tendency of the river is to rise over its banks in flood time and often to deposit silt on the flooded areas. Confined by levees, the silt load may still be deposited but within

Fig. 74 and chapter opening. Flood waters washing soil from an Idaho farm (photograph by Soil Conservation Service, U.S. Dept. Agric.).

the river channel. Each year the river may build its bed higher, and the next year's flood is consequently raised. To meet this threat, levees have been built higher until finally in some areas the river, confined by levees, flows well above the roof tops of cities and towns along its bank. Sooner or later comes the big flood which the levees cannot hold, and the results are disastrous. In a spectacular flood in 1852 the Yellow River in China broke through such elevated levees, took millions of lives, and found a new channel to the sea.[34] Along the Mississippi Valley similar catastrophes, but with less loss of life, have happened in much more recent times. In the great California floods of 1955 the Feather River poured through a levee break to do millions of dollars in damage and take many lives in Yuba City. In 1965 hurricanes and high water combined to send water over the Mississippi River levees in New Orleans and do millions of dollars worth of damage. To prevent this type of damage, spillways and bypasses are built along with a levee system to allow excess flood waters to pour out through channels across bottom lands, which can otherwise be used at nonflood times for agricultural purposes. However, even with these devices, levees break, and flood damage still takes place.

To give further flood control the tendency in the United States has been to emphasize large multiple-purpose dams. These dams, when built in a suitable location, can reduce floods as well as provide water for power, irrigation, and other uses. There are few conservation questions, however, about which more controversy has raged than the question of the value of these multiple-purpose dams. The most elaborate series of dams in the country thus far has been built along the Tennessee River, under the jurisdiction of the Tennessee Valley Authority. These have converted much of the river into a chain of fresh-water lakes. The T.V.A. has provided flood control, irrigation water, electric power, navigation, and water for domestic and industrial use through the dams built as part of a project to restore the badly eroded lands and to reorganize the damaged economy of the Tennessee River watersheds.[9] The T.V.A. has served as a model for many other nations and yet has been the target of more criticism than most other government agencies have received.

A still more elaborate series of dams is being established on the Missouri River system. The Columbia and Colorado rivers are being developed with similar chains of dams and reservoirs. The state water plan for California provides for one or more dams on every major river in the state (Fig. 75). As a nation we seem committed, perhaps somewhat unwittingly, to the principle that dams are worthwhile.

Objections to the big dams on our river systems have been many.

Dams are expensive. They flood lands at the reservoir site; they lose water through evaporation from the reservoirs; they destroy fisheries. Wilderness, wildlife, and recreational values are often sacrificed to dam construction. Dams may catch water which is heavily laden with silt. This silt normally settles to the bottom of the reservoir, and silt-free water is released at the outlet. Such silt-free water often has unanticipated damaging effects on the stream channel below the dam, scouring and eroding the river banks and picking up a new silt load which is then deposited in some previously silt-free area.[30,32] In addition, siltation of the reservoir may threaten the life of the structure and in some instances may result in the creation of a new alluvial plain at the former reservoir site. Water storage in reservoirs, with the consequent decrease in stream flow, can cause invasion of salt water in delta areas, creating new problems for agriculture in these regions.

It must be realized also that large dams do not prevent downstream floods. Each dam is built with a certain reservoir capacity, and, with the realization that under certain known flood conditions, flood waters will be in excess of what the reservoir can hold. Complete flood preven-

Fig. 75. An upstream dam in West Virginia. This earth-fill dam and reservoir is part of a Soil Conservation Project for watershed protection and reduction of flood damage (photograph by Soil Conservation Service, U.S. Dept. Agric.).

Fig. 76. Columbia River flooding at Vanport, Oregon. Downstream flood damage of this magnitude provides economic justification for large dams (photograph by Soil Conservation Service, U.S. Dept. Agric.).

tion, if it could be accomplished, would be so costly that it is not even contemplated for any major drainage area. At best dams are planned to hold back flood waters up to a certain rate of flow and to minimize damage from floods that exceed that rate.[30]

Yet despite these many objections, large dams on main river channels are the most economical way of minimizing downstream damage from the large, spectacular floods which have their origin in general rains covering a large portion of a drainage basin. Most cities, towns, and industries are located downstream and not high in the watersheds. It is downstream consequently that the greatest damage from single floods takes place (Fig. 76). Alleviation of such damage provides the economic justification for large flood-control dams.

Opponents of large dams have indicated that the same objectives can be accomplished at less expense by "stopping floods where they start" at the headwaters of streams. There is something to be said for this point of view. Under natural conditions of forest and grassland vegetation, soils in the watersheds of streams were protected by a sponge-like layer of litter and humus, and the structure of these soils favored water penetration and retention rather than runoff. Destructive use of headwater lands has increased the amount of runoff and in many areas has increased the frequency and severity of floods. Attention to proper conservation use of headwater lands would cut down on flood danger. Thus, along the Wasatch Front in Utah heavy summer rains in 1923 and 1930 caused severe flooding in many areas. In two adjacent canyons, however, the flood picture was quite different. Both watersheds received equally heavy rain, yet the watershed of Parrish Canyon produced severe floods, whereas the adjacent Centerville Canyon produced little or no flooding. Investigation showed that the Parrish Canyon watershed was heavily overgrazed; whereas the Centerville Canyon watershed was protected from excessive grazing. With this realization, the Parrish Canyon watershed was brought under protection from heavy grazing and fires, and the vegetation was restored. This has prevented further flood damage.[10] A dam in Parrish Canyon would not have helped. With the excessive erosion that was taking place it would soon have filled with silt, and the flood damage would have gone on. In this area the answer to floods was protection of the watershed.

In southern California in 1933 a chaparral fire burned 7 square miles of land in the San Gabriel Mountains. In the following winter a severe rainstorm occurred, and it was followed by a flood which caused an estimated 5 million dollars worth of damage. The flood issued from the burned-over watershed and had a peak flow estimated at 1000 second-feet per square mile. Nearby unburned watersheds which received the same amount of rainfall had peak flows measured between 20 and 60 second-feet per square mile and experienced little damage. In this area, vegetation protection rather than dams is the way to prevent such floods.[10]

To demonstrate the effectiveness of watershed management as a means toward flood control, the Soil Conservation Service has undertaken a series of watershed projects aimed at stopping floods high in the drainage basins, preventing erosion and siltation, and at the same time providing a better quality of land use. To date, these efforts have met with considerable success in some directions. Lands have been improved and made more productive and stable. Erosion has been cut down, and with this the silt load of streams has been decreased in some areas. Small local floods have been eliminated, and larger floods reduced to some extent. Flood damage to lands located in the upper watershed has been greatly reduced. However, land management practices alone have not accomplished all of these objectives. Flood control is still provided in part by dams but in these projects by many small dams on tributary streams (Fig. 76). In the aggregate these small dams are expensive and can be subjected to many of the criticisms also directed against the large downstream dams. Furthermore against certain types of floods they are ineffective.[30] For example, in December, 1955, heavy general rains fell for many days over much of northern and central California. Nearly every stream and tributary reached flood stage, and the major rivers poured into many cities and towns and inundated vast areas of agricultural land. In all, the damage was measurable only in hundreds of millions of dollars. Watershed treatment and small upstream dams would not have controlled these floods, although they would have alleviated much flood damage. However, the severity of the floods was reduced by the presence of the giant multiple-purpose dams at Folsom and Shasta. Such heavy rains as this can saturate the best-managed soils and exceed the water-holding capacity of the best-treated drainage basin.

It must be realized that long before civilized man appeared on the scene there were floods and that regardless of how much land-use practices are improved and whether we build small dams or large, floods will still occur. There is no single panacea to flood problems. In some places large dams alleviate flood damage; in others they are ineffective, and watershed management offers most promise. Lands must be preserved, and erosion must be prevented for reasons other than flood control. However, as long as we continue to build high-value structures, subject to damage by flooding, in areas where flood waters naturally accumulate, we will continue to experience damage from floods. To control such damage we seem committed to spend somewhat fantastic sums of money for dams and levees, upstream and down, but we cannot economically eliminate such damage so long as cities and industries remain on the flood plain. Under such circumstances, it seems reasonable to consider an alternative. Areas subjected to frequent flooding can be zoned to prevent their use for purposes that might involve excessive loss of property or life when floods occur. Such zoning can prevent the construction of additional structures in such areas. Outright purchase and removal of existing structures by government agencies would be less expensive than the efforts now directed toward flood control. Such lands could then be devoted to other uses less likely to be adversely affected by floods. Such flood-plain zoning has been tried on a small scale in a few areas but on the larger scene has not yet received adequate consideration. The possibility has been suggested also that in place of spending money for flood control the federal government should offer flood insurance to those using areas subject to flood damage. The cost of the insurance to the flood-plain user could be adjusted to the type of use and the likelihood that damage will be experienced. Such insurance costs would effectively prevent certain types of use for land subject to frequent flooding.[6,30,51]

## RECREATION

Water-based recreation is now big business in America. In many places—Reston, Virginia, and Columbia, Maryland, are examples—new towns and communities are planned around artificially created bodies of water in the expectation that these will make the site more attractive to the prospective home buyer. Waterfront property has become a scarce and expensive commodity. The costs of new dams and reservoirs are partially justified on the basis of the recreation use that they will attract. In a survey of America's outdoor recreation preferences, the water-based sports of swimming, fishing, boating, ice skating, water skiing, canoeing, and sailing ranked in the top twenty pursuits.[41] There is no doubt that the demand for access to recreation water is high and growing (see Chapter 12).

The need for natural bodies of water, untouched by development of any kind, is also great. Natural streams, lakes, and seashores that can be maintained in a near-primeval condition have become scarce in America, and have a value not only to those seeking a high quality of outdoor recreation but also for the study of hydrology, ecology, and other environmental sciences. These form needed reference points for comparison with those areas that man has changed (Chapter 11).

There is a tendency in water development projects to underestimate the value of an untouched stream or other body of water and to overemphasize the benefits in irrigation, urban water, power, or other quantifiable benefits in order to justify the construction of engineering facilities. Unless this practice can be reversed, America stands to lose much that is priceless and irreplaceable in outdoor resources.

## SOME FUTURE PROSPECTS

During the decades since World War II the growing demand for water has brought an increasing investment in research and development aimed at extracting fresh water from the sea. Such a source of fresh water could not only spare remote watersheds from development but make it possible for seacoast cities and islands to become independent of other water sources.

The feasibility of desalting water is related to the salinity of the water and the desired purity of the product. Sea water, because of its high salinity, 35 to 36 parts of salt per thousand, is far more difficult to purify than is brackish water of a much lower salinity. It is easier to purify water to a level equivalent to that of hard fresh water, with a salinity of perhaps 0.3 parts per thousand than it is to carry the process farther and achieve soft water with a salinity of 0.06 parts per thousand. Consequently the greatest successes, from an economic viewpoint, have come from the desalinization of brackish water rather than sea water. Nevertheless the desalting of sea water to produce urban drinking water is now past the theoretical stage and is being practiced in many areas.

Buckeye, Arizona, a town with a 1960 population of 2300, became the first American community to obtain its water supply from the desalting of brackish water. Its desalting plant produced 650,000 gallons of water per day at a cost of less than a dollar per thousand gallons.[29] Later, Port Mansfield, Texas, developed a plant which yielded 250,000 gallons per day. A large desalting plant was established in San Diego, California, in the early 1960's and later moved to Guantanamo Bay, Cuba, where it produces a million gallons of water per day. In the Virgin Islands a sea-water distillation plant yields 275,000 gallons per day at a cost of a $1 per 1000 gallons. A still larger sea-water plant in Kuwait, Arabia, using natural gas for power, yields 9 million gallons of water per day. In 1966 there were 200 desalting plants in operation around the world.[29,49]

In 1966 the Office of Saline Water of the Department of the Interior and the Atomic Energy Commission were cooperating with the Metropolitan Water District of Southern California to constuct a nuclear-power desalting plant that would produce 150 million gallons of fresh water per day at a cost of 0.27 cents per thousand gallons, and would also generate 900 megawatts of electricity per day. The Oak Ridge National Laboratory has carried out feasibility studies on a plant that would yield one billion gallons of water per day at a cost of 0.20 per thousand and would also produce 20,000 to 25,000 megawatts of atomic electric power. Such a plant could supply the water requirements of New York City.[18]

There is no doubt that desalting of ocean and brackish water holds great hope for supplying future water needs. However, there are problems to be overcome. The proposed Southern California plant, for example, will yield 23,000 tons of salt per day from sea water. This will include not only common sodium chloride but also many minerals of potentially high value, but at present the greatest challenge may lie in the disposal of the salt. Where nuclear energy is used to produce the power needed to operate the desalting plant, the safe disposal of atomic waste products presents another technological problem.

It is unlikely that desalting of sea water will be practical for producing the major amounts of water needed for irrigation. Arizona, for example, pumps 5 billion gallons of water per day from underground storage areas, but uses 4.7 billion of these gallons in irrigation alone, with all other needs supplied from the remaining 0.3 billion gallons. In federal irrigation projects the cost of water to the user is far less than the actual cost of delivering the water. The irrigation farmer is thus subsidized, indirectly. It is unlikely that the cost of desalted sea water will ever be within reach of the farmer. Furthermore, since sea water is available only at sea level it would be necessary to pump it, at a still higher power cost, in order to deliver it to irrigation projects located inland. The biggest hope for irrigation may lie in the desalting of brackish water located in inland sources or underground. Sea water is most likely to continue as a source for seacoast urban-industrial water supply.[29,49]

Despite the promise of desalinization, efforts to develop new sources of fresh water may be expected to continue. The most massive water development scheme yet proposed has been brought forward by the Parsons engineering firm of Los Angeles. This is the North American Water and Power Alliance (NAWAPA). It would tap the rivers of northern Canada and Alaska, pump water southward into a storage area in the Rocky Mountain trench of Canada, and deliver it as needed as far south as Mexico for a cost estimated at 100 billion dollars.[44] Obviously such a plan would reorganize the western countryside, have massive effects upon ecology, destroy great wilderness and wildlife areas. Wallace Stegner has described it as being potentially a "boondoggle visible from Mars, a project to make Rampart Dam look like something created in a sandbox."[46]

Regardless of what we do, the ultimate answer to water problems lies in population limitation. We could move water down the continent and irrigate all our deserts to provide more water and more food for more people. The people would then not have wild country or desert wilderness, but they would still have a population problem and growing water needs. We could, on the other hand, limit population growth at some point where we would have enough food, enough water, and enough wild country to satisfy anyone. We still have the choice.

# WATER CONSERVATION

It is difficult to take an over-all view of water-conservation problems because of their ramifications through all of civilized life. We have already noted some of the complex problems that are encountered in this conservation area. However, certain basic principles need to be formulated.

It is necessary that water-conservation plans be fitted into a general scheme of environmental conservation. They must include, as they have not always included in the past, adequate attention to proper land conservation in the watershed areas. Better soil conservation on agricultural lands can lead to better use of soil water, better storage of soil water, and increased yield to subsurface waters. This can diminish the demand for irrigation water for farm crops in some areas. Through soil conservation, erosion can be slowed down to a tolerable rate and silt problems downstream diminished. Better land-use practices on forest land and rangeland can also increase infiltration, stabilize runoff, and bring greater yields in timber and forage. Each region must take the responsibility for its own watersheds, streams, and rivers. Industries and municipalities must be held responsible for solving problems of water pollution.

All needs for flood control, irrigation, electric power, and municipal water cannot be met by sound land management and local initiative. The state and federal governments and thus the people as a whole are necessarily involved in the more complex water problems. Yet the expenditure of great sums of money at the state and federal level for somewhat doubtful gains in flood control, irrigation, and power cannot continue. Each day the decisions we make on the use of water involve the sacrifice of one value for the enrichment of another. When we commit ourselves to a policy of providing through engineering developments for unlimited urban, industrial, and agricultural development of one area, we are committing resources that might well be used to develop other values in other areas. We need to take a long look to the future before taking such steps. It is essential that the construction of large dams, water-diversion projects, numerous small upstream dams, or other structures be preceded by careful, unbiased research. In this the long-term, over-all effects of the structure on natural resources and potential ways of life for the future must be evaluated. Short-term gains must be weighed against long-term losses. The importance of fisheries and wildlife resources, wilderness and wild lands, recreational and aesthetic values must not be minimized, as they too often have been in the past.

Our two most basic resources, upon which our entire civilization depends, are water and soil. In their management we have too often taken the short view. With water in particular we have made conservation a political football and a source of contention between both the various government agencies and private industries. Local self-interest and political "axe-grinding" have often wielded more influence than the opinions of experts. For the resulting confusion the people have already paid heavily in tax money and perhaps more heavily in the loss of resource values. We cannot afford to allow such conditions to continue. We should never run short of useful water in America if it is carefully managed, but if it is not we can expect water problems to grow increasingly severe.

# | 7 |

# Timber and Man

Man has proved surprisingly illiterate in reading the lessons of history. Perhaps it is that, blinded by the glare of immediate profits, he sees the pages of the past as blank. Whatever the cause, the results are a discouraging repetition of mistakes. This has been noticeable in particular in man's treatment of forests. Properly managed, forests can enrich human life in a variety of ways, both material and psychological. Poorly managed they can be the source of disruption for the environment of an entire region. However, through the centuries we have seen a pattern repeated. The misuse of axe or saw, of fire or grazing causes forest destruction. This leads to disruption of watersheds, to erosion, and to flooding. Flood waters and silt in turn can damage or destroy the cities or farms of the lowlands. Yet, in many parts of the world, forest destruction continues.

The values of a forest are many. In this chapter, however, particular emphasis will be placed upon the role of forests as producers of timber, valued by man for wood or pulp.

## FOREST EXPLOITATION AND THE
## TIMBER INDUSTRIES

When the colonists came to America, the United States was one of the richest forest areas in the world (Fig. 77). It has been estimated that there were over 1000 million acres of forest in the United States, with over 8000 billion board feet of potential saw timber.[13] But to the early settler the forest was a nuisance, its limited value as a source of fuel and construction timbers outweighed by the fact that it occupied land wanted for his crops and grazing. The old, traditional fear of the dark woods as a dwelling place for real or imagined enemies was aggravated by the Indian wars, when hostile raiders swept from the forest

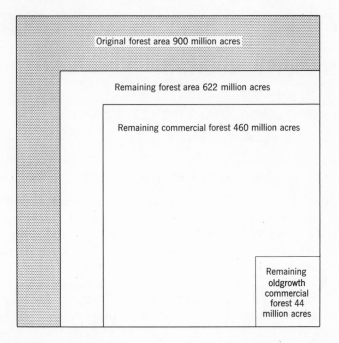

Original forest area 900 million acres

Remaining forest area 622 million acres

Remaining commercial forest 460 million acres

Remaining oldgrowth commercial forest 44 million acres

Fig. 77. Changes in the forested area of the United States from settlement to 1952 (source U.S. Forest Service.)

cover into the settled lands. Great areas of hardwood forest, which would be worth a fortune today, vanished, therefore, without contributing a single piece of furniture or a finished board.

With the increase in population and the need for wood for ships and cities, enterprising people were attracted by the value of the soft, easily worked, but strong and durable wood of the white pines, which grew in a belt separating the cold, northern spruce forests from the southern hardwoods (Fig. 78). We know now that these pine forests were an historical accident, successional forests grown up following some widespread catastrophe, perhaps fire or hurricanes, which had swept through the northern United States in the fifteenth century.[3,5,19] However, they were available for easy exploitation at the time when the surge of colonists into the prairie states created a major demand for timber. In the early nineteenth century white pine logging on a commercial basis began, centering in the New England states. The management practices used, if they can be called such, have been summed up as "cut out and get out." The future was little thought of when the supply of timber in relation to the number of people seemed limitless, and there was always more "out west." As the readily accessible forests dwindled, the center of the white pine industry shifted from Maine to New York to Pennsylvania and finally in 1870 to the great forests of Wisconsin and Minnesota.[22] With the destruction of the forests in the Lake States came the finish of the eastern white pine as a major commercial species, and the attention of the industry shifted to other species. Following on the heels of the loggers came fire (Fig. 79). The logging practices left much slash and debris on the ground; the rolling topography of the Lake States provided few natural barriers to fire. Fire starting in cutover areas can generate enough heat to leap to the tree crowns where, carried by the wind, it can spread at horrifying speed, almost impossible to escape or to control.

In October, 1871, a fire started near Peshtigo, Wisconsin, which swept over more than a million acres, burned out numerous towns and settle-

Fig. 78. White and red pine forest in Minnesota (U.S. Forest Service photograph).

ments, and killed 1500 people. In 1894 two major fires in Wisconsin and Minnesota burned hundreds of thousand of acres, killed over 700 people, and wiped out many towns. In 1918, a spark from an engine at a lumber mill in Minnesota started a fire which burned out Cloquet, a town with 12,000 inhabitants, swept over a large sector of country, and was stopped only at the outskirts of the city of Duluth. Four hundred people were killed, and timber and property worth 30 million dollars were destroyed.[12] These and many other fires during the same period finished off the damage that logging had begun. The virgin pine forests of the Lake States dwindled to a few scattered remnants, and in their place a scrubby growth of birch and aspen took over (Fig. 80).

Between 1900 and 1910 the lumber industry in the South occupied the center of the scene. Here the emphasis was on the hard, southern yellow pines. These trees, spreading from the area originally forested, had sprung up on abandoned and depleted fields left as the wave of cotton and tobacco planters moved west. Fast growing, quickly regenerating after logging, and favored by limited burning, the southern pine forests have proved highly resistant to destruction, and the South remains today the center of pine-timber production.

Fig. 79 and chapter opening. A forest fire. Fires sometimes move from the ground up tree trunks into the crowns where they are carried from tree to tree by the wind (U.S. Forest Service photograph).

Fig. 80. Birch-aspen woods in the Lake States. This type of forest replaced white pines after logging and fire (U.S. Forest Service photograph).

At the same time the southern pine industry was beginning to boom, the attention of other lumbermen shifted to the West. Here, the great stands of Douglas fir in the Pacific Northwest represented an immense storehouse of timber (Fig. 81). In 1905 the state of Washington took the lead as the chief lumber-producing state, and has held it since.[22] By the time the logging boom reached the West, however, sufficient force had been generated by the newly organized conservation movement to pevent the outright destruction that other areas had experienced. In forestry, this first took shape with the growth of federal concern over the hitherto unmanaged public lands. From the federal lead, the idea of conservation gradually spread to the large lumber companies. Left with no new worlds to conquer, these organizations realized the necessity of managing their own lands for permanent production. However, the original large wave of forest destruction has continued in numerous small ripples, represented by the smaller logging concerns with no lands of their own, which have moved through the woods country

Fig. 81. Douglas fir forests attracted the logging industry to the northwest coast (U.S. Forest Service photograph).

devastating remaining areas not brought under federal or forest-industry ownership. Many of these operators, too hemmed in by conservation laws in their homeland, have now moved into the forested lands of Latin America, hoping to repeat there the process of quick profits which means prolonged devastation.

## FOREST CONSERVATION AND MANAGEMENT

**Federal forestry.** The growth of federal forestry in the United States is associated with the name of Gifford Pinchot, one of America's first

Fig. 82. Destructive logging practices leave bare, eroding slopes, and stream beds choked with debris (U.S. Forest Service photograph).

professional foresters. He and other leaders were interested in bringing to a halt the "mining" of forests and in treating the forests for what they were, renewable resources capable of being both used and preserved for the future. Starting in 1891, President Harrison was enabled by Congress to withdraw federal lands from the general public domain and set them aside as forest reserves—Yellowstone Timberland Reserve, surrounding Yellowstone Park, was the first. With the election of Theodore Roosevelt as President, a naturalist and outdoorsman became chief executive. With the advice of Pinchot and others, Roosevelt managed to add a large new area to the forest-reserve system and to bring it to a total of 148 million acres by the end of his terms in office (Fig. 83). At the same time, he realized that these forests need not be "reserved" but could be used under careful forestry practices as permanent sources of timber. With their names changed to "National Forests" the old reserves were transferred to a new agency, the United States Forest Service, which was placed in the Department of Agriculture. Under the leadership of Gifford Pinchot, as the first Chief Forester, the Forest Service undertook the task of bringing management for use to the National Forests. Over the years, the Forest Service had developed an *esprit de corps* and a conservation philosophy which have persisted, despite many discouragements, to the present time.

The brand of forest conservation exemplified in the National Forest

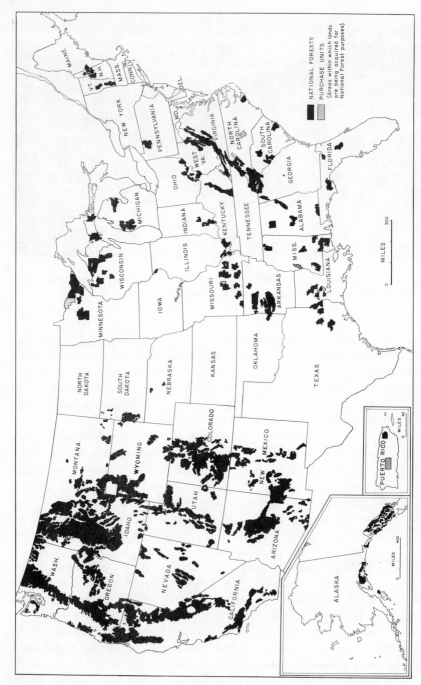

NATIONAL FORESTS

PURCHASE UNITS
(Areas within which lands
are being acquired for
National Forest purposes)

Fig. 83. National forests of the United States (map by U.S. Forest Service).

180

system can be summarized briefly as: (1) *Sustained yield*, the concept that timber harvest and growth must be balanced over a period of time so that forest yield will be continued into perpetuity. This leads to some popular misconceptions in its practice, for when a mature forest is being cut over, there is an initial period when harvest far exceeds growth. Thus in the Pacific coastal region where mature forests are still widespread, the timber cut in 1962 was 23 billion board feet; the net growth, 13.5 billion. Mature forests are slow-growing, so that almost any degree of cutting represents an excess over growth. However, if management is planned so that abundant reproduction takes place, the fast-growing young stands soon balance the rate of cutting. (2) *Multiple use*, the principle that the national forests should serve a variety of purposes and not just the single purpose of providing wood products. Grazing, wildlife, recreation, soil conservation, and, perhaps most important, watershed conservation are among the legitimate forest uses, the

Fig. 84. Block cutting of timber, with seed tree left to favor regeneration of the forest (U.S. Forest Service photograph).

ideal being to serve the community and nation in as many ways as possible. Although often receiving only lip service for lack of money or other reasons, this concept is one of great value for the future. (3) The general ideal of *"the greatest good for the greatest number in the long run"* has helped to guide Forest Service policy. The emphasis is here placed on the "long run" to avoid the short-term, high-profit philosophy which has influenced so many other activities in this nation.

**Some management practices.** Achieving sound forestry practice on private or public forests is a difficult job. It involves many different activities and skills. One of the first requirements is a thorough inventory of the forest resources. This means determination of the volume of timber in each area, broken down by location, species, age classes, condition of trees, and other criteria. Next a plan for harvesting the timber must be worked out that will permit timber removal while still guaranteeing good regeneration of the forests. In forests consisting of even-aged stands of trees, stands in which the commercially valuable species are of approximately the same age and size class, some form of *block* or *strip*

Fig. 85. Selective cutting. Younger trees and reproduction are left untouched (U.S. Forest Service photograph).

Fig. 86. Skill in falling trees is essential if a forest is to be harvested without damage to growing stock or other resources (U.S. Forest Service photograph).

cutting is usually practiced (Fig. 84). In this the timber is entirely removed from a block or strip of land. In some cases, a few healthy seed trees are left to provide seed for regeneration; in others, the trees in surrounding uncut areas must provide the seed. This method is useful in pine or Douglas fir forests, where the seedlings need light and thrive on open ground. It does not work with most climax tree species, in which the seedlings are best fitted to establish themselves in the shade and cannot compete well in full sunlight. In the usual climax forest, trees occur in uneven-aged stands, in which all age classes are represented. These are best harvested by a system of *selective cutting*, in which the older, mature trees are removed by the first logging operation, leaving the younger trees for a later crop (Fig. 85). In this system,

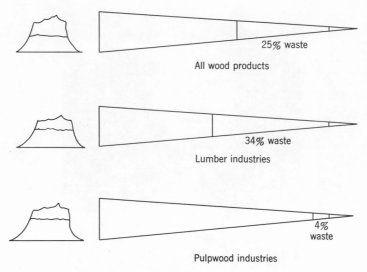

Fig. 87. Waste of forest products in harvesting and milling processes (data from U.S. Forest Service).

great care must be used not to damage young trees while removing older ones.

Skill in falling trees is essential to good management (Fig. 86). Careful location of tractor and truck trails for the carrying of logs to the mill is essential if damage to soil and timber, with consequent erosion, is to be avoided. Clearing of slash and debris to leave a good seedbed for forest regeneration is an important job. In intensively managed forests the trees should be thinned and pruned to provide best growth and yield. Diseased or damaged trees should be cut, and dense stands of production opened up. Lower branches of trees should be taken off to give clean, straight trunks for clear lumber. These maintenance operations can yield commercially useful products during the periods between harvestings of the main timber crop. A mixed, uneven-aged forest, with a variety of useful species, can provide some income, year after year, to its owner. All forests, however, cannot be so managed.

Prevention of waste is another important part of good forest management. Full utilization of the tree for lumber is not possible, but the remnant parts often have value for other wood products. The development of the pulp industry, producing paper and other products, and the plastics industries, has created a demand for practically the entire tree, as a source of wood fiber or cellulose rather than whole wood. These industries therefore make much better use of forest production

Fig. 88. Despite precautions fires still burn large acreages (U.S. Forest Service photograph).

than the lumber industries, unless these are connected with subsidiary industries using wood wastes (Fig. 87). As part of obtaining full utilization of forest products, there is a need to find use for a variety of trees not now utilized, instead of just the few preferred species that have been emphasized up to now.

Fig. 89. Repeated burning has changed this once-forested area to low-value brush (U.S. Forest Service photograph).

**Forest protection.** A job of major importance to forestry is still that of protecting the forest against the old enemies: fire, disease, and insects. Few areas of conservation have received greater publicity or made greater gains than the prevention of forest fires. The situation has changed markedly from the destructive days at the beginning of the twentieth century. Now a network of fire-lookout stations, fire roads, fire breaks, and suppression crews guard national forest lands (Fig. 90). Private lands also have been brought under increasing protection by state, county, and private fire-prevention and fire-suppression agencies. Despite this, extensive areas are still without adequate protection, and fire remains an important destructive force. In 1952 about 780 million board feet of saw timber in the United States were destroyed by fire.[9] Somewhat over 188,000 fires, averaging about 75 acres in size burned over 14 million acres of forest land. In 1962 an estimated 1.3 billion board feet were lost; however, only 4 million acres were burned. Expenditures for fire protection in 1962 were 153 million dollars com-

Fig. 90. Photograph showing the variety of equipment, from horses to helicopters. used in present-day fire fighting (U.S. Forest Service photograph).

pared with 78 million in 1952.[10] Dry weather and high winds can create conditions against which the most elaborate fire-suppression network is ineffective. Continued public cooperation and much more care on the part of the users of forest land are essential if fire losses are to be minimized. Most fires are still man-caused fires. Prevention remains the best way to stop fire losses.

Disease has been a less-publicized but, in recent years, a far greater enemy of the forests than fire. In 1962, over 3.8 billion board feet of saw timber were destroyed by this cause.[10] Even though some of this was salvaged through logging, much was a total loss. Among the most spectacular forest diseases have been chestnut blight, blister rust, and the Dutch elm disease. Chestnut blight, caused by a parasitic fungus, was introduced from the Orient early in the twentieth century. Within a short time it had eliminated the chestnut tree from the eastern hardwood forests. No effective way of controlling this disease has yet been found, and only through the introduction of disease-resistant strains of tree can the chestnut be re-established in this country. Blister rust, accidentally introduced from Germany, has prevented the eastern white pine from becoming re-established in the areas from which fire and logging had removed it; and it has spread through the western mountain forests of sugar pine and western white pine. This fungus disease spreads from pine tree to gooseberry or currant plant and from that back to pines. Control is a laborious process involving the eradication of the gooseberries and currants in areas close to white pine forests. The Dutch elm disease, spread from tree to tree by insects, threatens the existence of the elm tree component of the eastern hardwood forests. Thus far, the best hope for control of diseases lies in sound forestry practices, involving the removal of trees likely to become infected and the prevention of injury to young trees. However, where serious diseases are established, it is often advisable to encourage, through planting or the encouragement of natural reproduction, species that are not affected by the prevalent diseases.

Insects destroy more timber than fire and disease combined (Fig. 91). In 1962 the total insect destruction of saw timber in the United States amounted to 5.4 billion board feet, of which only a small part was salvaged. Among the more destructive insect pests are the pinebark beetle, which annually destroys large amounts of ponderosa pine in western forests; the spruce budworm, which attacks the spruce-fir forests of Canada; the pine weevil, which attacks white pine; and the larch sawfly, which has destroyed many of the mature tamarack stands of the North. With insects as well as disease, sound management aimed at maintaining a healthy growing stock, healthy soil, and a balanced

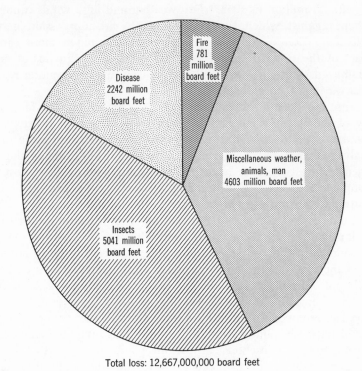

Total loss: 12,667,000,000 board feet

Fig. 91. Loss of saw timber to destructive agencies, 1952 (data from U.S. Forest Service).

biota is the best way to minimize losses. Where this fails, expensive special control measures must be used. Spraying forests with various chemical pesticides has brought some measure of pest control in some areas. Unfortunately, as we have seen in Chapter 5, most insecticides are not selective. Both useful and harmful insects are destroyed. The effects may spread to other animals, including highly valued wildlife. The net effect in some areas has been compared to burning down a house to rid it of termites.

## TIMBER FOR THE FUTURE

The United States situation. The forest situation in the United States now and the future prospects have been summarized by the United

States Forest Service.[10] Their 1965 report, although considerably more optimistic than similar ones prepared in earlier decades, still leaves little room for complacency.

We have lost about one-fourth of our original forest area, much of this having been converted into agricultural or other uses. Nevertheless, we still have a large store of timber. Within the United States, about 509 million acres are rated as commercial forest land, that is, land capable of producing commercial wood products either now or in the near future, and not withdrawn from commercial use in parks or reserves (Fig. 77). Only about 43 million acres of forest remain in old-growth timber; the rest has been cut over and is now covered with second-growth forest.[10] The balance between harvest and growth is favorable; the total annual cut of saw timber in the United States being estimated at 48 billion board feet for 1962, compared to 55 billion board feet in annual growth.[22] However, the total drain on saw timber from all causes, including fire, insect, and disease losses, still far exceeds the annual growth, with approximately 68 billion board feet cut or destroyed in 1962, compared with 55 billion board feet in growth. For all growing stock the total growth was 16 billion cubic feet, the total mortality was also 16 billion, including the annual cut.[10]

One of the most serious problems of forestry today, and for the future, results from the forest-ownership pattern (Fig. 92). National forest lands and lands controlled by the timber industries are fairly well managed for timber production. However, only 28 per cent of the commercial forest area in the United States is in federal, state, or local government ownership, and only an additional 13 per cent is under the control of forest industries. The balance, amounting to 59 per cent of our total commercial forest area, is in the hands of farmers or in other small miscellaneous ownerships.[10] These owners, often lacking adequate incentive, interest, or knowledge to practice forestry on their lands, have allowed their woods to deteriorate. A high percentage of them own forests that are judged to be poorly stocked, that is, supporting fewer trees per acre than they are capable of growing. The quality of timber on these areas is also poor, with low-value species taking over much area that could be growing better timber trees and with the growth form and wood quality of the individual trees falling below adequate standards. Many of the small forest holdings suffer from abuse or neglect, often being used for intensive grazing or other purposes that prevent adequate tree reproduction.[10]

One unfortunate fact, which has prevented sound forest management on much timber land, is that timber is often a long-term investment. The farmer or small owner who has timber land bearing mature timber is often handicapped by taxation based on the potential market value

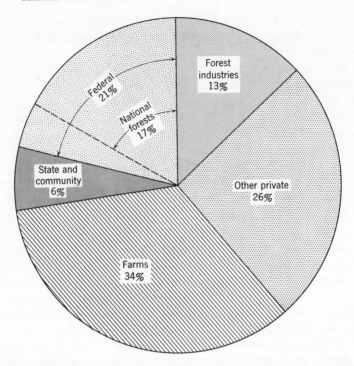

Fig. 92. Ownership of commercial forest land in the United States, 1952 (data from U.S. Forest Service).

of his timber stand. Under such circumstances he is tempted to sell to the highest bidder and to have the timber removed as quickly as possible. Once it has been removed he is free of the tax burden and may also be able to make use of the land for other purposes. Once a forest is cut over by clear-cutting methods, which remove all of the timber, it takes a long time to regenerate and yield further income. The average landowner may not be willing to hold his forest lands in trust for the future, knowing it will be at least several decades before any further substantial wood crop can be harvested. Instead he may be tempted to convert the former wood lot to pasture. Although recently forested lands make poor pasture, the facts are that livestock bring cash to the pocket each year, whereas timber would not. Considering that the average farm forest is less than 50 acres in size, long-term management for wood production may seem to make little economic sense to the owner.[10,18,19]

There are ways around the difficulties presented by small-sized forest ownerships. If taxation is based upon the amount of timber harvested rather than on standing timber, there is less incentive for harvesting the entire timber crop at once. Many states have changed their system of forest taxation to a yield tax, rather than a tax on standing timber. Community forest cooperatives have worked out well in many parts of the country. These permit many small owners to put their woodlands together to be managed as an economic unit under sound forestry principles with costs and profits shared. In the Scandinavian countries forest cooperatives have been developed to an encouraging extent. There, regional forestry boards, assisted by the government, provide technical assistance, arrange for forest planning, provide seedlings for replanting, and give loans and grants to assist in sound management.[24] Thus community and farm forest owner share the expenses and benefits of good forestry. Nevertheless, in the United States, it is perhaps unrealistic to include the forest area under farm ownership or miscellaneous private ownerships as part of the commercial forest land.[21] There is no guarantee that the owners will ever decide to treat their farm wood lots as commercial forests, for they may always prefer to use them for other purposes. With increasing demand for residential and industrial land, there is reason to expect that many farm wood lots in the eastern United States will be converted to these uses.[18]

The United States is in a favorable position at the present time with sufficient forests to meet its needs for wood products. There is every indication, however, that this will not be true for long. With a total of 509 million acres of commercial forest land in the United States, there are at present 2.5 acres of commercial forest per capita. With estimated population growth, however, there will be 1.6 or fewer forest acres per capita in 2000 A.D. In 1962 we used 12 billion cubic feet of wood per year, part of which is supplied by imports. By the year 2000 we will require an estimated 21 billion cubic feet. Between now and 2000 A.D. we cannot expect any increase in forest acreage; more likely there will be a decline as the demand for land for other purposes grows. It is estimated that by 2000 A.D. we will be unable to meet wood demands with available annual supplies. It is obvious that, by whatever incentive we use to accomplish it, we must somehow achieve a much better overall level of forest management and forest productiveness than we have today.[10] It should be remembered also that the 509 million acres of commercial forest land is largely in the hands of small private owners. Only 180 million acres of commercial forest is under the control of lumber industries, the federal government, or state governments and therefore is fairly certain to remain as commercial forest in the future.

**The situation in other countries.** Apart from the United States, the nations of the world represent all extremes in forest resources and forestry practices. In Canada, the timber situation is comparable to that in the United States. The timbered area suited to commercial forest production amounts to 529 million acres and contains an estimated 418 billion cubic feet of commercially useful timber, compared to 628 billion cubic feet in the United States in 1962. Thus, Canada has a larger commercial forest area than the United States but a smaller volume of commercially useful timber because of the lower productivity of the northern forest. The total yield in 1952 was approximately 3.5 billion cubic feet, compared to 10.8 billion from United States forests. The annual loss to fire, insects, and disease was less than in the United States. Thus the present timber situation and outlook for the future in Canada seem somewhat better than in the United States. Particularly favorable to future sound management is the ownership pattern, with 94 per cent of the commercial forest land in federal or provincial ownership.[25] Canada has been an important exporter of timber and timber products, particularly pulpwood, which is shipped to both Europe and the United States in large quantities. The United States can expect to meet some of its future timber needs by increased purchases from Canada. However, it will face competition from a growing internal market in Canada and from the timber-deficient countries of Europe.

In Europe the western concepts of forestry had their beginnings and have made their greatest gains. Europe's forests, although small compared to those of North America, are intensively managed and yield large quantities of wood (Fig. 93). The total timbered area in western Europe and Scandinavia, excluding the British Isles, is about 185 million acres. This area had an annual growth and potential yield of over 6 billion cubic feet timber in 1952, 55 per cent of the amount cut from United States forests, from an area less than 40 per cent as large.[14,24] West Germany, with about 17 million acres of forest, had a yield, in balance with growth, of over 700 million cubic feet of timber in 1954.[14] The same yield applied to United States and Alaskan commercial forests would be about 20 billion cubic feet of timber, compared to the 10.8 billion actually harvested. Although the forests are not directly comparable in terms of potential yield, this difference reflects the intensiveness of forest management in European countries.

Many of the early foresters of the United States were trained in Germany, and for many years German forestry practices have influenced American thinking. The trends in German forest management are therefore of particular interest. After 1840 German foresters engaged in a highly artificial form of forest management. Forests were clear-cut and

Fig. 93. An intensively managed beech forest in Germany showing dense reproduction of young trees following cutting (U.S. Forest Service photograph).

replanted to the species of trees that were in greatest demand, mostly to pure stands of spruce or pine. It was believed that by doing this the highest possible yields could be obtained from each forest acre without wasting soil productivity on the growing of "weed" species of trees or brush. The former broadleaved forests or mixed broadleaved and coniferous forests were replaced by uniform even-aged stands of conifers. However, it was found that the continued production of these single-species forests damaged the soil through increased podsolization and the breakdown of the circulatory system of soil minerals. Losses to such causes as insects, disease, and storm increased. The second and third generations from pure spruce or pine stands began to decline in yield per acre as growth rates and timber quality fell off. As a result, after 1918, there was a swing in Germany back toward a more natural type of forest. Mixed forests were planted, as comparable as possible to the original forests of the area. Clear-cutting was replaced by selective cutting with logging practices which did as little damage as possible to the remaining stand of trees. Under this natural system of forest management, known as *Dauerwald,* yields have increased, and forest land has been improved.[14]

The lesson from the German forests has not been taken seriously in other countries. In Australia, for example, where great damage has been done in the past by forest fires and the clearing of forest for grazing and agriculture, the tendency in recent years has been to emphasize the planting of pure stands of exotic tree species. The Monterey pine, from California, has been particularly popular and has been planted over large areas. Initially, growth rates and yields from these uniform forests have been high. However, the practice has not yet been tried for long enough to discover whether Australia will also experience the difficulties encountered in Germany.[21] Some Australian foresters are much in favor of putting greater emphasis on replanting with mixed stands of native species. In the United States also, most forest plantings are made without regard for the German lesson.

If we look at the forest situation for the entire world, it is found that there are an estimated 9.5 billion acres of forest land, i.e., that somewhat more than one-quarter of the total land area of the globe is forested. These forests are estimated to produce about 50 billion cubic

Fig. 94. A tropical forest in Puerto Rico in Caribbean National Forest (U.S. Forest Service photograph).

feet of utilized wood annually.[21] Much of this forest area is in the tropics where forestry problems are far different from those of temperate lands. Here the forests are undergoing destruction and are being replaced by permanent or temporary agriculture or grazing land at an accelerating rate, reminiscent of the clearing that occurred in the eastern United States in pioneer days. It is seriously questioned whether it will be possible to maintain the climax tropical rain forest for long enough to develop any understanding of its ecology and potential uses. At present such an understanding is lacking.[20] In tropical and temperate areas, many countries are almost devoid of forest resources either because of climatic conditions or because of past forest destruction. In these countries, even the simple needs for fuel wood are difficult to meet. Various optimistic outlooks for the future of the worlds' forests look to a day when all of man's needs for forest products will be met through management of the world's forests for sustained yield, and through free exchange between those areas which are well forested and those which are not. Such optimism must be viewed with caution. Although present levels of demand for forest products can perhaps be met for several decades, increasing demands and increasing populations present a problem for the future that the foresters alone will be unable to solve.

## THE USES OF FORESTS

Thus far we have followed the conventional treatment of regarding forests simply as sources of commercially useful wood. This value of the forests is indeed high, and the uses to which forest products are put are many. To one living in the United States, it is somewhat surprising to realize that the greatest use made of forest products in the world is for firewood. More than half of the total wood cut in the world is burned as fuel, and in some Latin American countries 80 per cent of the wood cut is used as firewood.[21] In the industrialized nations of the world, other uses seem more important. Lumber is still the major construction material, despite the wide use of concrete and steel. Pulpwood for paper is so important to western ways of living that it is difficult to imagine how civilized life could be maintained without it. The United States is the world's greatest user of pulpwood and greatest producer of paper. It has been estimated, for example, that to produce the Sunday edition of the New York Times for one year requires 125,000 tons of newsprint. This in turn utilizes the annual growth from 1250 square miles of Canadian forest land.[7] Despite the variety of wood substitutes that have been developed, the demand for wood products has increased. New uses for wood are being discovered with each decade.

Although the importance of wood products is great, it is essential to remember that forests are far more than sources of wood. The value of forests for watershed cover has long been recognized and, in many areas, is of first importance. Many forested areas can also provide forage for carefully regulated livestock grazing, even though unregulated grazing has been a cause of serious damage. Forests are homes for wildlife and scenes for outdoor recreation, values which we cannot afford to minimize. Long before forests were regarded as commercial resources, they were of great value to man. These other uses of forests will be given greater emphasis in Chapters 11 and 12.

Planning for sound forest management, therefore, involves the integration of timber growing and harvesting systems with the other uses of the land. Soil protection and the maintenance of soil-water relationships need more consideration than they have often received. The effects of timber-management practices upon wildlife production and recreational uses of the land are only recently receiving attention from foresters. Multiple use of forest land, in the full sense, has yet to be generally accomplished. Admittedly, on sites best suited for timber growing, the production of wood will continue to need emphasis; however, such an emphasis need not be incompatible with the other uses to which the land is suited. On some timber-growing sites, these other uses may be paramount. In planning for environmental conservation, we cannot emphasize wood at the expense of all other forest values.

# Livestock on the Range

The domestication of range livestock brought both opportunity and danger to man. The opportunity lay in the possibility for the material enrichment of man through use of lands too arid for farm or forest. The danger has materialized in the disastrous consequences of overgrazing in the lands of western Asia, North Africa, and Mediterranean Europe. Grasslands and dry shrub vegetation, in their native state, provide little food or products of commercial value for man. To become economically useful the native vegetation must be converted into animal protein through the agency of wildlife or domestic grazing animals. In America, the grasslands were used in prehistoric times by man as a source of meat and hides from the native big game—the buffalo, pronghorn, and elk. With the coming of the Europeans, the wild livestock were rapidly replaced by domestic cattle and sheep. Still later, the better-watered sections of the grasslands were plowed into farm lands for cereal-grain production. Farther west, however, in the drier regions, the grassland and shrub ranges have continued as grazing lands.

## THE RANGE LIVESTOCK INDUSTRY IN THE UNITED STATES

**Beginnings.** The first livestock probably reached America when the Norsemen landed in Vinland in the eleventh century. Neither the Vikings nor their livestock survived in this country.[35] It was not until the time of Columbus that livestock were again brought to the Americas, and it was probably Cortez who first brought cattle and sheep to the mainland of North America in the early sixteenth century. It was noted in an earlier chapter that livestock spread rapidly under Spanish methods of handling. Cattle and sheep came to New Mexico in the sixteenth and seventeenth centuries, and spread through California in the latter

199

part of the eighteenth century.[37] The horse must have escaped from Spanish missions and settlements in the seventeenth century, for by 1680 the Pueblo and Apache Indians had the horse, by the 1750's the horse had reached Montana, and before 1800 Canada. The feral mustang and Indian pony played an interesting role in the history of the American West.[39]

The livestock industry in the United States has had its most colorful history in the area known as the western range, the arid grassland, sagebrush, and scrub country lying westward of the 100th meridian, which bisects North Dakota and runs southward through Dodge City, Kansas. It should not be imagined, however, that the western range supports most of the livestock in the United States. The area east of the 100th meridian supports far more beef and dairy cattle than the area to the west, and it is only in sheep numbers that the west has a slight edge.[31] The livestock business had its beginnings in the eastern United States with the animals brought from Europe by the early colonists. From early colonial times livestock were pastured in forest clearings along the westward fringes of the agricultural lands. From here the animals were moved back into farm fields and pastures for fattening and from there to market in the towns and cities. As agriculture spread westward, the pastoral fringe of land moved ahead of it until the prairie states were reached.[9]

In the eastern United States, livestock had a profound influence upon the vegetation. With grazing pressure the native grasses and forbs were displaced from the pastures and fields. In their place came a mixture of exotics which had followed the settlers from Europe. The most important of these was Kentucky blue grass, a perennial which has followed agriculture and pasturing throughout its long history in Eurasia and which helped to stabilize the pasture lands of western Europe.[8] Blue grass is an excellent forage grass for livestock and well able to hold up under heavy grazing. With its aid the soils on eastern pastures were held in place and their condition improved.

**Texas cattle.** While livestock were gradually spreading with the American colonies, a major center of stock raising had grown up in the Spanish domain of Texas. Spanish land grants were liberal and favored the establishment of large ranches needed for the maintenance of a range livestock industry. The cattle in this region were the famous Texas longhorns, a breed originally developed in Spain, long legged, rangy, hardy, and well suited to foraging in a half-wild condition on the open range (Fig. 95). When Texas entered the Union there was little change in land-ownership policy. Texas retained ownership of pub-

Fig. 95 and chapter opening. Texas Longhorns. These descendents of the cattle that pioneered in the West are preserved in the Wichita Mountains Wildlife Refuge (photograph by Soil Conservation Service, U.S. Dept. Agric.).

lic lands within its boundaries and continued to follow the Spanish practice of disposing of them to encourage range livestock production. As a result the livestock business thrived. With abundant grassland range and little need for hay or pasture land, the costs of operation for cattlemen in Texas were low. Markets were difficult to reach, and many cattle were butchered for hides and tallow. Nevertheless, stock raising remained profitable. In the 1840's, trail herds of Texas cattle were driven to market in Louisiana and later to Ohio. With the California gold rush, a number of drives of Texas cattle to California were carried out.[9]

In 1860 Texas is estimated to have held over $4\frac{1}{2}$ million cattle. Following the Civil War, a greatly expanded market for beef led to the series of trail drives of Texas cattle immortalized in western song and story. The Chisholm trail between San Antonio and Abilene is the most celebrated route over which cattle were driven. Most of the cattle trails were developed to meet shipping points on the new railroads which were being built westward in the 1860's. These shipping points, Abilene, Newton, Dodge City, and others, soon developed into the wild and lawless cow towns famous in western legend. During the 20-year period between 1865 and 1885 an estimated $5\frac{1}{2}$ million head of cattle were driven northward from Texas, some to market, others to stock the newly opening rangelands to the north.[9]

The settlement of the grassland ranges in the central and northern prairies and plains was retarded for a time by the warlike tribes of Plains Indians. A few pioneer stockmen braved these dangers and established ranches in the north in early times. However, the biggest expansion took place in the 1870's, as the Indians were subdued and the herds of bison on which they had depended reduced and finally eliminated. In 1870 it is estimated that there were between 4 and 5 million cattle in the seventeen western states; by 1890 there were over 26½ million.[9]

**Sheepherding.** Sheep brought to New Mexico in the sixteenth century were to form the basis for the sheep industry in the West. In the seventeenth and eighteenth centuries sheep ranches were established in New Mexico, Texas, Arizona, and California. Along with cattle, sheep also spread westward in front of the American colonists from the eastern seaboard.[37] However, the greatest expansion of the sheep business in the plains and prairie states took place after the cattlemen were well established. The extent of this expansion is indicated by the figures for 1850 when there were 514,000 sheep in the West and 1890 when the numbers had reached 20 million. The greatest increase in the northern plains came in the 1880's when cattle numbers were beginning to decline. Wyoming carried 309,000 sheep in 1886 and over 2,600,000 in 1900, during which period the number of cattle declined by half a million. In Montana there was little increase in cattle between 1886 and 1900, but sheep increased from somewhat less than 1 million to over 3½ million.[9]

In California sheep spread with the Spanish missions, *ranchos,* and later with the American settlers. Great bands of sheep were moved westward to stock California in early days—over a half million between 1852–1857,[26] and later equally vast bands moved eastward to stock the ranges of the Great Basin states. Many of the early sheepmen in California used to carry on the old Spanish practice of nomadic or migratory sheep grazing. One route regularly followed took the sheepherders up the east side of the Sierra Nevada, across the high passes of the central mountains, and back southward along the western slopes of the Sierra.[37] The numbers of sheep on these long drives were large, and the damage has been made memorable in the writings of John Muir, who described the devastation in the Yosemite region, and in the findings of later surveys which described the almost complete destruction of ground vegetation in the Mt. Whitney region.[24] The spread of sheep in the West did not take place without arousing bitter feelings among the cattlemen. Cattlemen, with established home ranches, particularly resented the passage of migratory bands of sheep across the ranges, using forage which they had hoped to reserve for their own cattle. The bitterness broke out into the open cattle-sheep wars in some areas.

Fig. 96. Sheep on the western range, Idaho (photograph by Soil Conservation Service. U.S. Dept. Agric).

**Public lands and livestock.** The history of livestock in the West cannot be understood without considering the land-disposal policy of the federal government. As a result of numerous transactions, the United States government had obtained claim to approximately 1½ billion acres of land within the boundaries of the contiguous United States (Fig. 97). The policy of the government was to dispose of these lands as rapidly as possible. The philosophy of Thomas Jefferson has dominated land-disposal policies. He believed that the lands should be used to encourage settlement and development of the nation and thus to strengthen it against its enemies rather than sold for immediate gain to the treasury (Fig. 98). A variety of acts were passed by Congress providing for the sale or homesteading of federal land. Noteworthy was the Homestead Act of 1862, which provided title to 160 acres of land, free of charge, to legitimate settlers after 5 years of residence upon the land. The 160-acre limitation proved to be a major difficulty. In the farming lands of the East, 160 acres is more than adequate to support a family. In the arid West, where agriculture is not possible, 160 acres is insufficient for the raising of livestock. The acreage limitation, for the West, was later raised to 320 and then to 640 acres in 1916. However, even 640 acres does not provide adequate space for stock raising. Much unfortu-

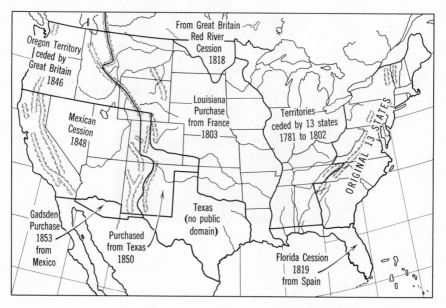

Fig. 97. The original public domain in the United States.

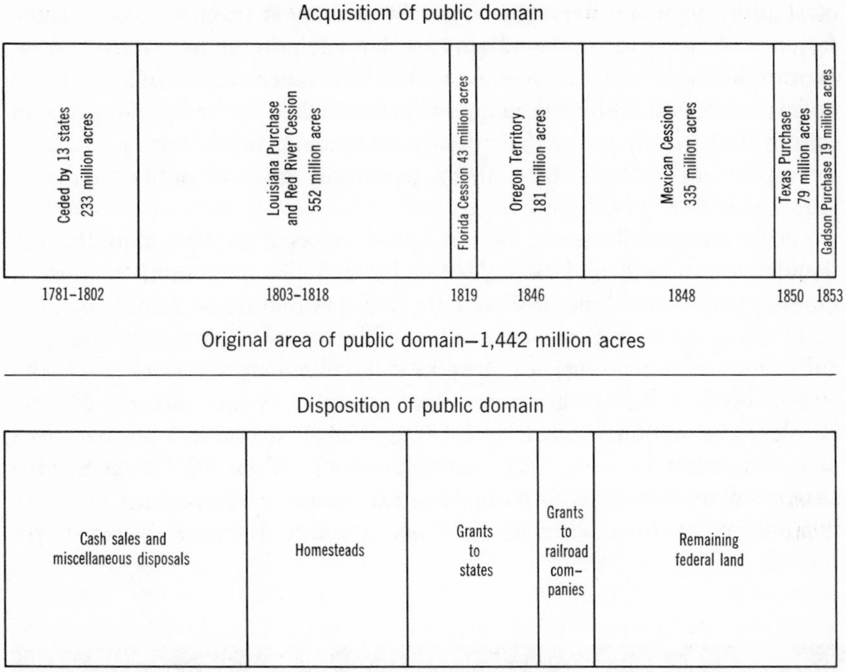

Acquisition of public domain

| Ceded by 13 states 233 million acres | Louisiana Purchase and Red River Cession 552 million acres | Florida Cession 43 million acres | Oregon Territory 181 million acres | Mexican Cession 335 million acres | Texas Purchase 79 million acres | Gadson Purchase 19 million acres |
|---|---|---|---|---|---|---|
| 1781–1802 | 1803–1818 | 1819 | 1846 | 1848 | 1850 | 1853 |

Original area of public domain—1,442 million acres

Disposition of public domain

| Cash sales and miscellaneous disposals | Homesteads | Grants to states | Grants to railroad companies | Remaining federal land |
|---|---|---|---|---|

Fig. 98. Additions to and disposal of the public domain in the contiguous United States (U.S. Bureau of the Census, statistical abstract of the United States, 1956).

nate publicity about farming opportunities in the West, accompanying the passage of the various homestead acts, encouraged settlers to attempt cultivation of much land that should never have been plowed. Ultimately this led to failure and land abandonment but not without much hardship to both land and settler.[9]

When the livestock industry expanded into the West, it moved into federal land. In favorable locations, stockmen established headquarters and attempted to obtain for themselves adequate range for their livestock. The limitations of the Homestead Act were evaded in various ways: by having friends or relations take up homesteads on adjoining areas and eventually dispose of them to the central ranch owner or by homesteading land in the areas where water was available and thus obtaining use of the surrounding, drier ranges. By one device or another, many ranch owners obtained title to considerable areas of land. Still, many were dependent upon the unpatented federal land, the public domain, for a large part of their range forage.[9]

The invention of barbed wire in the middle 1870's brought a measure of stability to western grazing lands by making it economically feasible to fence off areas of private range and thus exclude the migratory herder, or trespassing livestock. Some ranchers however, undertook to fence in large areas of public domain as well and had to be restrained from this by federal order. In the absence of fencing, ranch owners decided to respect each others rights to graze certain areas of public land and joined together to exclude trespassers.[9]

With the establishment of the forest reserves in 1891 and the national-forest system in 1905, additional stability was brought to western grazing lands. The land removed from the public domain and reserved as national forest included much valuable mountain grazing land. Initially, misunderstandings led to efforts to eliminate livestock from the forest reserves. Later, however, local stockmen were allowed grazing privileges on national-forest land, being charged a nominal fee per head of livestock grazed (Fig. 99). Difficulties arose when the Forest Service attempted to improve the national-forest ranges by restricting livestock numbers or seasons when grazing was permitted. Many stockmen re-

Fig. 99. Tallying sheep as they enter a national-forest range, Idaho (U.S. Forest Service photograph).

sented what they believed to be unwarranted government interference with their grazing rights.[37]

After the national forests were established, much federal land still remained as unreserved public domain. Most of this was suitable for grazing land. In 1934 the Taylor Grazing Act was passed by Congress as a measure to bring this federal range under proper management. Eighty million acres of public domain land were placed into grazing districts to be managed jointly by the federal government and committees of local stockmen. The Grazing Service was established to administer the new grazing districts. From the start, however, it was handicapped by the opposition of stockmen, who resented interference with long-established practices, and by lack of support from other federal agencies. In 1946 its functions were taken over by the newly created Bureau of Land Management, which since that time has had responsibility for both the Taylor grazing districts and the other unreserved public-domain lands. This agency has responsibility over 160 million acres of federal land in western grazing districts and has been attempting to restore them to productivity (Fig. 105).

Since the 1880's western stockmen with access to federal land have been dissatisfied with its administration. Since the time when they were ordered to remove all fences from public-domain land, they have attempted to bring pressure to bear on Congress to make it possible for them to obtain outright leases of federal land for grazing purposes. Grazing privileges on the national forests and the more liberal grazing allowances on Taylor grazing lands have not been sufficient to satisfy those who want permanent grazing rights on federal land. Stockmen's associations, with a powerful lobby in Washington, have brought pressure in many sessions of Congress to have grazing lands removed from the jurisdiction of the Forest Service and other federal agencies and turned over to the use of cattle and sheep interests.

**Restriction of the western range.** The westward movement of agricultural settlement rapidly cut down on the amount of land available for grazing. Originally the rich chernozems, prairie soils, and the deeper brown soils of the plains states supported range livestock. Early livestock owners in the northern grasslands once found the forage so abundant and nutritious that cattle could thrive on it throughout the year. Some reported that cattle were able to gain weight on natural feed during the winter and become fat enough for market in early spring.[9] But as the better soils were taken by farmers, livestock were forced into drier lands and less-fertile upland soils. This combined with deterioration of the vegetation made it no longer possible to carry livestock through

Fig. 100. Cattle on short-grass range in Texas (photograph by Soil Conservation Service, U.S. Dept. Agric.).

the year on natural forage. Furthermore the market for grass-fed beef began to decline as the cornbelt states were settled and corn-fed cattle were shipped to market. A lasting relationship developed between western cattle owners and the mixed farm-livestock economy of the corn belt. Cattle were shipped young from the western range, fattened to market age on corn and other forage, and moved to market. This practice, in turn, led to a change in the type of cattle in the West. The hardy Texas longhorns could thrive on rough range forage but failed to fatten into choice beef in the corn lot. They were gradually replaced on the western ranges through shipment of other breeds from the East— Herefords mainly (Fig. 101), but also Aberdeen-Angus, Shorthorns, and others. The newer cattle breeds required more care and were less able to fend for themselves. The rancher with a permanent establishment and available hay or irrigated pasture lands (Fig. 102) was favored over the older type of operator who depended entirely on native forage.[9] Western sheepmen, who were primarily interested in wool production, were less dependent upon the farming states. The Merino sheep, a wool breed, came with the Spanish and for long remained the preferred sheep of the west. Later, a new Merino-type sheep, the Rambouillet from France, became more popular for wool production. In the farming states, generally, the emphasis shifted from wool to mutton breeds as the industry became established.[37]

**Damage to the western range.** Severe winters, drought, and the uncertain market conditions of the late 1880's and the 1890's put an end to the great expansion period of the livestock industry. During the period of expansion the western United States was settled, but it was settled at a high cost to the nation. This cost was revealed in the first general survey of the western range carried out by the Forest Service in the early 1930's.[18] This survey revealed that the original capacity of the native range vegetation to support livestock had been cut in half during the few decades that the range had been grazed. The original capacity of the native vegetation was estimated at 22½ million animal units (1 animal unit equals 1 cow or horse or 5 sheep or goats). As a result of overstocking by livestock the vegetation had deteriorated to the point where in 1930 the range capacity was only 10.8 million animal units. However, in 1930 the western range was still carrying 17.3 million animal units instead of the 10.8 million that it could have supported without

Fig. 101. Purebred Hereford cattle, New Mexico (photograph by Soil Conservation Service, U.S. Dept. Agric.).

Fig. 102. Cattle on irrigated pasture (photograph by Soil Conservation Service, U.S. Dept. Agric.).

further damage. The damage was therefore continuing. It was believed that if stocking were reduced to a level below the range capacity, it would take approximately 100 years to restore the ranges to their original condition. In about 60 years of use, therefore, enough damage had been done to require a century to repair.

The survey also found that of the 728 million acres of range in the West, 589 million acres were suffering from serious erosion, thus both reducing their future productivity and adding to the silt load of the streams (Fig. 103). Only about 95 million acres were found to be in satisfactory condition, and these for the most part were either privately owned or national-forest lands. The lands that were in by far the worst condition were the great stretches of public domain, the no-man's lands of the West that had received neither administration nor care.[18] This Forest Service report was received with great distaste by stockmen, who admitted local overgrazing but denied the widespread severity of the damage and labeled the report as seriously biased.[37] However, both sides would admit that much was needed to restore or build up the grazing capacity of western rangelands.

The factors that have contributed to overgrazing of rangelands are several. First, in the early days, was ignorance. Stockmen from the East, inheritors of European traditions, were familiar with livestock management on the well-watered pasture lands of these regions. They had no experience with the arid lands of the West, where the capacity of the land to support livestock is often extremely low. The Spanish, with experience with arid ranges, had learned mostly how to exploit them, not how to conserve them. As permanent ranches were established and men settled down to the business of earning a living on a long-term basis, some proved to be good observers and managers. They learned to recognize the better forage plants and the conditions that favored them and handled their livestock accordingly. Through practical, trial-and-error management they developed the systems which later-day scientific range managers were to adopt or modify. Others, less capable or more handicapped by economic or environmental circumstance, failed to learn the lessons and continued to try to carry more livestock than the range would support.

Climate has been, and remains, a major cause of range damage,

Fig. 103. Erosion following overgrazing on a formerly productive range in Arizona (photograph by Soil Conservation Service, U.S. Dept. Agric.).

Fig. 104. Effects of drought (photograph by Soil Conservation Service, U.S. Dept. Agric.).

although it is often blamed for man's mistakes. Droughts are normal on western ranges, and grazing capacity fluctuates with wet years and dry. A range properly stocked for a high rainfall year, may be dangerously overstocked if drought follows. With dry years, livestock numbers must be reduced, or supplemental feed in the form of hay or food concentrates must be purchased to carry them without pressure on range forage. However, a widespread drought often brings falling market prices and higher prices for hay or grain. If the rancher is short of cash, there is a strong temptation to try and hold excessive numbers of livestock in the hopes that better conditions will return. Damage always results (Fig. 104).

Economic factors remain a major cause of range damage. High prices for beef, mutton, or wool encourage heavy stocking; falling prices make it difficult to dispose of animals without great financial loss. Ranchers, like everybody else, are in business to make money. There are easier ways. It is easy to blame the cowman or sheepherder for ruining the West, but only if one forgets the circumstances under which these pioneer stockmen tried to survive.

## RANGE ECOLOGY AND MANAGEMENT

Carrying capacity. Much range damage has occurred because of failure to realize that each area of range has a carrying capacity. This can be defined as the number of animals that can be carried on it

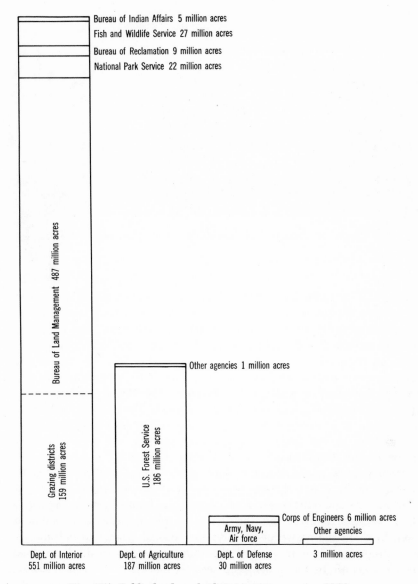

Bureau of Indian Affairs 5 million acres
Fish and Wildlife Service 27 million acres
Bureau of Reclamation 9 million acres
National Park Service 22 million acres

Bureau of Land Management 487 million acres

Other agencies 1 million acres

U.S. Forest Service 186 million acres

Grazing districts 159 million acres

Corps of Engineers 6 million acres
Army, Navy, Air force
Other agencies

Dept. of Interior
551 million acres

Dept. of Agriculture
187 million acres

Dept. of Defense
30 million acres

3 million acres

Fig. 105. Public lands and administrative agencies, 1964.

and kept in good condition without damage to the range forage. Carrying
capacity depends on the soil and climate, the type of native vegetation,
and the ability of the vegetation to hold up under grazing. It varies
greatly from one site to another, being very high in well-watered areas
with deep soil and extremely low on rocky, arid ranges.

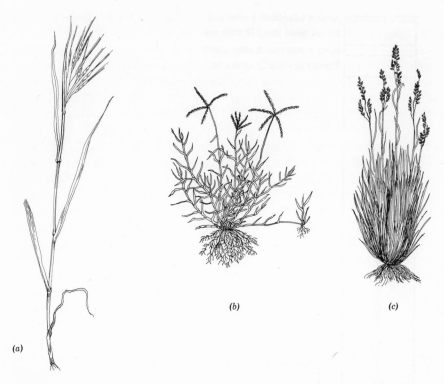

*(a)*

*(b)*

*(c)*

**Fig. 106. Growth forms of grasses: (a) annual, (b) sod forming, and (c) bunch.**

Grass can stand only a limited amount of grazing pressure. Each perennial grass plant produces each year a certain surplus of growth which can be safely grazed without injury to the plant. Each plant also has a metabolic reserve, a certain minimum area of leaves and stems needed to carry out the necessary photosynthesis to build and store foods in the crown or root system. Annual grasses, which die each year and regenerate from seed the following year, could theoretically be cropped off to the roots once seed has been cast without damage to future generations. Actually, with annuals as well as perennials a certain minimum amount of leafage and stem must be left on the ground to provide soil protection and a more favorable bed in which seeds will germinate. The number of animals that can be carried safely on the range depends therefore on the surplus of leafage and stems put on by the vegetation. If too many animals are kept on the range, not only the surplus is eaten, but also the reserve portions of the plant.

If this process is repeated for long the plants become weakened and die out.

Species of range plants differ greatly in their ability to withstand use. The taller grasses that make up the climax vegetation of the prairies are not able to withstand heavy grazing. Under heavy cropping they disappear, and their place is taken by more resistant, often sod-forming, grasses, which have leaves and stems that grow more nearly horizontal to the ground surface and are therefore less easily cropped (Fig. 106). With continued heavy use even these sod-forming grasses will disappear. On the resultant bare ground, relatively unpalatable weeds of various kinds will seed in. If the range is protected from fire, woody plants of less palatable varieties will move into former grassland areas.

In a widely used classification, put forward by Dyksterhuis,[16] range plants are placed into three categories: *decreasers,* the tall climax grasses, nutritious and highly preferred by livestock, which decrease in number under moderate grazing; *increasers,* species also present in the climax but in a lesser amount or subordinate position. They are often sod formers and are also nutritious and eaten well by livestock but better able to stand up to grazing use. These species increase in number or in space occupied as the tall climax grasses diminish. With very heavy grazing pressure, even the increasers are killed out, and their place is taken by *invaders,* native or exotic weeds or woody plants of low forage value, little used by livestock and generally not as well adapted to maintaining or holding the soil as the original vegetation. Proper range management then includes maintaining a balance on the range

Table 8. Successional Changes with Grazing and Protection on the North American Prairie[36]

| | | Decreasers | |
|---|---|---|---|
| Climax | Grazing | Big bluestem (*Andropogon gerardi*) | No grazing |
| | | Little bluestem (*A. scoparius*) | |
| | | Lead plant (*Amapla canescens*) | |
| Middle succession | | Increasers | |
| | | Kentucky blue grass (*Poa pratensis*) | |
| | Grazing | Blue grama (*Bouteloua gracilis*) | No grazing |
| | | Yarrow (*Achillea millefolium*) | |
| | | Invaders | |
| Early succession | | Western wheatgrass (*Agropyron smithii*) | |
| | | Plantain (*Plantago spp.*) | |
| | | Russian thistle (*Salsola kali*) | |

Fig. 107. An overgrazed range compared with one reseeded and protected (U.S. Forest Service photograph).

Fig. 108. Sheep trails "contouring" an overgrazed slope in southern California (U.S. Forest Service photograph).

216

between increasers and decreasers and keeping the invaders to a minimum.

In terms of plant succession, overgrazing leads to a replacement of climax species or species high on the successional scale by plants low on the successional scale or pioneer species. Conversely, the absence of grazing pressure if the damage is not too great will usually allow normal successional processes to operate and will permit the climax species to regain the ground.

**Range condition and trend.** Range managers are trained to judge ranges on the basis of *condition,* which on many range types is simply a way of measuring the extent to which a range has departed from a climax state towards lower successional stages as a result of grazing use, and *range trend,* which determines whether under existing conditions of management the range is returning toward a climax condition or deteriorating further.

Fig. 109. A Texas range in excellent condition. Bluestem and grama grasses predominate in the cover (photograph by Soil Conservation Service, U.S. Dept. Agric.).

In the Soil Conservation Service system, five classes of range condition are recognized, varying between excellent and very poor[20] (Figs. 109–111). An example of the criteria used is provided in Table 9. It will be noted in the bottom row of this table that the acres required per animal unit month, that is, needed to support one cow or five sheep for one month, vary between 0.75 for a range in excellent condition and more than 5.0 for a range in very poor condition. Obviously then, a rancher who keeps his ranges close to excellent condition will be able to carry more livestock and make greater profits than a rancher who allows his ranges to deteriorate. It should be remembered, however, that range condition is a measure of the degree to which a particular type of range approaches its maximum potential yield of forage. It is something quite apart from range and soil type. Thus, a well-watered prairie range with tall climax grasses on deep soil, rated in excellent condition, would have a higher carrying capacity than a range in excellent condition in the desert grassland region of the Southwest.

**Range pests.** Although it is true in a general way that in the absence of grazing or with a reduction in livestock numbers ranges will improve in condition, there are many exceptions. Some of the invaders which occupy depleted ranges are not native plants and occupy no place in normal successional processes. Under some circumstances these invaders will continue to hold the ground even when the range is completely protected. Normal successional processes are halted, and the cover of exotics is said to form a *disturbance climax*. Thus, in California, the exotic grasses and weeds that arrived with the Spanish now form a disturbance climax which maintains itself. Studies at the San Joaquin Experimental Range in California have shown that even with complete protection from grazing over a long period of years, the native perennial grasses do not replace the exotics. Elsewhere in the West, large areas of rangeland have been covered by a blanket of cheat grass (*Bromus tectorum*) which has completely replaced the original vegetation.[22] Both its soil-holding ability and forage value are low compared to the native grasses, but it maintains itself effectively even in the absence of grazing.

In Pacific coast states the poisonous Klamath weed has invaded overgrazed ranges, and for a long period it seemed impossible to control. Finally a species of beetle, which feeds only upon Klamath weed, was introduced from Australia and has proved to be an effective agent of control. Unfortunately the beetle does not tolerate the disturbance in the vicinity of roads and highways. Here a fringe of Klamath weed persists, ready to reinvade the ranges when beetle numbers decline. Beetle and weed thus live in a precarious balance.

Fig. 110. A Texas range in poor condition. Only remnants of bluestem and grama grasses remain (photograph by Soil Conservation Service, U.S. Dept. Agric.).

Fig. 111. A Texas range in very poor condition. Very little vegetation remains (photograph by Soil Conservation Service, U.S. Dept. Agric.).

## Table 9. A Range Condition Score Sheet

| Factors Evaluated | Excellent | Good | Fair | Poor | Very Poor |
|---|---|---|---|---|---|
| 1. Relative potential forage yield (in per cent) | 90–100 | 75–90 | 50–75 | 25–50 | 0–25 |
| 2. Important desirable forage plants (percentage of ground surface covered by each species): Wild oats, *Avena* spp. Soft chess, *Bromus mollis* Calif. bunchgrass, *Stipa pulchra* Cutleaf filaree, *Erodium cicutarium* Bur clover, *Medicago hispida*, etc. | 85–100 | 65–85 | 35–65 "DECREASERS" | 10–35 | 0–10 |
| 3. Less desirable forage plants (percentage of ground covered): Ripgut brome, *Bromus rigidus* Annual fescue, *Festuca megalura* Foxtail, *Hordeum murinum* Yarrow, *Achillea millefolium* Blue dicks, *Brodiaea capitata*, etc. | 0–15 | 10–30 | 15–50 "INCREASERS" | 25–65 | 40–90 |
| 4. Undesirable forage plants: Medusahead grass, *Elymus caput-medusae* Nitgrass, *Gastridium ventricosum* Star thistle, *Centaurea melitensis* Dwarf plantain, *Plantago erecta* Tarweed, *Hemizonia* spp., etc. | 0–15 | 5–20 | 10–40 "INVADERS" | 25–75 | 40–100 |
| 5. Plant residue or litter per acre | Abundant | Adequate | Moderate | Scarce | Very scarce |
| 6. Erosion | None | None to slight | Slight to moderate | Moderate to severe | Severe |
| 7. Acres per animal unit month | .75–1 | 1–2 | 2–3 | 3–5 | 5 plus |

For California Annual Grass Range in North-Central California. Adapted from Grover (1945).

Along with an invasion of weeds following overgrazing comes an invasion of animal pests. Under climax conditions in grasslands a variety of rodents and other types of animals live without creating serious problems. When low successional weeds replace the climax, a different group of animal species also moves in and usually increases in numbers to pest proportions. The kangaroo rat (*Dipodomys*), jack rabbits (*Lepus*), and ground squirrels (*Citellus*) are among the range invaders. Vast amounts of money and time have been spent upon their control, often under the theory that the rodents were the cause rather than an effect of range damage. However, numerous studies have shown that the most effective means of control is a three-strand barbed-wire fence, which keeps out livestock. When grazing is excluded, and the grass grows tall and dense, ground squirrels, jack rabbits, and kangaroo rats must either move out or perish.[19,23]

**Handling of livestock.** Range management would be relatively simple if all that were needed to solve range problems was a simple reduction in livestock numbers. Unfortunately, the problem is much more complex. Livestock, like wild animals, have behavior patterns of their own, which often lead to actions quite contrary to the rancher's desires. An annual grass range of 10,000 acres in good condition could theoretically carry 800 head of cattle for a 6-month grazing period without any damage to range forage. Yet, such a range with 800 head could also show signs of serious overgrazing. The difficulty is that livestock of their own accord do not distribute themselves evenly over a range and graze every acre equally. There is a normal tendency to concentrate and spend much time around watering places. Similarly, livestock like salt and will congregate in the vicinity of salting grounds. The topography will also influence their distribution. Level ground will usually receive heavier cattle use than slopes. Even on an area of level range cattle may prefer to graze in one place in preference to others. Minor soil differences, resulting in better tasting or more nutritious forage can attract livestock to one area instead of another. Habit is also a strong factor. The result is that on the theoretical 10,000-acre range, areas that the livestock prefer may be overgrazed, whereas other areas will remain untouched. Proper range management must take this into account. Fencing, although expensive, is an essential tool. With fences, livestock can be moved from one area to another and kept in each until the forage is properly utilized. Where fencing is not practical, good results sometimes can be obtained by the strategic location of salting grounds and watering places (Fig. 112). The location of salt blocks near the water hole is usually an indication of careless range management.

Fig. 112. Proper distribution of salt blocks can force cattle to utilize range that they might otherwise avoid (U.S. Forest Service photograph).

Choice of livestock is another important factor in range management. Some breeds are better adapted for one range than another. Sheep normally do better on steep-hill ranges than cattle and are better adapted to ranges where forbs and shrubs predominate over grasses. Sheep breeds that band closely together require a herder and must be kept moving to avoid range damage. Where predatory animals are common or where ranges are unfenced, these breeds are preferred. On fenced ranges where there is little danger from predators, the breeds of sheep that tend to scatter rather than band together will usually give more even utilization of the range.

To restore damaged ranges a reduction in stocking is often needed, and sometimes that is all that is required. In some instances, however, a reduction is not the answer, but rather a difference in the method of handling livestock. Thus, if it is desired to shift the vegetation from fast-growing, early-maturing annual grasses to slower-growing, later-maturing perennials, it may be desirable to graze an area heavily early in the season, thus preventing the early-maturing species from setting seed. The livestock are then removed to another pasture until the later-maturing species have time to mature and cast seed. The stock may then be returned to the area, to moderately graze the desirable species and to trample the seed into the ground. Such a system, of course, requires that the rancher have enough feed elsewhere to carry the stock during the period when the desired grass species are maturing. A variety of similar systems have been devised to meet various problems of range management. All of the answers are not yet known, but we know enough now to do a much better job of range management than is being done.

## RANGE PROBLEMS IN OTHER COUNTRIES

Throughout the world, in prairie, steppe, pampas, and veld, ranges are still being damaged and deserts are encroaching on formerly useful land. The more productive ranges with high carrying capacities usually receive more adequate care, but the more arid and marginal rangelands are frequently exploited with little apparent concern for the future. Abuse of rangelands carries not only the consequences of lowered live-stock-carrying capacity and a diminished economic return from the land but affects all other natural resources as well. In some areas a valuable wildlife resource is destroyed to make room for livestock; the range is then damaged so that it is no longer suited for either wildlife or livestock. Such damaged areas are a source of erosion and disruption of watersheds, which can in turn affect still wider areas than those originally damaged.

In many areas of Africa among peoples such as the Masai and the Zulu, cattle have a traditional social value that far exceeds any market value that they may have. Traditionally, the worth of a person has been measured by the number of cattle he owns. The animals are killed and eaten only on rare, ceremonial occasions and are not regarded as a source of meat, although their milk may be used. Under such circumstances the usual incentives for animal husbandry or for careful management of range and pasture are lacking. Under primitive circumstances, livestock numbers were limited by predators and a variety of other natural causes. With civilization, however, many of these limiting factors have been removed and the numbers of livestock have increased rapidly. With this has come widespread overgrazing and severe erosion. Large areas of Africa in the past have been rendered uninhabitable to cattle by the presence of the tsetse fly, some forms of which carry human sleeping sickness, but which more commonly carries the livestock disease *nagana*, fatal to cattle. Efforts to extend grazing land through elimination of the tsetse fly have involved bush clearing and use of insecticides.

However, since wild species of African game serve as hosts for the tsetse fly, campaigns have been directed against the wild game, and hundreds of thousands of head of spectacular and valuable wild mammals have been slaughtered in the name of fly control. Ironically, more recent studies have shown that the game animals being removed have a higher economic value and produce more meat than the livestock with which they are replaced (Chapter 9). The most economically efficient utilization of the dry, rough rangelands of Africa in the future will probably prove to be some combination of use by existing domestic breeds and species of grazing and browsing mammals that are at present wild, but are amenable to some degree of domestication.[12,13]

In India, as in Africa, the noneconomic value of cattle has handicapped range-management progress. The cow, introduced by the invading Aryans over 3000 years ago is an object of religious veneration to many Hindus. Sacred cows, unrestricted and unconfined, damage both range and agricultural lands. India is a country that normally would support forest. But over much of the peninsula, forests have been completely eliminated to make room for grazing or cropland. Overgrazing, combined with gathering of vegetation for fuel, have done further damage so that, in an area that would have supported productive vegetation, barren desert exists and is spreading. George Schaller has stated: "India had an estimated 204 million cattle and buffalo and 94 million goats and sheep in 1956, of which 21 million of the former and 13 million of the latter grazed exclusively in the forests (Venkataramany, 1961). Livestock is permitted to graze without restrictions in virtually all forests and most sanctuaries, and serious damage to the vegetation culminating in widespread erosion is common particularly in the thorn and deciduous forests."[33] Efforts on the part of the government in 1966 to reduce the numbers of cattle caused riots and the threat of political upheaval.

In the Middle East and the Saharan region, deserts have been spreading and becoming more barren through overgrazing. Writing of Iraq, Bryan and Springfield[1] have described the virtual elimination of vegetation from the rangelands. Larson has described devastation in the Libyan desert, and sees no hope for range improvement until such time as the numbers of livestock moved about by nomads can be brought under some control.[21]

Australia has been a world leader in the management of pastures in its better watered lands but, in the semiarid lands of the interior, rangelands have been allowed to deteriorate extensively. The presence of exotic pests has handicapped range improvements in many areas. At one time the prickly pear cactus, introduced from Mexico for livestock feed, overran millions of acres of range, forming dense, impenetrable

Fig. 113. Prickly pear in Texas. In the United States as in foreign countries this plant has been a vigorous invader of overused range lands (photograph by Soil Conservation Service, U.S. Dept. Agric.).

thickets. All efforts at control failed until a biological method was attempted. An insect enemy of the prickly pear was brought in, which fed on and destroyed the cactus. Its extent was thus reduced to manageable proportions. In 1928 and 1930, several million eggs of the *Cactoblastis* moth were brought from Argentina and the larvae hatched out in prickly pear territory. By 1933 the last big area of prickly pear had been cleared out.[12,28,29]

The introduction of the European rabbit to Australia greatly aggravated range problems. Originally brought in by those who felt nostalgic for the rabbit hunting of the Old World, the rabbit spread rapidly throughout much of temperate Australia. Free from the predators and other limiting factors of its homeland, it had no difficulty displacing the native, marsupial mammals. On the arid ranges of the interior the combination of sheep and rabbit grazing was more than the vegetation could withstand. Drifting sand dunes and blowing dust marked the eastward march of the desert into the already narrow belt of productive land. Great sums of money were spent on rabbit control. A fence was built completely across the border between New South Wales and Queensland in hope of confining the rabbit. The effort failed.[28] A new answer was then sought, a biological one. Myxomatosis, a virus disease endemic among cottontails in South America, but fatal to the European rabbit, was introduced. Spread from one rabbit colony to another by mosquitoes, it proved to be initially highly effective in reducing the rabbit population. Undoubtedly tens of millions of rabbits died. Rangelands, held back by rabbit grazing, began to recover. But the rabbit did not disappear. Here and there rabbits survived, apparently disease-resistant, and these are building up a new strain of hardier rabbits against which some new, more virulent strain of the disease will undoubtedly be applied.[30]

With rabbits temporarily under control, their place as a pest on the arid lands was taken by the native kangaroos, the red kangaroo in the steppe, the grey kangaroo in the scrub, the wallaroo or euro in Western Australia. A war against kangaroos was under way before the war against rabbits had ceased. Arid lands are unstable ecosystems. Further simplification of their biota from grazing pressure of domestic livestock increases their instability. Pest problems and range abuse go together everywhere.

It would be possible to go on for pages, reciting stories of man's successes and failures in managing rangelands. It is enough, perhaps, to emphasize that, throughout the world, livestock have a place in balanced land use. With increasing populations in an already meat-hungry world, this place will grow in importance. It becomes urgent therefore to institute effective range management in all lands, before rangelands are pushed downhill on the successional scale to a point of no return.

## LIVESTOCK IN ENVIRONMENTAL CONSERVATION

The future of the range livestock industry is a matter of debate. F. F. Darling, for example, after intensive studies of livestock management in Scotland and a more general survey of other areas, concludes that livestock cannot be permanently maintained on arid grazing lands, unless we use grazing systems that more closely approximate the type of grazing pressure applied by native big-game animals.[10] One basic difference between the two is that big-game herds feed selectively and keep moving and thus do not put sustained pressure on any one area. Livestock under current systems of management are usually more or less confined and use a single area of range continuously and heavily. Darling's suggestion is that some form of livestock handling that approximates the old nomadic herding and allows each area of land a period of rest following selective use may be an answer to the problem. Yet, the lands grazed by the herds of nomadic peoples in the Old World have suffered perhaps more than other lands from overgrazing.

It has been seriously questioned by some whether livestock have any permanent place on arid rangelands or whether any but the lightest degree of stocking will not eventually lead to serious range damage. Livestock have a definite place on agricultural lands and pastures in the more humid parts of the world and on irrigated farm and pasture lands in the drier regions. In such a role livestock contribute toward a balanced land-use and farm economy. On arid rangelands they have been, too often, forces for destruction. Yet most range managers today believe that livestock, if properly handled, can continue to have a place on range as well as farm lands.

The rangelands of the world vary between good grassland and desert or barren mountains where forage is produced only in favorable localized areas. All of these lands have a variety of uses, of which the support of livestock is only one. Many deserts and mountains have incomparable values as wilderness recreation lands and homes for rare forms of wild-

Fig. 114. If properly managed, livestock can maintain their place on the rangelands of the West (photograph by Soil Conservation Service, U.S. Dept. Agric.).

life. Outdoor recreation, wildlife production, and watershed protection are the chief uses that compete with livestock use of ranges. These uses are not necessarily incompatible. It is neither desirable nor necessary to draw strict lines between recreation and livestock land, so long as livestock are carefully managed. In the West, cooperative agreements have opened areas of private rangeland to public recreation, and many stockmen have found wildlife to be a profitable by-product of sound range use. Further study of the forage needs of game and livestock and of the extent of competition between them, as well as the extent to which one complements the other, may lead to increasing livestock use of certain lands now reserved for wildlife or recreation. Thus, Buechner's studies of the pronghorn antelope in Texas revealed that moderate range use by cattle creates forage conditions more favorable to the pronghorn. Admittedly in certain areas one type of land use must necessarily receive a higher priority than another, but it is questionable whether we can afford to devote large areas of land for one exclusive use. It is certain, however, that we cannot tolerate for much longer the type of range misuse that has contributed to destruction of vegetation, erosion, and increased flood damage in the dry lands of the world. Uncontrolled grazing has no place on any land area.

# The Management of Wildlife

## CONSERVATION BEGINNINGS

**Depletion.** There is no area of conservation with a longer history in America than wildlife conservation. From early times, colonists became concerned with the dwindling numbers of wild animals and took measures to preserve them. Laws intended to preserve game appeared on the books as early as the seventeenth century.[19] But to the pioneers cutting a swath through the American wilderness, conservation laws meant little. Species after species of wild animals decreased in numbers or disappeared. Leading the list of vanished species is the passenger pigeon, once present in vast flocks that darkened the skies. About its passing, Aldo Leopold has written:[20]

There will always be pigeons in books and in museums, but these are effigies and images, dead to all hardships and to all delights. Book pigeons cannot dive out of a cloud to make the deer run for cover, or clap their wings in thunderous applause of mast-laden woods. Book pigeons cannot breakfast on new-mown wheat in Minnesota, and dine on blueberries in Canada. They know no urge of seasons; they feel no kiss of sun, no lash of wind and weather, They live forever by not living at all.

In the West the bison saw the march of progress. In herds numbering in millions they roamed the vast grasslands from Canada to Mexico. For generations they had supported hundreds of thousands of Plains Indians, and uncounted wolves, coyotes, and bears.[1] But a market for meat and hides, the buffalo rifle, and the westward-moving railways brought their doom. A few carefully guarded herds in parks and refuges are survivors. Perhaps the near extermination of the buffalo was part of a concealed national policy to subdue the Indians, perhaps not. At any rate, with the buffalo went the last hopes of the warlike Indian tribes. Soon after the Indians were vanquished, the prairie itself mostly disappeared with its biota.

Still farther west the path of progress crossed the trail of the great grizzly bear of California. The Spanish *vaqueros* had hunted the grizzlies, even testing their courage and skill by capturing them and later matching them in combat with their range bulls. With less color but more dogged persistence, the settlers who followed the lure of gold westward, hunted the grizzlies down. By the start of the twentieth century, hope for California species was finished, and in the following two decades the last few survivors were destroyed by persons whose names, in this connection, are best forgotten.[16]

At the start of the twentieth century, despite volumes of paper conservation laws and the passionate pleas of conservationists, wildlife in North America had reached a low ebb.[17] The hope of most naturalists was that, somehow, in refuges and preserves and through carefully enforced laws, we could preserve the remnants of once vast wildlife populations. Few foresaw the change that was to come, although at the time the forces that would bring the change were already at work.

**Restoration.** Wildlife occupies the anomalous position among our resources of belonging to everybody and therefore, under the earlier interpretation, of belonging to nobody. The ownership of other resources usually goes with the land, and it has been the responsibility of the landowner to preserve or destroy them as he sees fit. But the title to wildlife does not go with the land. Centuries of British tradition, under which wildlife belonged to the Crown, led to the American concept that wildlife belonged to the American equivalent of the crown, the sovereign people.[18] However, it was a long time before the people, through their representatives in the state governments, assumed their full responsibility. There are many turning points in the history of wildlife conservation in America, but a significant one came in 1878 when California and New Hampshire first established fish and game commissions, charged with the duty of conserving wildlife.[19] Soon the other states followed.

The establishment of agencies concerned with wildlife conservation gave hope that the many game-preservation laws already on the books would be taken seriously. A further step in this direction was taken in 1887 when Michigan, Minnesota, and Wisconsin went into the business of hiring permanent salaried game wardens to enforce the game laws.[19] These early game wardens had a difficult task, for the pioneer spirit tolerated little interference with traditional rights to hunt and fish. In the backwoods, if a game warden were to be shot, nobody knew who pulled the trigger. But, gradually, respect for law and order and interest in game preservation became more widespread. The warden's job was made easier.

The amount of protection offered to wild animals through enforced game laws had grown steadily. First, hunting seasons were set with a view to protecting game during the breeding seasons and at other times when they were most vulnerable. Then the means by which game could be taken were limited, with the more obvious methods of mass destruction outlawed. Bag limits, restricting the number of animals that a single hunter could take, were passed to prevent the wagon loads of game which early hunters used to cart away. Hunting for the market was outlawed in many states and was effectively stopped when the federal government entered the game-protection struggle through the newly formed Bureau of Biological Survey (now U.S. Fish and Wildlife Service). For species of little value for meat or sport, complete protection became the rule, with the result that by the early twentieth century most wild animals that classified as neither game, predators, nor pests were added to the protected lists. For game, additional protection came with the institution of wildlife refuges, intended as resting areas or breeding grounds, from which game could issue forth to restock hunted lands.

The idea of protection for game spread from the limitations placed on human hunting to that of eliminating the natural foes of game, the predatory animals. It seemed a simple rule, to the biologically uninformed, that, if a coyote ate quail, fewer coyotes would mean more quail. Predator-control practices spread from the simple hunting and trapping of predators by private individuals to the participation of

Fig. 115. The California quail, one of the important upland game birds of the West.

county, state, and federal governments. Hunters, trappers, and poisoners were hired to conduct a ceaseless war against those animals which, like man himself, preferred meat.

As game departments became better endowed financially, the idea spread that, where nature had failed, man should do the job. When protection from hunting and predators failed to increase game, artificial propagation of game appeared to be the answer. It seemed to make sense that game should be produced on farms, reared to a size when they could shift for themselves, and then released in depleted habitats. Among the native game, quail, cottontails, deer, and other species, were reared on game farms, hauled about the country by wagon, train, or truck, and released in what appeared to be suitable locations. Interest of the game farmers shifted early to exotic species. The ring-necked pheasant, native of eastern Asia, was well adapted to life of agricultural lands, where native game failed to thrive. Reared on game farms, and later introduced throughout America, it spread to become the country's number one upland game bird. Similarly, the Hungarian partridge and the Chukar partridge were introduced and liberated from game farms to become permanent additions to the wildlife of America. But for every success, there were countless failures, when the liberated game failed

Fig. 116. Brush rabbit. This and its close relative the cottontail are heavily hunted throughout the United States.

Fig. 117. The black-tailed deer. Two species of deer in the United States, the white-tailed and the black-tailed or mule deer support most of the big game hunting.

to survive. To balance the record, some introductions were too successful; the English sparrow and starling were added to the list of urban and agricultural pests.

With all of these conservation efforts and sometimes in spite of them, some kinds of wildlife began to increase. To these the game conservationists "pointed with pride," as proof that their methods produced results. But at the same time, other species on which equal or greater efforts were lavished, continued to decrease to the point of extinction. And to further confound the picture, species regarded as pests, predators, and enemies of man and game in many instances increased more rapidly than the carefully protected game animals, despite countless dollars and man-hours of effort spent toward their eradication. We can now evaluate these apparent paradoxes and the worth of early game-conservation measures in the light of new ecological knowledge.

## ECOLOGICAL IDEAS

The Kaibab story. In northern Arizona, in the Grand Canyon country, lives a herd of Rocky Mountain mule deer which has achieved international fame. Here in the Kaibab National Forest the deer are not different in appearance from their relatives elsewhere in the West. What distinguished them was their phenomenal rate of increase and equally rapid decline several decades ago. They were one of the first American wildlife populations to put on a demonstration of what has since been called a population *irruption*. Thus they achieved a measure of immortality in conservation annals.

Before 1906 there were not many deer in the Kaibab country. Nobody knows how many, for sure, but the best guesses say about 4000 animals. Supported in part by this deer population was an abundant population of predatory animals, plains wolves and coyotes, mountain lions and bobcats, and some bears. Sharing the range with them were sheep and cattle in addition to various other wild animals. In 1906, President Theodore Roosevelt, acting in the name of wildlife conservation, proclaimed the Kaibab region a federal game refuge. To make room for more game, the livestock were moved out. To allow the game to increase, trappers were put to work removing the predatory animals. Operating with great efficiency these men exterminated the wolf and greatly reduced the numbers of other predators.

Without further livestock competition for forage, with complete protection from hunting, and with few remaining natural enemies, the deer population responded. At first the forest rangers and others noted with satisfaction a healthy increase in the number of deer. Soon, a different note was sounded in the Forest Service reports. There were deer everywhere. Tourists could count hundreds in a short walk. Shrubs began to take on a heavily hedged appearance, as though overefficient gardeners had been pruning them. On the aspen trees a browse line was noticed, with all the leaves and small twigs removed as high as a deer could reach. Next, highly valued timber-tree reproduction began to suffer and to be killed out from heavy deer browsing. Forest Service reports sounded a warning and requested that the deer population be reduced in numbers.

Elsewhere in the country, conservationists and sportsmen were waging what they sometimes thought was a losing battle to save wildlife from extinction. The idea that there could be too many deer, anywhere, was strange and frankly unbelieveable. The Forest Service reports were ignored, even by the game department of Arizona, which should have known better. Meanwhile, the Forest Service was becoming desperate

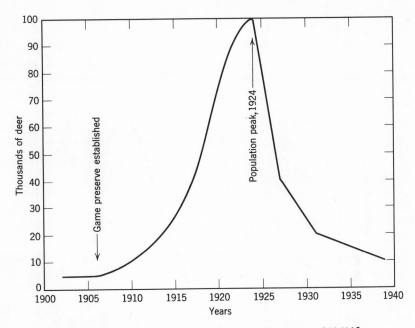

Fig. 118. The Kaibab deer irruption [from Rasmussen (1941)].

in its efforts to prevent forest damage and what seemed to be inevitable mass starvation for the deer herd, and they attempted to initiate a large-scale hunt to eliminate the excess deer. A wrangle about the rights of the federal government over wildlife as opposed to states' rights developed that went to the high courts of the land. While the controversy went on the deer problem solved itself, the deer died.

Between 1906 and 1924 it is estimated that the Kaibab deer herd had increased from 4000 to 100,000 animals (Fig. 118). Between 1924 and 1930, 80,000 deer died from starvation. Between 1930 and 1939 further die-offs reduced the herd by another 10,000. The rest managed to survive.[30]

**Some population dynamics.** The Kaibab example taught some people that protection for wildlife can be carried too far. It demonstrated to game biologists some facts about animal populations which have since been confirmed by numerous studies. One basic fact is that most game animals have high reproductive rates. Given favorable conditions an animal population can multiply rapidly. In nature a balance is reached between reproductive capacity and the drains upon the population by

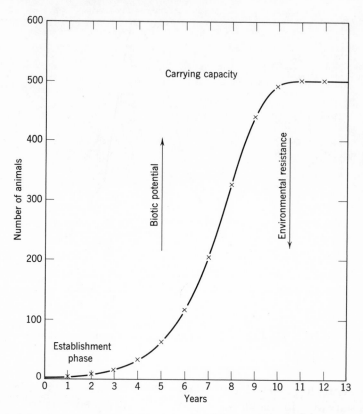

Fig. 119. Theoretical population growth curve showing the increase in a deer population in a new environment with a carrying capacity for 500 animals.

all of the many factors that bring loss. The number of animals present at any one time depends upon the balance between two forces: the *biotic potential,* or maximum rate at which a species can increase if unchecked, and the *environmental resistance* (Fig. 119), the sum of all the forces that cause death or lower reproductive gains.[29] If the environmental resistance is lowered, in one way or another, animal populations increase. If a species, such as the Kaibab deer, is freed from natural checks by a great expansion in its habitat or reduction in the numbers and kinds of enemies, it can increase for a time at a rate determined only by its maximum reproductive ability.

Every habitat, for wildlife as well as for domestic livestock, has its *carrying capacity,* which sets firm limits on population increase. No wild-animal population can be maintained permanently at a level above

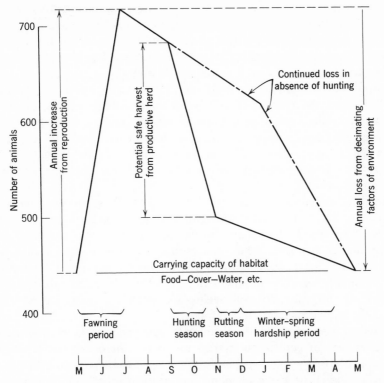

Fig. 120. The annual fluctuation in a deer population and the shootable surplus.

the carrying capacity, which is determined by the available food, cover, water, and other essentials for life. Yet each year, a population at carrying capacity will produce young. This crop of young will represent, therefore, an excess above what the environment can support. Either the young must perish or older animals must die to make a place for them. The annual crop of young, therefore, represents a surplus number of animals which cannot be maintained by the environment (Fig. 120). This surplus each year may safely be harvested by man, without in any way decreasing the numbers of animals that the environment will maintain.[19] If man does not harvest it, natural causes will bring about the reduction.

The carrying capacity for any species in a complex, climax environment may be relatively stable from year to year and, consequently, the number of animals will not change greatly. If the environment is generally favorable for the support of a great variety of animal species, then there will be predators, parasites, diseases, and competitors present in numbers adequate to remove the excess produced annually by any one species population. In the more simplified environments in cold or dry ecosystems, carrying capacity can be expected to fluctuate greatly. Following wet years in an arid region an abundance of plant life may be produced and provide a high carrying capacity for a species such as the chukar partridge that will build up to a high population level. However, in such areas, dry years follow wet and, at such times, the carrying capacity for most species may drop to an extremely low level. Thus we see great fluctuations in the numbers of animals that inhabit arid regions, and we cannot count on any particular level of abundance being maintained.[10]

In successional environments the carrying capacity changes from year to year in a direction either favorable or unfavorable to a particular species. Thus the habitat may absorb the annual surplus of young produced during the time when succession is proceeding in a direction favorable to that species. However, once a turning point is reached and plant succession is no longer in a direction favorable to the animal species, carrying capacity will decline in each succeeding year and die-offs in the animal population will follow.

Among the various kinds of animals, some species in some environments appear to control their own numbers. These are the territorial animals. A territory is now generally considered to be an area inhabited by an individual or group of animals of a given species and maintained for the more or less exclusive use of that individual or group. Other individuals or groups are excluded either by direct aggression toward them, or by various behavioral devices that lead to mutual respect of each other's territories. Some animals (the robin, for example) maintain territories during the breeding season but then come together in large flocks for migration and the winter. Other animals, the wren-tit for example, maintain territories throughout the year. Some species, such as many of the colonial-nesting seabirds, have territories that consist only of the immediate area surrounding the nest. Others, such as the California quail, include within their territory feeding, nesting, roosting, and escape cover. The roe deer, in some environments, maintains a territory for the exclusive use of the single family group. The wolf maintains a pack territory within which all members of the pack may breed and rear their young. In all species that are territorial, this form of behavior results in spacing of individuals and thus in limitation of the numbers of individuals that are permitted within a particular environment. Excess individuals, unable to find a suitable territory, are driven out or otherwise are forced to move out from the particular area.[10,25]

Among nonterritorial animals, some appear to be controlled in numbers by various predators or by some combination of predation, parasites, and disease so that their numbers remain fairly stable as long as their natural enemies are present. If the enemies are removed by man's activities or by some natural catastrophe, then populations of such species may increase for a time to high levels before other environmental factors, food shortage, lack of cover, adverse weather, etc., operate to cause a decline in their numbers. Many of the smaller game animals, quail, pheasants, cottontails, tree squirrels, appear to have their overall levels of abundance controlled in these varied ways. Those that are to some degree territorial assist through their own behavior the operation of other limiting factors in their environment. The animals that cannot *find* suitable territories become more vulnerable to predation, adverse weather, or other causes of death.[10]

Among animals such as the mule deer or white-tailed deer, territorial behavior is at best weakly developed. Where natural enemies are reasonably abundant, these animals can exercise some control over numbers. Where man has removed most natural enemies, however, these species soon begin to increase to a point where they press upon the food supply of their environment. Thus the Kaibab deer increased to a level beyond the carrying capacity of their area, overbrowsed and destroyed the shrubs and other food plants on which they depended, and thus ultimately crashed to a much lower level than might have been maintained if their numbers had been controlled by man.

It is now recognized as one of the tasks of wildlife management to control animal numbers. In natural environments little disturbed by man this may not be necessary, but even in our national parks the numbers of deer, elk, and other large mammals often reach a level above what the habitat can support and, in order to protect the vegetation and the habitat of other animals, it becomes necessary to reduce and control the numbers of the overabundant species. In areas where public hunting can be permitted, the process of control and regulation of animal numbers can be a pleasurable exercise for those who like to hunt.

**Habitat needs.** Control of animal numbers is a major task of wildlife management. Even more important, if we are to have wildlife at all, is creation and maintenance of suitable wildlife habitats. Habitat needs vary for each species. Failure to understand these needs has led to many mistakes. A study carried out in British Columbia helps illustrate this point.

R. Y. Edwards has told the story of Wells Gray Park and its caribou herd.[11] Before 1926 this was a primitive area, of high, glacier-topped mountains, breaking off southward to foothills and valleys. The valley floor and lower mountain slopes were covered with a dense, humid, cedar-hemlock forest. At higher elevations this was replaced by a drier, boreal forest of spruce and fir, breaking way at about 7000 feet into alpine tundra. On dry, south slopes at lower elevations was a forest of Douglas fir, with grassy openings.

The original animal life was varied but without excessive numbers of any one species. The mountain caribou were the most spectacular animals present. They wintered in the damp cedar-hemlock forest, where they fed upon the abundant supply of lichens which grew there, and in summer traveled to the higher tundra and spruce-fir forest. There were a few mountain goats at higher elevations and a small number of mule deer that wintered in the dry, Douglas fir forest and grassland. A few mountain lions and coyotes followed the deer. Small numbers of black and grizzly bears were present, as were wolverines and martens in the heavy forest. Beaver were well distributed but not abundant.

In 1926, the scene changed. A fire started in the Douglas fir forest and spread northward along the river valleys sweeping into the cedar-hemlock forest. The fire was intense and destroyed the humus of the forest floor, and even burned out the large stumps of trees. Over 200 square miles of forest were destroyed. After the 1926 fire, another 80 square miles burned in 1930–1931 and another 100 in 1940. Together these fires reduced the great extent of climax forest to early successional stages. On the burned area fireweeds and willow invaded, followed by birch and aspen. A completely new habitat was created, with a much simplified type of vegetation. In this habitat a different type of animal life was favored, not the rich abundance of many species that had been present but great numbers of a few adapted species.

Deer became numerous in the burn, and with the increase in deer the mountain lion and coyote increased also. White-footed mice and ground squirrels invaded the burn and increased to high levels. Beaver and black bear, favored by the successional growth, increased and thrived. Most strikingly, moose, previously unknown in the area, colonized it 4 years after the first fire. Favored by the abundant willow, birch, and aspen browse, they became numerous. With the moose, timber wolves invaded the area. By contrast, all of the species which had been favored by the climax forest growth decreased. Most striking was the decrease in the caribou. The decline started in 1926, was noted with alarm by 1935, and was accentuated by the 1940 fire. In the early 1950's only a small remnant of the caribou herds existed, and these animals were to be found in winter in the three small remaining patches of mature, cedar-hemlock forest. They were absent from the burn. With the fire had gone the dense cover and abundant growth of lichens and other climax plants on which they had depended for food.

Throughout North America, the decrease in numbers of caribou in recent decades has been a matter of concern to wildlife conservationists. In Alaska and Canada the barren-ground caribou of the tundra have declined in numbers.[3,21] The woodland caribou has vanished from the forests of the northeastern United States and has decreased greatly in Canada. Wolves have been blamed for the decrease, climate has been blamed, competition with moose and deer has been blamed. It is now generally recognized, however, that the basic cause is fire or fire plus logging. Fire has destroyed the lichen-covered forest over great areas of caribou range. With the climax forest the caribou have gone. At the same time the great increase in moose in both Canada and Alaska has caused comment. Fire, with the successional growth of willow, birch, and aspen, is a basic cause. Conservation efforts aimed at decreasing losses from hunting or eliminating predation by wolves have had little effect on numbers of moose or caribou. Habitat is the controlling factor.[21]

If the list of wildlife species now extinct or threatened with extinction is examined, it will be found that a high percentage of these species are like the mountain caribou. They are wilderness animals, dependent upon the maintenance of climax or near-climax habitat conditions. The now-rare fur bearers of the United States, the marten, wolverine, and fisher, appear to be among these forms. They are now scarce in most areas of their former range, despite almost complete protection from hunting or trapping. For such wilderness animals it is now apparent that maintenance or restoration of their numbers depends, with our present knowledge, on maintenance of extensive wilderness areas in which they can survive. As we learn more of their habitat requirements, we may be able to single out those special features which favor their survival and through management to increase these habitat features. Until then protection of wilderness is the only answer.

The species of wildlife that form the bulk of our huntable game populations and those which have become pests of farm lands, forest lands, and rangelands are the successional forms. They have been favored by our use, and misuse, of the land and have exercised their biotic potentials in expanding into newly created habitats left by fire, loggers, or excessive numbers of sheep and cattle.

Looking at the wildlife situation now through the eyes of ecologists, we can easily see the importance of habitat and the capacity of game populations to expand when habitat is provided. Yet through the long years of effort towards wildlife conservation, these facts were not obvious.

**The role of protection.** Protection from hunting once seemed to be all that was needed to bring game back to previous levels of abundance. We know now that all of the protection in the world cannot lead a game population to increase when the habitat is not adequate. For the wilderness animals strict protection from hunting or trapping is required if their numbers are to be preserved in the few remaining areas where they survive. But protection will not increase them; for that, we need more wilderness.

Waterfowl, while not climax species, have been hard hit by the expansion of settlement. Their migratory habits and tendency to congregate in large flocks have made them particularly vulnerable to hunting. Veritable armies of duck hunters set forth each year in pursuit of waterfowl. Without rigidly enforced game laws, the numbers of ducks, geese, and swans would soon be reduced to the vanishing point. Many waterfowl breed in the pothole country of the Canadian prairie and the still largely undisturbed tundra of the Arctic. From breeding grounds they migrate along well-defined routes, or flyways, to wintering grounds in the southern United States or Central or South America (Fig. 121). Those wintering in the United States have been affected by the drainage and reclamation of formerly extensive marsh or slough areas. In California, major wintering ground for the Pacific flyway, high land values have resulted in the drainage of much of the former winter habitat. Flocks of geese and ducks concentrate on the few remaining water areas and move out to feed on rice, barley fields, and truck gardens, causing extensive damage. Management has attempted to provide, through land purchase and development, more extensive wintering grounds and feeding areas apart from the croplands.

Drainage and urban development have removed large areas of marsh along the East and Gulf Coasts, wintering grounds for birds of the Atlantic, Mississippi, and Central flyways. Some of these birds are also affected by the disappearance of breeding grounds. The ducks and geese of the Mississippi flyway breed in large part in the marshes and potholes of the North Central United States and Canada. The great land-reclamation program of the federal government in the early decades of this century led to the drainage of many important breeding areas. Waterfowl-conservation measures have included reflooding of formerly drained marshes, where these are of low agricultural value. Rigid protection from excessive hunting remains important if the numbers of waterfowl

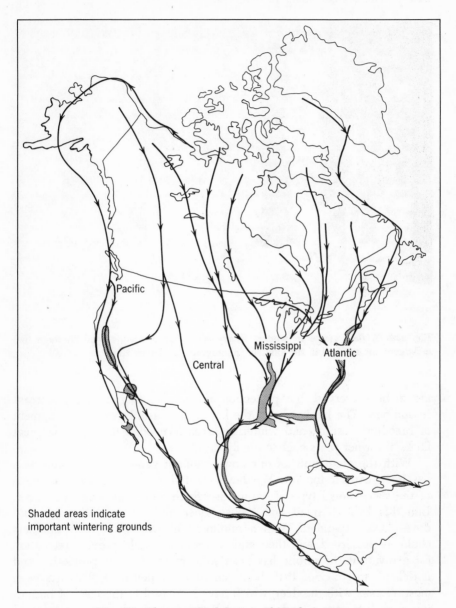

Pacific

Central

Mississippi

Atlantic

Shaded areas indicate
important wintering grounds

Fig. 121. The waterfowl flyways of North America.

Fig. 122. A deer range in winter. Heavy snow has created a food shortage that endangers the survival of the animals (photograph by Thone Riney).

are to be preserved, but protection alone will bring no great increase in numbers. The habitat holds the key to increase. Further development of breeding, resting, and wintering areas is needed to bring the great flocks of former years back to the flyways.

With the great bulk of our now-abundant game animals, protection has been carried too far. We have created what is almost an excess of the successional type of habitat in which most game animals thrive. Into this habitat, quail and grouse, deer and rabbits, pheasants and doves have expanded. With a minimum of protection their numbers could be preserved, and their annual surpluses could provide recreation for many. But the public has been sold on the idea of protection and is difficult to convince that there can be too much of it. This has been most obvious with the deer, which have increased to the level of becoming a pest of forest land, rangeland and farm land in many areas of the country. With deer, early in wildlife-conservation history, hunting was restricted to the male sex only. This was done with the realization that under normal levels of hunting enough bucks would survive for reproductive purposes. The female animals, protected from hunting, could produce enough young to permit the population to increase. The law protecting does was a measure to provide for population growth, not a measure of chivalry. However a tradition has grown around it among sportsmen until the doe deer has been elevated to the position of "America's sacred cow." Some simple mathematical calculations will show that removal of part of the bucks each year will never keep a deer population from increasing. Yet, it has been extremely difficult to obtain the necessary changes in hunting laws essential if excess deer populations and the consequent die-offs and waste are to be prevented. By overprotection of species with abundant habitat we waste game, destroy range, and endanger the future of wildlife.[24]

More so than protection from hunting, the importance of predator control has been oversold to the public by zealous conservationists. It is difficult to find records of any serious studies which show where predator control has accomplished anything of value. Where livestock are concerned, it is a different matter. Major predators must be thinned out where sheep are to be run free on the range. Smaller predators can be an expensive nuisance when overly abundant in farming areas. But where game alone is involved, predators are part of the ecological balance. In the biotic pyramid it is the number of prey animals that determine the number of predatory animals, and not the reverse. Predators help to harvest the annual surplus and thus to keep populations from overrunning the food supply of their habitat. Predators help to

Fig. 123. The coyote, one of our most heavily persecuted predatory animals, yet a traditional part of the western scene.

eliminate the old, and sick, and weak from a population and make room for younger and more vigorous animals. And above all, perhaps, predators have a place in a balanced biota, as part of the natural scene. Their recreational value and aesthetic worth is immense. Wildlife to be worth preserving should be wild, and to remain wild it should be rich and varied, with predators as well as prey. If wildlife management is to concentrate on the sheer production of meat, eliminating all that conflicts with or feeds upon the cherished herbivores, it becomes then only another form of animal husbandry, a useful and profitable pursuit, but lacking those qualities associated with the word "wild."

## AN ENVIRONMENTAL APPROACH

We have passed through two major phases in wildlife conservation in America. Intially, preservation and restocking dominated thinking. This led to confusion and bafflement when carefully protected species declined or liberated animals from game farms failed to survive. Next we moved into the age of the wildlife specialist, when emphasis on habitat management and population dynamics led to some spectacular gains and a greatly widened understanding. But this period has also been the age of the hunting-license buyer, the hunter who demands an ever-increasing supply of those species which he prefers to shoot. Using the new techniques, the game specialist has been able to produce great crops of deer, pheasants, or ducks but at a cost. In dollars alone this cost is excessive. Game departments are supported entirely by income from hunting-license fees. Too often the sportsman who buys a 3-dollar license expects to shoot a brace of pen-raised pheasants which cost 5 dollars for the game department to produce and still get his deer, ducks, and quail shooting thrown into the bargain.[22] Sometimes, also, the gain in shootable game has been at the expense of other natural resources. Increasingly it has been at the expense of wildlife itself, neglected or destroyed in the effort to increase numbers of already too abundant game.

It is necessary to re-examine basic thinking about wildlife problems and enter a new era of wildlife conservation, of the conservation of balanced biotas in place of specialized concentration on increasing numbers of huntable game. It should be an era in which the needs of the people as a whole, for natural environments with abundant and varied animal life, are given precedence over the wants of the hunter.

In the past, wildlife has been relegated in the thinking of conservation

Fig. 124. The pronghorn antelope.

workers in other specialties to those land areas not suited for more economically valuable products. The Class VIII land of the soil conservationist has been called wildlife land. We realize now that wildlife, like all life, requires deep, rich soils and does poorly on sterile, barren areas where soil nutrients are lacking.[28] If wildlife is to remain abundant, it must be fitted into farm plans, range plans, and forest plans. Only a small percentage of our lands can reasonably be reserved for wildlife alone. However, it is *wildlife* that must be fitted into land-use plans, not an unhealthy monoculture of a favored game species. The hunters of the future must pay for this in decreased game bags. They must also pay in higher costs, for in most parts of the country game is produced on private lands. Money is still the main incentive for encouraging private production, whether that production be of machines, corn, or pheasants.[22] The shootable annual surplus of currently favored game animals will be smaller as game are fitted back into a balanced biota. But for the hunter who seeks a type of recreation which is not found in taverns or on skeet ranges, the rewards of being active on wild or well-managed lands which have a rich and varied animal life should far outweigh the decrease in hunting take.

## A BROADER VIEW

North America has, to a marked extent, led the way in wildlife conservation on wild lands. Although we still have problems with threatened species and natural areas (see Chapter 12), wildlife conservation has been generally successful, and the skills of wildlife management have been developed to a high degree. Elsewhere in the world, however, such success is rare. Wildlife is being decimated by the same combination of destructive forces that were operative in 19th-century America, aided by the extreme pressure of human populations upon the habitat that still remains.

Europe, with a long tradition of wildlife conservation, has gone farther in some respects than have the United States and Canada. The European emphasis has been on the intensive production of game on limited areas. In many European countries, responsibility for wildlife rests with the landowner. Those who take an interest have often done a creditable job; those who have had no interest in wildlife have done poorly. Despite the density of population in most European countries, the more popular game animals have been maintained on private estates and sometimes on public land in fair numbers. Away from farm and urban areas, in forests and mountains, the numbers and variety of wild animals are often quite high. Although there has been in the past a trend toward the extermination of predators, the wolf and bear still remain in the mountains of the Balkans and in northern forests. Considerable success has been achieved with saving and restoring some species that were once on the point of vanishing. Thus the European bison has been maintained in the forests of Bialowicza in Poland, despite the hazards and devastation caused by two world wars in that general region.[37]

In the Soviet Union the protection and management of wildlife has made enormous strides in recent decades, and Soviet wildlife scientists are now among the world's leaders. Despite the practical orientation of Marxist political philosophy the preservation of wildlife for aesthetic, recreational, and scientific values is well accepted. The economic exploitation of wildlife resources, however, has been developed to a degree exceeding any efforts in North America, and progress has been made in the domestication of wild species such as the African eland. One of the most spectacular successes has been in the preservation and commercial use of the saiga antelope, a species that once abounded on the steppes of Eurasia but was reduced to near extinction in the early decades of this century. Under management it once more numbers in the millions and yields quantities of meat and hide for the market through sustained-yield cropping.[4]

South from the U.S.S.R. the lands of Asia present one of the more discouraging spectacles for wildlife conservation. The situation in India, once a land that could equal Africa in the scenes presented by great herds and flocks of wild animal life, is representative. George Schaller has summarized the information on the primitive abundance and present scarcity of large mammals in India. Where once elephant, rhino, buffalo, lions, tigers, and many kinds of deer and antelope roamed in great numbers, extinction, near-extinction, and scarcity are now the rule. Much of the damage has occurred in recent decades, particularly since independence was achieved in 1947. Indiscriminate slaughter, direct shooting campaigns aimed at protecting crops, and a general inattention to protective game laws have been involved. Most serious however has been the continued and growing pressure of people and livestock on the remaining wildlife habitat. Without better planning and control over land use, without modern and more efficient agriculture, and without control of human population growth, there is little hope for the maintenance of wildlife in India.[31]

By contrast, the situation in Africa is more hopeful. Here are the world's greatest existing wildlife resources and here not long ago was the bleakest prospect for future preservation. Fortunately, many of the new governments of Africa, despite economic difficulties and political turmoil, have recognized the value of the wildlife resource and have taken steps to preserve it. The economic impact of tourism in East Africa has been a marked factor leading to effective wildlife preservation. A major attraction to the tourist from Europe or America has been the sight of great game herds roaming wild in the East African national parks.[18] In Southern Africa the protection of wildlife in national parks has a long history and, more recently, the management of wild animals

Fig. 125. Studies in Africa indicate that wild species such as the impala (A) and the kudu (B), living in mixed herds with many other species under natural conditions, can produce more meat per acre and bring in a greater economic return than could be obtained from domestic livestock in the same area.

252

outside of parks has proceeded on a rational basis. The commercial production of wildlife on ranches for sale as meat, hides, and other by-products is now well established. Springbuck and blesbuck have replaced sheep on many South African farms; mixed game ranching has proved more profitable than cattle ranching in many areas of Rhodesia.[9,34]

Although conditions for wildlife vary enormously around the world, in most areas wildlife has been neglected. Where population pressure is great and resources are few, there has been little room for wildlife conservation. Lee Talbot, after a survey of world wildlife problems, has stated that wildlife can be used as an index to the condition of the biotic resources of an area.[33] Where wildlife is abundant, other renewable resources are usually well preserved. A scarcity of wildlife accompanies destructive exploitation of resources with all of its unfortunate consequences.

Where wildlife still remains, it is essential to take early steps toward conservation and management. With present rates of human-population increase it is unlikely that any area will remain unaffected by man for long. It would be unfortunate if future generations were denied first-hand knowledge of the variety of wild animals which have accompanied and influenced man throughout his evolution and spread over the earth. There is an increasing feeling also that wild land and wildlife may be strangely important for the preservation of man himself. With the unbridled growth of technological civilization, with its regimentation, specialization, and tensions, the pressures on the human spirit grow more intense. Until a more sane way of life can be achieved, man needs a refuge, a place for escape from artificiality and confinement, where he can come to grips with his own still-primitive self. So long as wild places and animals are preserved, a sanctuary for man also remains.

# Fisheries Conservation

## FRESH WATERS

The fisheries of the fresh-water lakes and streams of North America attract annually an army of anglers numbering well over 20 million.[10] Dangling a hook and line into a quiet pond or flashing a trout fly over a splashing stream is a form of recreation with a traditional, and almost irresistible, appeal to a large segment of the American population. Because it is a form of sport open to participation by both sexes and all ages of people, it has a much larger group of followers than the more strenuous sport of hunting. The history of fish conservation, in America, has closely paralleled that of conservation of game. In most instances responsibility for management of fisheries resources rests with a joint fish and wildlife agency.

**Beginnings.** The history of fresh-water fisheries in America can be traced through a period of early abundance when streams ran clear and fish could be easily taken, to a time of serious depletion. The causes of depletion were basically the same as those which have affected other natural resources. Forests were cut over, and streams that once supported abundant fish life deteriorated. Farm lands were mismanaged and erosion silted up lakes and streams. Debris washed from overgrazed slopes choked stream channels below. Pollution from mill or factory wiped out fisheries for miles below the source. Eventually, the situation became serious enough to cause alarm and action. In the 1870's the Federal government entered the picture when a Bureau of Fisheries, forerunner of the present U.S. Fish and Wildlife Service, was created. State governments began to form fish-conservation commissions or agencies to look into the problem of restoring and improving fisheries.

Like game conservation, the conservation of fisheries went through a period of emphasis on protection through restrictive laws and of concern with the control of wild predators and then moved much more thoroughly into the field of artificial propagation and the introduction of exotic species. Most of the early state fish commissions were charged initially with the task of setting up fish hatcheries, where fish could be reared and then released to stock streams and lakes. They were also charged with looking into ways of improving fisheries through the introduction of new species from other areas. Only much later did an ecological approach begin, with attention to providing suitable habitat for existing fish populations and research toward discovering actual causes of fisheries depletion.

The effect of the hatchery program on fresh-water fisheries was far reaching. Whereas a good share of America's game birds and mammals are still truly wild animals reared in more or less natural habitats, America's fresh-water fisheries are increasingly artificial. A wild fish in a natural stream or lake is becoming more difficult to find, except in the still-existing wildnerness of Canada and Alaska. The early history of fish conservation saw the mass movement of species from one side of the continent to the other, plus the introduction of many additional kinds from Europe and Asia. Even those streams which still support native species of fish are often stocked with hatchery-reared fish or their descendants.

**Fresh-water ecosystems.** Fish are end products of food chains in aquatic ecosystems. The base on which fish populations are supported consists of microscopic floating green plants, usually algae, which are collectively termed *phytoplankton.* These plants are the photosynthetic organisms which maintain the other life in streams and lakes. The ability of the water to supply nutrients to these plants varies with the fertility of the soils in the watershed and determines in large part the productivity of the phytoplankton. This in turn determines the productivity of the water in terms of pounds of fish per acre. If the water is low in nutrients, it will support either a few large fish or many dwarfed or stunted fish, depending on the type of lake or stream and the conditions within it. Fish rarely starve to death as quail or deer do. In the presence of a diminished food supply, they respond by slow growth rates and small size.[16]

Lakes vary with age and the condition of their surrounding watersheds. At one extreme are the *oligotrophic* lakes, clear cold lakes of the high mountains or the glaciated region of northeastern America (Fig. 126). These lakes, with rocky bottoms and barren infertile watersheds, are low in productivity. Low water temperatures and the lack of dissolved nutrients prevent an abundant bloom of plankton. On the rocky bottoms, rooted vegetation has difficulty in becoming established.

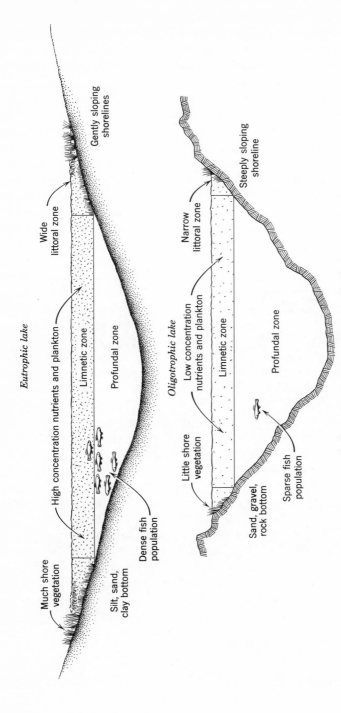

**Eutrophic lake**

Gently sloping shorelines

Wide littoral zone

High concentration nutrients and plankton

Limnetic zone

Profundal zone

Much shore vegetation

Silt, sand, clay bottom

Dense fish population

**Oligotrophic lake**

Steeply sloping shoreline

Narrow littoral zone

Low concentration nutrients and plankton

Limnetic zone

Profundal zone

Little shore vegetation

Sand, gravel, rock bottom

Sparse fish population

**Fig. 126. Cross sections through oligotrophic and eutrophic lakes.**

Such lakes will support few fish. At the other extreme are the *eutrophic* lakes. These lakes are warmer, with muddy or sandy bottoms, rounded contours, and gently sloping shorelines, and usually are surrounded by watersheds in which soil has developed and matured (Fig. 127). With warmer water and an abundance of dissolved nutrients, these lakes support much plankton and a high fish population.[2,16,21]

Similarly, streams can be divided into two classes. Rapid, cold, upland or mountain streams are like the oligotrophic lakes, low in nutrients and consequently low in plant life and fish. The slower-moving streams and rivers of the lowlands, which drain areas of rich soil, are warm, and high in nutrients and fish life.

Fresh-water fisheries, consequently, can be roughly divided into two general categories: those of the warmer, rich environments and those of colder, more sterile streams and lakes. Among the cold-water fish

Fig. 127. A dense growth of emergent vegetation around the edges, abundant floating vegetation in the water, and a high concentration of microscopic plankton characterize eutrophic lake edges and ponds (photograph by Soil Conservation Service, U.S. Dept. Agric.).

are those most highly regarded by sports fishermen, such as the brook, cutthroat, and rainbow trout, the muskellunge and northern pike. The warm-water fish include the black bass, the various sunfish, and, at the extreme of tolerance for warm turbid waters, the catfish and carp. The problems of conservation and management vary with the two groups. One general rule is apparent—the trout fisherman must remain content with lower yields per acre of stream or lake than the man who fishes for sunfish or carp.

**Fisheries management.** In earlier days of fish conservation, the approach to the management of warm-water fisheries was much the same as that for trout fisheries, with increasing restrictions on angling which limited gear, seasons, numbers and size of fish that could be legally caught, combined with the development of a hatchery program. After a time, experience began to show that this approach did not make sense. Some lakes, heavily stocked with hatchery fish, began to produce less than other unstocked lakes. Fish populations, increased without reference to the food supply, were stunted in size and provided little incentive for angling. Some restrictions on take are obviously necessary—dynamite, poisons, and nets can finish off any population. However, once a general rule was established limiting sports-fishing gear to hook-and-line, further restrictions were often unnecessary. Studies in the reservoirs of the TVA and of various warm-water species in Midwestern lakes and ponds, where hatchery stocking and rigidly enforced seasons and creel limits had been the rule, showed that these measures were unnecessary. It was found that these lakes could be fished as heavily as anglers wanted to fish them and would still yield an abundance of fish from natural reproduction alone. The question was raised whether a warm-water lake could be overfished when recreation was the only incentive. With these studies came a shift in the emphasis of management, from artificial propagation and restrictions on take to improvement of habitat and relatively unrestricted fishing.[14]

It has been apparent that fish have a remarkably high rate of reproduction. One adult female fish may lay thousands of eggs. Given adequate spawning grounds, proper water conditions for hatching, adequate food, and enough weedy cover for protection, natural reproduction will produce increasing numbers of catchable-size fish. If the habitat is adequate, hatchery propagation of fish is unnecessary. If the habitat is protected and improved, nature will supply the fish.

With trout and other cold-water fish, it has also been realized that too much emphasis has been placed on hatchery production and not enough on habitat improvement. Nevertheless trout fisheries often present a different problem, for the demand for fishing and the capacity of the habitat often do not coincide. With the best of management, natural propagation cannot meet the demands placed on some of the heavily fished cold-water lakes and streams. Although it is generally true that these waters are not "fished out" in the sense that the last fish have been caught, they can be "fished out" in the sense that all of the easily caught fish have been hooked. When this happens they no longer provide adequate recreation to fishermen. To meet popular demand, fish and game departments are forced to remain in the hatchery business, stocking streams and lakes with trout on a "put-and-take" basis. Trout are reared in hatcheries to legal or "catchable" size and then released in suitable places before the start of the fishing season. It is not necessary that these fish be able to survive permanently in the stocked waters but only that they survive long enough to be caught. Heavily fished areas may be restocked several times in a single season. Similarly, intermittent streams, sterile lakes, and reservoirs which could not support permanent fish populations can be stocked. These fishing grounds, if located near centers of population, will attract fishing pressure which would otherwise fall on the natural fish populations of productive lakes and streams. The more remote areas are thus preserved for the enthusiast who prefers more natural conditions.[2,11]

Deterioration of streams and lakes through failure to practice conservation on watershed lands remains a major problem to be solved by fisheries managers working with all others who can be interested in sound land management. Logging in some areas, despite laws to the contrary, often results in the choking of streams with debris or the pollution

Fig. 128 and chapter opening. Opening day of fishing on Grand Coulee Reservoir. Although high dams often destroy sea-run fisheries, the reservoirs can provide a different type of fishing and are popular recreation areas (U.S. Bureau of Reclamation photograph).

Fig. 129. This fish ladder takes fish over the Rock Island dam on the Columbia River (U.S. Bureau of Reclamation photograph).

of streams with organic wastes. Industries and cities still contribute to stream pollution. Poor farming practices, overgrazing, mining, and lumbering still cause increased erosion with consequent deterioration of watercourses. In addition, many practices advocated in the name of conservation, have caused much damage to fisheries. The construction of high dams on rivers creates impassable barriers to migratory fish. Admittedly, the reservoirs formed behind the dams can provide a different type of fishing which may have equal or greater value, but this does not always occur (Fig. 128). Low dams can be by-passed by fishways and ladders; high dams such as Shasta in California and Grand Coulee in Washington cannot (Fig. 129). Although mature fish can be lifted over these dams by one device or another, young fish returning downstream experience high mortality during the trip over the dam. In addition to dams, irrigation canals prove a major hazard to fish life. Where possible these must be screened off to prevent fish from entering them and perishing. Unfortunately, the design, installation, and maintenance of adequate fish screens is expensive.

**Farm ponds and food fish.** One of the important developments that has come with the rise of the conservation movement has been an interest in farm fish ponds. Small ponds developed on farming lands not only serve in water conservation but, when stocked with fish, can be a permanent source of recreation, food, and sometimes income to the landowner. Many farm owners in the Middle West and South have developed their own home fishing grounds, stocked with bass or sunfish.[2]

In most other parts of the world, fish are important not so much for recreation as for food. Where populations are dense and space for livestock limited, much of the animal protein in the diet of the peoples comes from fish. The farm ponds of the United States have their counterpart elsewhere in the world. Where these contribute importantly to the local food supply, they are usually more intensively managed than in the United States and produce higher yields. German fish ponds, stocked with carp and fertilized, are reported to yield up to 1400 pounds per acre per year; whereas some of the fish ponds in southeast Asia, where both fertilizer and fish food are added, give yields of as high as 13,500 pounds per acre.[16] Such high protein yields offer considerable promise for enriching the diet of the world's peoples. However, reservoirs, natural lakes and streams, canals, and swamps also contribute fish to the world food supply. It was estimated in 1967 that 15 per cent of the world's commercial fish catch, or about 7 million tons of fish, was contributed by inland fisheries (FAO statistics).

The importance of fish for food is high and will become higher. There remains something to be said for a way of life where the fish of lakes and streams are important chiefly for recreation and only secondarily for the pot. It is the objective of the conservation movement to maintain that way of life in North America. It should be the objective of conservation also to restore the possibility of that way of life to all lands.

## MARINE WATERS

**Ocean ecology.** The oceans cover some 70 per cent of the globe. They represent an area still little known and, in a broad sense, little modified by human activities. Even the vast amounts of sediment washed from the continents by erosion, greatly accelerated by human use of the land, have brought little change in the composition of the oceans. Sewage and industrial wastes, a major concern in inland waters and along coasts, have had little overall effect upon the wide seas. Yet the areas of the ocean of greatest interest and concern to man and the products of the ocean most valued by man have been greatly affected.[9,13]

Life in the oceans, as in fresh waters, is dependent upon the chemical properties of the water. Water must provide the nutrients from which living substance can be built. It must also contain oxygen to support most forms of life, and it must be sufficiently clear for light to penetrate. At the base of the pyramid of life in the ocean, as in lakes and streams, is phytoplankton. The production of plankton depends on light penetration and on nutrient concentrations. Although the depths of the ocean extend more than 30,000 feet below sea level in the great oceanic troughs and much of the ocean lies more than a mile below sea level, these depths are not productive. Light can penetrate as much as 400 feet but usually reaches less than 100 feet in ocean waters (Fig. 130). It is only in this lighted zone of surface water that green plants can live and food can be produced. This surface zone, however, produces such

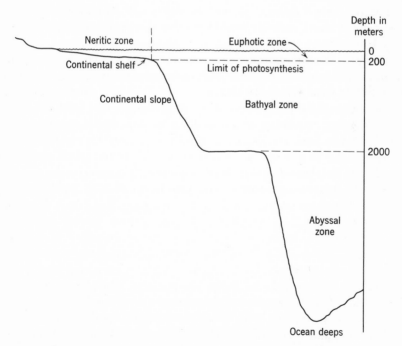

Fig. 130. Zonation in the ocean [data from Odum (1953)].

abundance of life that animal life can exist almost throughout the ocean, either moving to the surface layers to feed or depending on materials moving downwards from the productive surface layers. Animals of various kinds have been dredged from even the greatest ocean depths.[6,16]

The abundance of plankton in the oceans is so great that it is often pointed to as a source of food for man. It is already used for that purpose but only when processed through the bodies of larger marine animals, just as grass provides food for man when processed through wildlife or livestock. However, plankton and the organisms which feed on it are not equally abundant throughout the oceans.[3]

There is a normal tendency in the oceans, similar to that of erosion on land, for nutrient materials to be carried from surface waters, where they can be used in plankton production, into the depths, where they are of little use. As animals and plants die, their bodies sink downward, carrying with them the stores of nitrates, phosphates, and other nutrients that they have gathered during their lives. Were there not a counterbalancing tendency, over the centuries the surface waters would become depleted, and life would cease to exist except where nutrients were entering from the land. Fortunately, the waters of the ocean are in continual circulation. Surface circulation in the major ocean currents is brought about by forces generated through the earth's rotation and by the differences in water temperature between tropical and polar seas (Fig. 131). Cold water, being heavier, sinks downward in polar regions to be replaced at the surface by warmer water moving from tropical regions. The cold water, moving in the ocean depths, works toward the equator. In areas where the earth's rotation and consequent atmospheric currents keep the surface water moving away from the edges of continents, the cold water from the ocean depths can reappear again at the surface. This movement of cold water from depths to surface, known as *upwelling*, takes place along the west coasts of all continents that lie within those latitudes known as the trade-wind belts, as well as in certain other shore areas. In areas of upwelling, nutrients from the ocean floors are brought again to the surface. These areas, therefore, are highly productive of plankton and consequently support great numbers of marine organisms, including important populations of fish. The nutrient-rich waters from these areas move in surface currents to other parts of the ocean, where they continue to support abundant life.[11,19]

Addition of nutrients to ocean waters also takes place along the edges of all of the continents. Here is to be found a submerged portion of the continent known as the continental shelf, toward which move all of the soil and minerals washed from the land. Although this deposition of chemicals has little effect upon the ocean as a whole, it is impor-

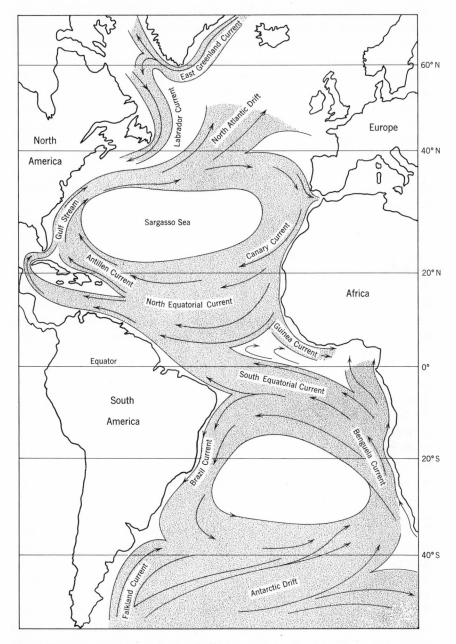

Fig. 131. Major currents of the Atlantic ocean. These currents may carry nutrients from areas of upwelling to other parts of the ocean.

265

tant in raising the level of nutrients in these shallow, offshore waters. Similarly, pollution can be a serious problem in this area.[12,13]

The fisheries of the world are located, for the most part, either on continental shelfs, in regions of upwelling or in currents carrying enriched waters from areas of upwelling. These marine fisheries are exploited primarily for commercial purposes, although sport fishing is becoming important. They have been and will remain major sources of food for mankind and of vitamins to replace those lacking in foods grown from depleted soils. Because they are exploited for food and profit, much attention has been given to devising efficient gear for catching fish quickly and easily. Like the livestock industry on land, the commercial fishing industry wants maximum quantities of meat for a minimum of effort.

**Exploitation and conservation.** Increasing demands for fish have caused the fishing industry to grow, and developing technology has brought more efficient means of exploiting fish populations. Fish schools are sometimes located by radar, and planes may guide fishing boats to the most productive grounds. Such factors have led to a growing danger of overfishing, a danger that varies with the type of fishery. Contributing to the danger is the fact that the oceans, like the public domain lands of the past, belong to no one. The jurisdiction of state and federal governments has traditionally extended only 3 miles offshore. Beyond that point the water has been international. More recently the tendency has been to extend territorial limits to the edge of the continental shelf, although international law has been vague on this point. Beyond the limits of state or national control the ocean is open to exploitation by whoever gets there first. Thus, in the productive waters of the north Pacific and Bering Sea the interests of the United States, Canada, Japan, and the Soviet Union may conflict. Only through interstate and international agreement has fisheries regulation been possible.[7,8]

**Marine mammals.** One group of marine organisms known to be seriously depleted through continuing efficient pursuit consists of the various marine mammals. Three major groups of whales, the right, humpback, and sperm whales, have been threatened with extinction. Other more rare species are now seldom recorded. The whaling industry had a colorful history in the eighteenth and nineteenth centuries. Whaling ships from many nations pursued their prey from the tropics to the ice-bound polar seas. With the twentieth century, whaling became less romantic but far more efficient and destructive. Factory ships were equipped to hunt, kill, dismember, and process whales and return home with the finished products ready for sale. Various international agreements intended to establish safe harvest levels, still fall short of providing necessary protection.[12]

By contrast, another marine mammal, the Alaskan fur seal, was saved from extinction by adequate international agreement signed in 1911. Prior to this, the fur seal, which breeds on the remote Pribilof Islands, attracted hunters from Russia, Japan, Canada, and the United States. With the entire population concentrated on a restricted, rocky breeding area, continued unrestricted hunting threatened quick extermination. Since the signing of the fur-seal treaty, the seal population has recovered to its original numbers and is being harvested at a level that permits its continued existence.

**Anadromous fisheries.** In a particularly vulnerable position are the anadromous fish, which migrate from fresh-water streams to the ocean. These fish must face not only the hazards of ocean life but for reproductive purposes have to pass the dangers encountered in streams and rivers. One example is the Atlantic salmon. Originally salmon were abundant along the northeastern coast of the United States and supported a commercial fishery. A combination of dams along streams with commercial and urban pollution are thought to have been major factors in their decrease. Now they remain abundant only in Canadian waters.[18] On the Pacific coast, the Pacific salmon, of several species, compete with the tuna for first place among commercial fish. Heavy exploitation has led to some depletion, but the major threat to their existence has come in the home streams. The construction of Grand Coulee dam on the Columbia blocked the upper reaches of that river to Chinook salmon spawning. Shasta dam and other high dams on the Sacramento river and its tributaries have cut off large areas of spawning ground in California. To partially replace the reproduction lost through dam construction, major hatcheries have been constructed below the dams, and, to date, these hatcheries have helped to maintain the fishery. In the Sacramento, as a result of improved water conditions below the dam, the salmon population is believed to have increased. However, increasing demand for power, irrigation, and flood control will result in a series of dams on all of the main rivers in California, and many more dams on the Columbia River system. These developments will force increased dependence on the remaining open streams and a much greater effort to develop and improve habitat conditions, as well as an increase in hatchery production, if salmon fishing is to be perpetuated.

A major struggle has been waged between those who wish to maintain open streams for fisheries and recreation and those who wish to dam them for flood control, power, and irrigation. With few exceptions, the representatives of the people in state legislatures and Congress have voted for dams. Increasing demands for water for other purposes leave less water for fish protection. The fisheries manager has tried to meet this by increased efficiency of production in those waters that remain available, but he cannot work miracles.[8]

**The sardine story.**[5,9] Management of the main ocean fisheries is free from the troubles of coastal streams, but it is plagued by the difficulties of finding facts about animal populations that cannot easily be counted or watched as they go through their life cycles. It is faced by the mysteries of a highly complex and little understood oceanic environment. To date, fisheries management in ocean waters has been largely a research endeavor, a continuing attempt to find the basic information on which a sound management program can be based. When this is discovered and the fishing industry convinced of the necessity for management, laws can be passed and agreements made which will help to perpetuate fish resources. Until then, we will continue to face crises such as the one that has confronted the sardine-fishing industry of the Pacific.

In 1936–1937, along the Pacific coast of North America between San Diego and British Columbia a total of nearly 800,000 tons of Pacific sardines were landed. The sardine industry had risen to the point where it was the first-ranking fishery in North America in pounds of fish caught and the third-ranking commercial fishery in value of catch, surpassed only by tuna and salmon. The value of the take was in excess of 10 million dollars annually. The sardine found its way to market in many forms, as bait for fishermen, as the familiar canned sardine for the pantries of the nation, as dog food, oil, and fertilizer for the fields. In 1953–1954, the catch of sardines had fallen to a total of 4460 tons (Fig. 132). Sardine-fishing fleets were sold for other uses; canneries and reduction plants were idle. The failure of the sardine fishery illustrates many of the questions that puzzle those who depend on the resources of the sea for a livelihood and biologists who seek to maintain those resources.

The sardine industry in the Pacific began during World War I in California, with a catch of over 27,000 tons reported in 1916–1917. In succeeding years it spread northward to the waters off Oregon, Washington, and British Columbia. Soon it supported a major fishing fleet and processing industry. In 1924 the catch jumped to 174,000 tons and continued upward to its peak in 1936–1937. The fishing fleet grew to 300 vessels, each taking 100 to 200 tons of fish per day of fishing. After 1936 the take remained at a fairly high level until 1944. Biologists, however, could see that trouble was developing long before the total catch

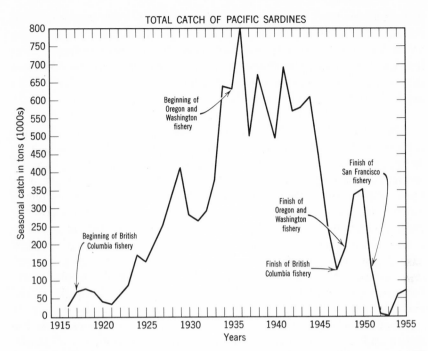

TOTAL CATCH OF PACIFIC SARDINES

*(Chart. Y-axis: Seasonal catch in tons (1000s), scaled 0 to 800 in increments of 50. X-axis: Years, from 1915 to 1955. Labels within chart: "Beginning of British Columbia fishery", "Beginning of Oregon and Washington fishery", "Finish of Oregon and Washington fishery", "Finish of British Columbia fishery", "Finish of San Francisco fishery".)*

Fig. 132. The rise and fall of the sardine fishing industry (Calif. Dept. of Fish and Game, 1957).

started to decline. Under heavy fishing the older fish were removed from the population, and the annual take began to depend upon the yield of younger fish. The average catch per boat and per night of fishing declined. This was masked by the fact that more boats were putting to sea and fishing longer, so that the total catch held up. The symptoms of trouble caused the biologists to attempt to regulate the fishing industry in order to balance the annual catch against the productivity of the population. These efforts at regulation were not successful.

The first fishery to fail was in Canadian waters. Between 1945–1946 and 1947–1948 the Canadian catch dropped from 34,000 tons to less than 500. The Washington and Oregon fisheries soon followed. After the 1948–1949 season the northern fishing fleets stopped operation, and the sardine canneries of the Northwest closed down. For a few more years the yield off California remained high. In 1951, however, the San Francisco fishing fleet returned with a disastrously low catch of 80 tons. With this, the main center of the industry closed down. Catches remained high in southern California waters for one more year, and then this fishery too collapsed.

Throughout all of this period the sardine industry remained unrestricted and refused to tolerate any limitation upon its take. Whether or not such restriction would have prevented the sardine disaster remains open to question, but it is most likely that the fishery could have been better maintained with intelligent regulation.

The final collapse of the sardine industry in United States waters is associated with failure in reproduction and survival of young fish. The expected addition to the population provided by the growth of young sardines to catchable size has not occurred in recent years. Offshore waters in southern California, which were major spawning grounds in the past, are no longer producing young fish. A sardine fishery still exists in Mexican waters off the coast of Baja California, but it is not large enough to support a major fishing industry. Movement of sardines from Mexican to California waters, which occurred in the past, took place in 1955–1956 and allowed for an increase in catch in those years. However, this movement alone is not sufficient. There is evidence that changes in the condition of the ocean, resulting from shifts in currents or other causes, are involved in the depletion of the fishery. If this is true, little can be done except to hope that former conditions will return. However, since overfishing and the resulting depletion of breeding populations is a contributing factor, there is less excuse. Overfishing can be prevented. Fortunately, in 1955, the California legislature passed its first law limiting the catch of a marine, commercial fish. This law, intended to protect the anchovy fishery, on which the former sardine-fishing pressure has descended, may set a precedent for future laws that will provide needed protection for the sardine and other ocean fisheries.

## WORLD OUTLOOK

It is often pointed out that the world's oceans represent a major source of food, particularly protein, for the future. It is less often recognized that they represent a major source of protein now, and that they are already being heavily utilized. Statistics from FAO indicate a world ocean-fisheries yield in the middle 1960's of over 40 million metric tons, or over 600 pounds for every square mile of surface water. This has been calculated by Georg Borgstrom to represent a protein yield equivalent to that of all the world's cattle.[3] The bulk of this production is obtained by Asian fishermen. Europe and North America also harvest a high percentage. The southern hemisphere nations harvest relatively little. Japan and the Soviet Union are the world's great fishing powers, with high-seas fleets that roam over the world's oceans. The great centers of commercial fisheries have been in the northern hemisphere near the centers of human population, but in the 1960's the fisheries of the southern hemisphere are being heavily exploited also.[3]

The oceans are sometimes considered as a great source of plankton, which potentially could be harvested and used for human food. There is no doubt that vast quantities of phytoplankton are produced each year in the oceans. This serves in turn to support the zooplankton, the floating microscopic or near-microscopic sized animal life of the oceans. In turn this supports larger animal life on up through what are sometimes unusually long food chains. When we harvest the larger forms of sea life we are already indirectly harvesting the plankton, concentrated into more readily obtainable forms of animal protein. Georg Borgstrom has pointed out the nature of several of these marine food chains. Around 500 pounds of phytoplankton can produce at best 100 pounds of zooplankton. This could in turn yield a maximum of 10 pounds of herring and this in turn could provide the food supply for 1 pound of mackerel. Should tuna feed upon the mackerel, the pound of mackerel would produce approximately an ounce and a half of tuna. A tuna weighing a hundred pounds, therefore, could represent a phytoplankton production of 500,000 pounds. By contrast, the food chain ending in the giant blue whale represents relatively few links. The blue whale feeds directly upon the larger zooplankton and may process three metric tons of this per day, converting it into whale meat. Man has yet to construct any device more efficient than the blue whale for the harvesting and conversion of plankton and, rather than exterminate these creatures, we should be cultivating and increasing them as highly valued marine livestock.[3]

Considering the nature of the marine environment and the limited extent of highly productive waters, it is overoptimistic to expect that the seas will provide any vast new supply of food for the future. Undoubtedly the yield from the oceans can be increased, but there is also the need to restrict and limit the take from those species and areas that are being overharvested today, and these are many. Apart from natural fisheries, high yields have been obtained by fish-farming in estuaries and bays, using the same principles as those applied to freshwater ponds. The marine environment, if properly managed and utilized, offers the opportunity to support people in ways of living that to some will be more interesting and pleasant than land-based ways. The oceans can enrich the life of limited human populations in the future; they can never be viewed as a means for supporting unlimited human population growth.[7,20,13]

# | 11 |

# The Natural Environment

## INTRODUCTION

Thus far in this text the emphasis has been upon the management of those lands and resources that are extensively or intensively managed for commercial or sport use. There is, however, more to conservation than the efficient and sustained production of species and things of economic or recreational value. There are qualities and aspects to the environment that must be considered without reference to any increment that they might add to the gross national product or any fluctuation that they might create in indices of economic growth. There is a need in the human environment for wild nature, untouched or little modified by man's activities.

In the pursuit of science most people have come to realize that there is a difference between basic and applied scientific research. The physicists who first sought to explore the nature of the atom did so without thought of the eventual destructive and constructive uses to which the knowledge they acquired might some day be put. They were seeking only to explore the mysteries of nature, to add to the understanding of its structure and functioning, to increase our awareness of the universe in which we lived. Viewed from any perspective of human values, their inquiry was worthwhile, regardless of whether or not we feel that the application of their knowledge has been a benefit or a curse. Similarly the work of L. S. B. Leakey in searching for early man in Olduvai Gorge was not motivated or supported through any desire for economic gain. It was enough that we might learn more about human origins and evolution. This is the nature of basic research. By contrast, the scientists who developed a new strain of rust resistant wheat may well have been motivated in their research primarily by the need for expanding the human habitat and increasing the efficiency of agricultural production. They may well have by-passed many fascinating avenues of genetic research that had no obvious practical application. Such applied

Fig. 133. There is a need in the human environment for wild nature, untouched or little modified by man's activities (U.S. Forest Service photograph).

research, by its nature, is directed toward practical goals. It is true, of course, that the line between the two kinds of research is not clear; one may well turn into the other. It is important that we recognize the need for supporting the pursuit of knowledge for the sake of knowledge in itself. This has been a traditional role of the university.

In the pursuit of conservation we must also recognize the value of nature in itself, apart from any value it may have for future exploitation. There is a need to set aside areas only for the purpose of having them available for the purpose of present or future pursuit of knowledge about the natural world. There is a need to set aside natural communities only for the quiet, aesthetic appreciation some people may get by viewing them. There is perhaps also a need to set aside other places only for the sake of the wild creatures who live, unstudied and unpraised, within them. There should be room on earth for all of these areas. We should grant the right of existence to species other than man, without even being threatened by the obvious truth that man's future existence may well depend on them.

## THE VALUE OF WILD SPECIES AND NATURAL AREAS

Those who are already convinced hardly need further arguments about the value of nature. Those who are not convinced, unfortunately, include many who hold the future of the American environment in their power, among them legislators, planners, and the men who control the decisions of business and industry. It is necessary, therefore, to consider some reasons, basic and applied, why it is important to preserve wild things.

## "PRACTICAL VALUES"

The rhesus monkey has probably been on earth as long as man himself. Since man and monkey came into contact, the monkey has been viewed as a pest or a pet or as something to eat, depending on which person was viewing it. In the 20th century, however, the monkey became an important medical ally of man. As an experimental animal it has made possible major advances in biology and medicine, including knowledge about human blood groups, that has permitted the survival of many people who might otherwise have died. Man could have survived without the monkey, but the monkey has increased the welfare of man. In the 19th century, however, a practical man might well have asked "what good are monkeys?" Few could have given him a convincing reason why monkeys should be preserved.

In the early years of this century, *Penicillium* was a nuisance mold on bread. Nobody could have convinced a congressman that this genus of molds should be saved, even after Alexander Fleming in 1929 discovered that it had an antibiotic effect upon bacteria. But the many soldiers who did not die in World War II because of the availability of penicillin and the millions of people since then who have been saved by it or its various antibiotic descendants should be willing to vote for the preservation of "useless" species.

The list of previously wild species that have suddenly made major contributions to human survival and well-being is long: from the wild grasses that were to become corn and wheat, the wild mammals who were to become our domestic animals, on through to the sea urchin and the house mouse. We do not know what previously unnoticed creature, living perhaps in some rain forest or at the bottom of the sea, may hold the key to protection against some disease or environmental predicament that besets mankind. The value of saving wild things as a sort of "life insurance" for humanity should be obvious.

The wild species of this earth represent a reservoir of genetic materials. Each species is irreplaceable, we cannot create it again if it is lost. Each, however, is a storehouse of genetic information that we cannot afford to lose, since we cannot predict or in any way foresee the ways in which this information may someday prove valuable.

It is comparatively easy to maintain an awareness of the relative abundance and distribution of the larger or more conspicuous species of plants or animals. We have a fairly good idea of the number of rhinos and elephants on earth, and of the acreage of old-growth redwood trees. It is impossible to keep track of the presence or abundance of the great variety of small and inconspicuous creatures. We don't know if some species, once described and studied, still exist. However, each species exists as part of some ecosystem or natural community. As long as representative areas of the earth's different kinds of communities and ecosystems are preserved, we have a strong likelihood of maintaining those species that comprise them. It becomes important, therefore, not only to give attention to the preservation of those species of which we are aware but to preserve an adequate representation of the different kinds of environments and communities on earth.

A community or ecosystem can in itself make a contribution to our knowledge that none of the individual species within it can do. Through

Fig. 134. A community or ecosystem can in itself make a contribution to our knowledge that none of the individual species within it can do. Roosevelt elk in redwood forest (photo by J. Bernard).

studies of the structure and functioning of ecosystems that have not been modified by man, we can gain a better understanding of those that man has modified and is using to practical ends. If small areas of intact vegetation had not been preserved in the mountains of Lebanon we might never have guessed that trees could still grow there, and the process of reforestation might not yet have started. The existence of natural communities in Africa made possible the studies of the economic values of wild mammals and the relative advantages that these have as meat producers compared to domestic livestock breeds. The existence of undisturbed watersheds makes possible the study of the role of vegetation and soils in water yield and flood control that could not be carried out were such intact ecosystems not available.

The presence of natural areas in a region can further be of benefit through maintaining the stability of lands that are used for direct commodity production. In part this can be through contributions to the stability of watersheds, in part through contributions to overall biotic diversity. There is a distinct need for comparative studies of *long-term* yields from areas of diversified biota compared to simplified or monocultural areas. Thus far our emphasis has been on short-term gains.

## AESTHETIC AND ETHICAL VALUES

There is no general agreement on the meaning of beauty, but there is widespread agreement on the nature of ugliness. Most people prefer a beautiful environment to an ugly one, and most would agree that a major element of environmental beauty is contributed by the natural scene, either in itself or in some blend with the man-made. In 1965, national attention in America was focused on the aesthetics of the environment by a conference called by President Johnson and held at the White House. This touched off a national beautification campaign under the leadership of Mrs. Johnson. Although major attention was given to the removal of man-made ugliness, billboard removal, removal or screening of junkyards, the construction of scenic highways, etc., the major underlying theme was that man had inherited a beautiful world and had done much to destroy that beauty.

The contribution of natural areas and wild species to the aesthetic quality of the environment is obvious. The untouched wild land provides an opportunity for man to contemplate and enjoy a portion of the world as it once was. Wild species enrich the quality of those lands that man is using. A city park without wild birds is a sterile place. Farming lands from which all wild things are removed are little better than rural factories.

One cannot state the degree to which man is dependent upon some contact with wild nature and natural environments. Although we are becoming increasingly an urban people, this is a recent phenomenon, and there is no evidence by which we can judge what kind of people would be produced after many generations of separation from a more natural world. We are after all a wild species, only recently separated from environments that were mostly wild. Our behavior was conditioned by life in the wilderness, and later for thousands of years in rural villages and fields. The extent to which people flee the cities to seek outdoor recreation whenever the opportunity is presented may itself be an indication of our need to have contact with environments that are not entirely shaped by man.

We go to great lengths throughout much of the world to preserve monuments and historical sites that tell us of man's past accomplishments, his cultural heritage. The difficulties of being without history have been faced by many of the developing nations of the world, where the oral traditions once passed on by the tribal elders have been forgotten and written records are few. Some attempt to create their own history by telling of what might have or should have happened. But there is also a need to preserve the environments in which history took shape. A person who has not seen wild country can hardly appreciate the experiences of his pioneer ancestors.

Perhaps even higher than the values that have been discussed are the ethical reasons for preserving wild nature. These vary from culture to culture. Here in America they have been stated by many people from Henry Thoreau to Aldo Leopold.[16,28] Perhaps Leopold's concept of an extension of ethics from people to the land, mentioned in Chapter 5, states adequately the philosophical issue involved. Do we concede a right of coexistence to the other species that have evolved with us on earth, or do we insist upon our prerogative to kill and destroy anything that stands in the way of our immediate and assumed material well-being? Some would insist along with Walter Lowdermilk on the need for an 11th commandment, concerned with conservation;[19] but considering how inadequately we observe the other ten it seems that adding another would give little further protection to wild creatures.

To the followers of some religions, forms of Hinduism and Buddhism for example, life is sacred and one avoids taking it. Such a restriction, however, has been applied only to animal life and not to the vegetation that supports it. Without habitat, animals do not last long, despite religious protection. In the Western tradition the concept of a "reverence for life" has been a strong feature of the philosophy of Albert Schweitzer and of St. Francis of Assisi.

One cannot legislate religion or ethics, or force people to assume a sense of responsibility for their fellow beings. Neither can one force an appreciation for beauty. One can only hope that such feelings toward the human environment will grow. Meanwhile, to convince the Philistines, it may be necessary to fall back upon harder economic weapons. Recreation and tourism are part of this arsenal and will be discussed in the succeeding chapter.

## STEPS TOWARD PRESERVATION

**The national park system.** America, through its national park system, has in many ways led and set an example for the rest of the world in setting aside extensive natural areas to be preserved in a primitive condition. Although the roots of the ideas of natural area reserves go far back into the past, the first beginnings of the American park system came in the 1860's when Yosemite Valley in California was first set aside as a reserve.[27,29] The credit for this must go in large degree to Frederick Law Olmsted, the designer of New York's Central Park. Having visited Yosemite and having been impressed with its grandeur he managed, with the assistance of others, to persuade Congress to pass a bill preserving Yosemite Valley "for public use, resort and recreation." This occurred in 1864, with the Civil War still raging. Since no federal organization existed to accommodate such a reserve, it was ceded to the state of California to become the first state park. Under state control, however, it suffered from extensive mismanagement, and the area above the valley of Yosemite was subjected to extreme abuse from excessive grazing. John Muir, the famous California naturalist and founder of the Sierra Club, led the fight to have Yosemite proclaimed a national park and placed under army protection. In 1890, partial success was achieved as the Yosemite watershed was proclaimed a national park. It was not until 1905, however, with the intervention of Theodore Roosevelt, that Yosemite Valley was removed from state jurisdiction to become part of Yosemite National Park.[29]

While the Yosemite battle was going on, Judge Cornelius Hedges and several other explorers visited an area of incomparable beauty in the mountains of northwest Wyoming. Impressed by the grandeur of this region of geysers, hot springs, waterfalls, lakes, and mountains, they worked to have the area set aside for the future enjoyment of the Ameri-

Fig. 135. Our remnant herds of bison remain in national parks and wildlife refuges (National Park Service photo).

can people. In 1872, with little debate or understanding of what was happening, Congress passed a bill which President Grant signed into law, proclaiming the Yellowstone region as America's first national park, to be administered by the Secretary of the Interior. The beginning of a system that now includes much of America's finest and most scenic country was achieved.[29]

Into the national park system however was built contradictions that were ultimately to cause trouble. Yellowstone was designated as a "pleasuring ground" for people. Public recreation was stressed when Yosemite Valley was first reserved. In the background, however, was the belief that the natural values that were the focus of this public use must be fully preserved. In 1916, when an agency was finally formed within the Department of the Interior, the National Park Service under the leadership of Stephen Mather, the congressional act stated the need to conserve the scenery and wildlife in such a way that they would be "unimpaired for the enjoyment of future generations." The parks thus had a dual purpose, to preserve nature and to make it available for public enjoyment. These two purposes have come into conflict. Furthermore, the need to preserve "unimpaired" natural areas forced the park service to adopt initially a policy of complete protection and preservation. Applied to certain ecological situations such a policy may be completely successful. However, a pine forest protected completely from fire or other disturbance may cease to be a pine forest. Plant succession will lead toward a climax of other conifers. A deer or elk herd, protected completely, may increase to the point of destroying their habitat and threatening the survival of other wild species.[29]

In the 1960's the National Park Service was forced to seek a resolution to these dilemmas. A committee headed by A. Starker Leopold studied wildlife in the national parks and issued a report stressing the necessity for managing wildlife and wildlife habitat within the parks.[17] With this direction the park service moved to cut back the numbers of the troublesome, overabundant elk herds in Yellowstone National Park. In the late 1960's the Park Service is in the process of designating, within the national parks, areas to be protected against people, to be maintained as wilderness or natural reserves.


## WILDERNESS PRESERVATION

Apart from the national park system, a second major step was taken toward the preservation of natural areas when in 1929 the United States Forest Service recognized the importance of designating certain portions of the national forest system as "primitive areas," to be maintained free from development or disturbance. In this act they were following the leadership of such men as Aldo Leopold and Robert Marshall, who believed that there was a need to maintain large wilderness areas to which men could go and live under primitive conditions and experience a completely natural environment, remote from civilization and its adjuncts.[22]

Further protection for Forest Service primitive areas came in 1939 when some of the more scenic and spectacular regions were designated as wilderness areas. However, these administrative decisions on the part of the Department of Agriculture did not give the protection to wilderness that many of those who were strong believers in the wilderness concept thought was necessary. Consequently, a drive began to give full legal protection to wilderness by having Congress act to designate a National Wilderness System, from which all forms of development would be restricted—roadless areas, within which only primitive means of transportation would be permitted—areas within which vegetation and animal life would continue to exist in an undisturbed state.

In 1958, Congress established an Outdoor Recreation Resources Review Commission with the duty to study the outdoor recreation resources of America with consideration of the measures needed to provide for future recreation needs of the people. Among other projects this commission studied the wilderness resource of America and in its 1962 report recommended that Congress enact legislation designating, for permanent preservation, a national system of wilderness areas.[23] In the course of this study it was revealed that there were only 64 large wilderness areas, over 100,000 acres in size, remaining in the contiguous United States. The total area in such large wilderness tracts was 28 million acres. Most of these, fortunately, were on federal lands, but under the jurisdiction of a number of separate agencies.[18]

After long debate in Congress, in 1964 a Wilderness Act was finally passed establishing a national wilderness system, but designating as part of the system only the wilderness areas and smaller wild areas that had already been designated by the United States Forest Service. Provision was made for the addition of other appropriate areas to the system after future study and review.[20] At the time of writing, wilderness hearings are being held throughout the United States with a view to including within the wilderness system the still wild areas included in national parks, wildlife refuges and other areas of public land, including those Forest Service primitive areas that had not been designated as wild or wilderness areas before the bill was enacted. Nine million acres were included in the wilderness system established by the 1964 act.[20]

## SMALL NATURAL AREAS

Further steps toward the preservation of natural areas, including many that are of smaller size than could logically be included in the wilderness system, are being taken by both government and private organizations. Among the latter, the Nature Conservancy and the National Audubon Society have been leaders in the purchase and preservation of important wild areas that had been in private ownership.

In 1959, in discussions between the International Council of Scientific Unions and the International Union of Biological Sciences, it was agreed that it would be worthwhile to establish an International Biological Program to study certain urgent biological problems as part of a joint world effort. A committee was established to study the problem. In 1963 the International Council agreed to establish an international program (IBP) to study the "Biological Basis of Productivity and Human Welfare." Among the various activities of IBP it was recognized that the establishment of protection over a system of natural reserves for scientific study was of great importance, since many of the more interesting biotic communities were rapidly disappearing in the face of population growth and development. A subcommittee to develop a program for conservation of natural environments was therefore established. By 1967, thirty-eight nations had agreed to participate in the IBP and had established national committees for that purpose. In the United States the IBP was sponsored by the National Academy of Sciences through a national committee, and the various federal agencies agreed to participate in the program.[30]

The IBP has given further stimulus to a program to designate and to protect natural areas for scientific study. In 1967 such areas were being reserved in suitable locations on federal lands, and it is expected that a national system of natural areas will result, to be added to an

Fig. 136. Unique natural communities such as this grove of ancient bristlecone pines deserve special protection in a system of natural reserves.

international register of natural areas designated primarily for scientific study.

The struggle to retain bits and pieces of the old, wild America is well advanced, but can hardly be considered a victory. Each area gained must still be held against the encroachment of those who would develop it for mass public use and those who wish to extract some resource that it contains. There is still a job to be done in designating, within the wilderness system, a special category of protection to be extended to large blocks of undisturbed land needed for the study of extensive communities containing far-ranging species of animal life. The International Union for the Conservation of Nature has provided a special title for such areas, Strict Nature Reserves, not to be used even for wilderness recreation if this will interfere with the long-term preservation of the natural biota. In 1967 there are few areas in the United States that fit this category, although some national parks and portions of others meet the necessary criteria.[1]

Perhaps most disturbing is the continued onslaught against areas supposedly set aside "for all time." The drive to build dams that would flood part of the national park area of Grand Canyon is an example. The struggle to obtain needed water for the Everglades National Park, in the face of urban and agricultural requirements that each year grow larger, is an even more desperate situation.[26] Efforts to set aside new national parks, such as the Redwood National Park in California, have encountered major opposition from the private interests involved and from local governments that feel that their tax base would be threatened by any extension of federal ownership.[21]

## RARE AND ENDANGERED SPECIES

Although the United States is a world leader in wildlife management, the emphasis of this profession has been traditionally directed toward producing game for the hunter rather than the protection and restoration of game that is not available for sport. Early in history, some species (the passenger pigeon, Carolina parakeet, heath hen, and California grizzly among them) became extinct. Today many species are rare and in a highly endangered status. Other once-abundant species are decreasing for reasons that are not understood.[11]

A concern for endangered species has led to acceptance of responsibility over them by the United States Fish and Wildlife Service, and active interest and protection by private groups such as the Audubon societies. For some, strict protection from hunting or other disturbance seems the only measure needed to bring back populations. For others, habitat restoration is essential. The establishment of a Federal Wildlife Refuge system, starting with the Pelican Island in Florida in 1903 and since extended to 300 refuges by 1967, has been an important step.[11]

Good success has been achieved with some species. The trumpeter swan, once near extinction, is now relatively secure. The sea otter of the Pacific Coast, once thought to be extinct, is once more abundant. The Key deer of southern Florida is, for the present at least, secure. The wild turkey and the Alaskan fur seal are now abundant creatures, although they were not long ago considered to be endangered.

Among the many species for which special protection is still required are the California condor, black-footed ferret, ivory-billed woodpecker whooping crane, grizzly bear, Everglades kite, Hawaiian geese, Florida panther, timber wolf and red wolf. A list prepared by the Fish and Wildlife Service in 1965 included 55 species or races of mammals whose status was endangered, rare, or unknown and probably rare, along with a much longer list of birds. Continued vigilance is extended over the small remnant populations of condors, cranes, and Hawaiian geese. Equal vigilance must also be extended to other species if they are to remain on this earth.[11]

## WORLD VIEW

As in most areas of environmental conservation the prospects for preservation of natural environments and wild species are far less promising in most of the world than they are in the United States. The critical nature of the problem has been brought into focus by such organizations as the International Union for the Conservation of Nature, which in 1966 published a two-volume Red Book that listed hundreds of rare and endangered species over the world. The International Biological Program has helped focus world attention on the need to set aside major areas of undisturbed vegetation and animal life for future scientific study.

Perhaps the situation in underdeveloped countries is best exemplified by consideration of Peru. A survey of the Peruvian interior in the 1960's, intended to locate an area to be designated as a national park, found only two areas in the entire Amazonian headwaters region that were at all satisfactory. Over most of this rain-forest area the influence of shifting cultivation, exploitation of timber, commercial hunting of animals for furs or meat, and other human activities had seriously interfered with the native biota. Of the two areas, one located on the Manu River northeast of Cuzco had remained undisturbed only because of a small, but highly warlike, group of Indians who had kept all strangers out. The other, located around the Cutibireni River, northwest of Cuzco, was satisfactory in many respects, but appeared to be lacking in animal life, perhaps as a result of continued hunting.[24]

In a report to the 11th Pacific Science Congress in Tokyo, 1966, the situation in the Philippine Islands was described as critical.[5] Although national parks had been set aside, they had not been protected. Lumbering and other activities threatened to destroy all remaining natural areas of significant size in the islands. Throughout Asia and Latin America, with a few exceptions, similar problems prevail. National parks often exist on paper, but receive no effective protection in the field. The pressure of population, of people living on the edge of poverty in lands with little technological development, threatens environments in areas that were not long ago considered far remote from any likely disturbance.

A first World Congress on National Parks, held in Seattle in 1962, did much to focus world attention on the problem and defined criteria for parks, nature reserves, and similar areas.[1] However, the implementation of its recommendations will require a major international effort, with the wealthy countries assisting in every possible way so that those undisturbed environments of major world interest can be preserved. There is little doubt that such an effort should receive a high priority and, probably, the highest priority in any conservation planning. The time in which it can be accomplished is critically short. Failure to take the steps needed to prevent a vanishing species or an undisturbed environment from disappearing from the earth will mean irrevocable change in the human environment. We will not be able to remedy the loss later on.

# The Demand for Recreation

Following World War II, as national prosperity soared to new levels and leisure time for Americans became more abundant, it became clear that a new industry of major national significance had arisen, the outdoor recreation industry. Although related to the old area of conservation, recreation provided a new banner under which groups not previously interested in conservation could rally. Furthermore, recreational needs and wants could be quantified, expressed in terms of man-hours or recreation days, or assigned dollar values based on actual cash expenditures. One cannot assign such a dollar value to a natural area or wild species that few people see, that is reserved for unspecified scientific study at some time in the future, or that simply exists for itself alone.

The increasing national interest in recreation was given focus with the creation of the Outdoor Recreation Resources Review Commission (Chapter 11) and, in particular, with the publication of its report in 1962.[15] New facts were revealed on recreation demands by the general public, new data were presented on the availability of recreational space and facilities, and new questions were raised, such as "Why do people do what they do, and would they rather do something else?"

## THE OUTDOOR RECREATION RESOURCES REVIEW[15]

The major recommendations of the recreation commission fell into five categories:

1. Establishment of a national outdoor recreation policy.
2. Establishment of guidelines for the management of outdoor recreation resources.
3. Improvement of outdoor recreation programs to meet increasing need.

4. Establishment of the Bureau of Outdoor Recreation in the Federal Government.

5. A federal grants-in-aid program to the states.

Congress responded favorably to the report and in essence the government accepted the statement that "It shall be the national policy, through the conservation and wise use of resources, to preserve, develop, and make accessible to all American people such quantity and quality of outdoor recreation as will be necessary and desirable for individual enjoyment and to assure the physical, cultural, and spiritual benefits of outdoor recreation." The commission report specified further the role of the federal government to be:

1. Preservation of scenic areas, natural wonders, primitive areas, and historic sites of national significance.

2. Management of federal lands for the broadest possible recreation benefit consistent with other essential uses.

3. Cooperation with the states through technical and financial assistance.

4. Promotion of interstate arrangements, including federal participation where necessary.

5. Assumption of vigorous, cooperative leadership in a nationwide recreation effort.

In 1962 a new federal agency, the Bureau of Outdoor Recreation, was established within the Department of the Interior. In 1964 the federal grants-in-aid program was assured with the passage of the Land and Water Conservation Fund Act. This permitted the charging of fees to users of national parks and other federal recreation lands with the money to go into the federal fund. The fund would also receive money from the sale of federal real property and from taxes on motorboat fuels. The fund would provide money to the states on a 50–50 matching basis for recreation planning, land acquisition, and land development for recreation. To receive federal funds, however, the states were required to submit to the Bureau of Outdoor Recreation a suitable recreation plan, before money could be used for land acquisition or development. Thus overall planning to meet outdoor recreation needs was provided for.

The recreation commission further recommended as guidelines for management the classification of lands into six categories of outdoor recreation resources:

Class I. High-density recreation areas.
Class II. General outdoor recreation areas.

Class III. Natural environment areas.
Class IV. Unique natural areas.
Class V. Primitive areas.
Class VI. Historic and cultural sites.

Through such a classification it was hoped to guarantee not only the provision of mass-recreation facilities, but also the reservation of wild and remote natural areas for the highest quality of outdoor recreation. Hopefully, if the needs of the many could be met close to home, the remote areas could be preserved for the use of the few who really preferred and appreciated their qualities.

# RECREATION ACTIVITIES[15]

In its analysis of American outdoor recreation activities the commission found that pleasure driving ranked first, walking for pleasure second, and the playing of outdoor games or sports third, in a tally of the average number of days spent per person each year. Water-based activities of all kinds, from swimming to skin-diving, ranked very high. Activities that, by their nature, were related to wild country or natural areas (for example, nature walks, hunting, hiking, mountain climbing) did not rank as highly as those activities that required only open space or water space for their exercise. The American people were revealed as having a high demand for outdoor recreation, but not necessarily a high demand for those forms of recreation based upon wild country. Nevertheless, because of the lack of more generalized mass recreation facilities, the pressure upon wild country facilities was enormous. The need for development of recreational space in or near the cities to meet the daily or weekend recreational demand was stressed by the committee.

Of the various categories of state and federal outdoor recreation land, the state parks received the greatest number of visits (nearly 255 million in 1960), national parks received nearly 80 million visits, and national forests nearly 93 million visits. The greater pressure upon state parks reflects their location closer to the major urban centers of population. To the Easterner in particular, the national forests and parks are often far from home and require a major vacation trip if they are to be visited. State parks can often be reached easily in an afternoon or weekend.

Unfortunately, statistics can be misleading and there is some cause to wonder in 1967 whether both state and federal recreation agencies are not being misled by the statistics provided by the various recreation surveys. Thus the statistics on the preference of people for automobile driving as a form of outdoor recreation leads to the expansion of highways and, in particular, to a scenic highway program, since these are apparently what the people want. People drive, however, for a variety of reasons: because they know how, have a car, can afford to operate it, it gets them away from their usual environment, and it brings the family together, while providing some degree of privacy from other people. In driving they see different areas, get to know new places, have the opportunity to enjoy whatever roadside beauty is available. Many people also get considerable pleasure out of the sheer ownership and operation of a motor vehicle. But people may also drive because there is nothing else to do within easy reach that they know how to do, how to appreciate, or can afford to do. Given an equal choice between driving and skiing, which is relatively low on the list of outdoor activities, and assuming that an area was available (along with skiing

Fig 137. Although it was built primarily for power and water regulation, Shasta Dam has created a lake that is now a major recreation area for northern California.

Fig. 138. The enormous demand for recreation space is now a major factor determining the use that will be made of our lands.

lessons, skis and other equipment), and that the person could equally afford skiing, there is little doubt that skiing would climb much higher on the list of activities among all of the younger and more active people.

Relatively few people go on nature walks or hike in wild country compared to those who drive or walk about the city. But the comparison is again open to question. Relatively few people have been taught anything about nature or how to appreciate wild country. Relatively few people have the same opportunity to participate therefore in activities that include a personal involvement with wild nature, as in activities that involve only a motor car and a road.

Should we spend federal and state funds more for building highways and swimming pools, because these are what people will use, or should we spend the money for building the skills and appreciation needed for better use of wider and more natural environments? There are those who say we must not make value judgments about recreation, that nobody can say that a hike in the wilderness or the operation of a sailing craft on the ocean is a higher form of recreation than driving a car or sitting by a swimming pool. However, we are accustomed to making such value judgments, and we do not spend federal money to build bigger and better equivalents of Las Vegas, even though gambling is a highly popular form of recreation. Undoubtedly, those who understand the values of wilderness, the skills of skiing or sailing, or the adventure of hunting are in a better position to make judgments about them than those who know of these things only from seeing them in television advertisements.

## URBAN OPEN SPACE

Few would question that one of the greatest needs in our society is for open space in or near the cities that is developed and available for various forms of outdoor recreation. With 70 per cent of our population living in urbanized areas, and with the amount of leisure time growing in each decade, the demand for recreation space close to urban areas is both large and increasing.

In addition to its value for recreation, open space, in the form of areas growing trees or other plants and supporting various forms of wild animal life, adds beauty and variety to cities, gives them a definition, shape, and identity that they might otherwise lack, and generally adds to the pleasure of living in them.[13]

One of the first big steps toward the reservation of urban open space in the form of city parks came in New York in the 1850's. At this early date, the pressure of urban populations upon land in or near the cities was already great. Few people could afford a long train or boat journey to a distant recreation area. Most were forced to spend all of their time within the city and seek whatever recreation it had to offer. William Cullen Bryant could foresee a future when the need for public parks in the city would be intense. Consequently, through his efforts in what was to become the middle of Manhattan, a major area of 700 acres was purchased for very little and was developed by Frederick Law Olmsted into New York's Central Park. The value of the land in Central Park would today be beyond the reach of government purchase if it had been at any time opened for development. But Central Park has stood through the years and New Yorkers would not tolerate its development as real estate. It is impossible to measure the ways in which it has contributed to the welfare and enjoyment of New Yorkers.[15]

Fig. 139. Open space adds beauty and variety to cities, gives them a definition, shape, and identity that they might otherwise lack.

Not to be left far behind, San Francisco in the 1870's set aside and later developed a still larger Golden Gate Park in an area now surrounded by urban housing and high-value real estate. In the 1890's in Boston, Charles Eliot and others went a step farther and developed not just a park but a park system, providing a variety of kinds of urban open space and room for many types of recreational activity. In the second decade of this century, Chicago also developed a park system including the outstanding Cook County Forest Preserve.[15]

It was once relatively easy to purchase and set aside open space in or near cities and to develop it for parks and recreation. Now with increasing populations and skyrocketing land values it is extremely difficult. As the need for open space grows, the possibility of a city or county government being able to afford to buy it appears to decrease. Most cities today have open-space plans showing the areas they would like to open up, keep open, or develop for recreation. Few have great success in putting the plans into operation, since the pressure for real-estate development can usually persuade the landowner to sell to the developer and convince the city government that it is in their best interest to allow development to take place.[2,18,19]

One of the greatest problems has come, not from the acquisition of open space but the preservation of that already required. Parks and other open areas seem an easy answer to the location of public facilities. The land can be used at no charge and requires no clearing away of existing structures. Consequently, there has been a regrettable tendency to locate freeways in parks, sometimes disguised as parkways or scenic highways, as well as to locate other urban facilities that are incompatible with the use for which the park was intended. There is also an unfortunate tendency to locate highways in areas that might otherwise be acquired with relative ease for future parks or other urban recreation space. Each such proposal must be vigorously opposed by those who favor parks or, simply, would rather have a beautiful city than one that is easy to get to and easy to leave. Battles against freeway development are fought and have been fought in nearly every major city from San Francisco to Washington.[6,19]

It has been suggested by some planners that one approach to the urban open-space problem would be for planning authorities to give it highest priority in planning, to regard it as a fixed quality, and all other urban elements as relatively more movable. Such a procedure is needed, but its implementation will depend on the resolve of the citizenry of each town and city and their desire to maintain their communities as environments suitable in all respects for their inhabitants.[19]

## OTHER NATIONS

The demand for outdoor recreation in other nations appears to vary with their state of urbanization and technology. People who live year-round in the country are inclined to go to town for their vacation. They make daily use of the open space around them, but often view this activity as part of the daily routine rather than as recreation. People who do not have enough to eat are little inclined to seek recreation. Consequently, the apparent internal demand for outdoor recreation space in most of the developing nations is small. The potential demand, however, as the circumstances of the people improve and as they become more urbanized, is probably great. It would be easy for these countries to save open space now when the demand is small. It may be quite difficult to obtain space for recreation in the future when the demand is great.

In Japan, for example, with increasing prosperity following World War II, the demand for recreation has grown enormously. The nation has a respectable national park system, but the parks are overcrowded. Millions of visitors seek them out during vacation and on weekend trips and, to an American, almost unbelievable numbers of people toil up the mountain trails and climb the high peaks. Still greater numbers crowd the available beaches. The weekend journey from Tokyo to Mount Fuji is a nightmare to one who is used only to a New York level of overcrowding.

In England there has been a long tradition of using the countryside for hiking, cycling, riding, shooting, and other outdoor activities. With increasing prosperity, outdoor space has become crowded. The Nature Conservancy, a government body equivalent to the National Park Service in the United States, has done an excellent job of establishing and preserving a system of national parks and other outdoor areas, but it has been a difficult struggle, since pressure on lands for other uses has also been increasing. The same picture prevails in most of the other developed countries in Europe, and there has been an increasing flow of European tourists to recreation areas abroad.

The interest of people in the wealthier nations in preserving and in visiting the natural treasures and outdoor resources of the developing nations has been an unexpected boon to the economies of some of these countries. In Kenya, for example, tourism is a major industry and, throughout East Africa, it has had an economic impact far greater than was expected when these nations were first being prepared for independence. The support for the preservation of outdoor recreational space in the developing nations can be expected to come, to a large extent, from outside their boundaries until such time as the economic welfare of their own peoples has improved.

# | 13 |

# The Urban Environment

There is little doubt that in the 1960's, unlike the 1930's, many of the major conservation battles are being fought, not on the farmlands and the wildlands, but in the cities. It is in the cities and their environs that the greatest deterioration of the human environment is taking place. It is the influence of urban populations and urban growth that results in many of our major land-use conflicts. It is in the cities that the decisions about land use throughout America will be made.

To put the issue in proper perspective with the use of 1960 census data, the bulk of the United States population (70 per cent) is urban. This does not mean, however, that most people live in cities, since the census figures include among urban populations all people who live in towns of 2500 people or more. Only 28 per cent of the population lived in cities of 100,000 or more. The suburbs, spreading out from the city proper, contain additional people and various smaller communities adjacent to the city but, with separate governments, contribute to city-centered urban populations. Such metropolitan areas, containing a central city of 50,000 or more, or central "twin cities" of 50,000 or more, along with adjoining suburbs and smaller communities, contained 64 per cent of the total United States population. By 1967, this had increased to 66 per cent. Thus nearly two-thirds of the American people live in "citified" areas and share in the problems of the city environment.

Perhaps the most remarkable statistics involve the growth of urban populations in the United States during the past half century. In the period 1910 to 1960 the population of the United States doubled. The urban population, however, tripled. The percentage of people living in urban areas was 46 in 1910 and 70 in 1960, and conversely rural populations declined from 54 to 30 per cent in that period. The growth of some cities in that period has been enormous. The population of Los Angeles increased eightfold from 1910 to 1960. There were close to 20 people in Albuquerque in 1960 for every 1 person in 1910, whereas Phoenix increased nearly fortyfold in the same period. This rapid growth

Fig. 140. It is in the cities and their environs that the greatest deterioration of the human environment is taking place. Here in New York, smog and congestion create problems that are exceedingly difficult to solve (photo by Litton Industries— Aero Service Division).

and the sheer mass of people in some metropolitan areas has not only complicated old problems unbearably, but has added a whole new dimension of environmental problems.

In the 1960's in many, if not most, large American cities, the city heart had deteriorated, and the core city was characterized by deteriorating housing or slum conditions in which minority ethnic groups were crowded. The metropolitan edge had deteriorated by the unplanned spread of suburbs, most of which offered a minimum of environmental amenities; by the spread of unplanned highway strip towns; and by a fringe area, neither farm nor city, but of neglected land in transition from one state to another. Traffic congestion in and around cities had become extreme. In an effort to solve traffic problems, freeways, parking lots, and other automobile-oriented enterprises, had cut into and often shattered the earlier city framework, sometimes destroying scenic and historically significant areas as well as urban open space in the process.[11]

Pollution of both air and water had become severe. In many areas, shortages of water existed or threatened.

In the 1960's also it was apparent that the greatest problem was presented, not by the existing situation but by expected future growth. It was expected by some in 1965 that urban populations would double in size by the year 2000, leaving a scant 35 years to build new housing and urban facilities equivalent to all that had been constructed in all of the previous centuries of American history. At a minimum, we were faced with the necessity of building the equivalent of one city as large as metropolitan Washington each year. The questions to be answered were where we should build and how we should build, as well as how we should repair or rebuild that which was already faulty.

## URBAN PATTERNS AND PROBLEMS

It is impossible here to do more than give a sketchy outline of some of the problems involved in planning and developing new urban areas and improving the old. Most of our towns and cities grew originally with little overall planning or control. They reflect thousands of individual decisions and hundreds of partial plans. These have contributed in some areas to a rich texture of interesting urban diversity, in others to ugliness and confusion. Past efforts to achieve some order in the cities have to a large degree taken the line of separating urban functions through zoning. Zoning laws have separated the industrial areas where people work in producing goods; the commercial areas where people shop or work at office jobs; and the residential areas where people sleep and carry out much of their social life. The latter are further divided into areas of single-family detached homes and areas of multiple-family housing represented by high-rise apartments or other high-density housing.[15] Such a separation of urban functions was inhibited originally by transportation facilities. In the 19th century and earlier, it was necessary to be within walking distance of work and shopping areas. With the development of individual transportation by private automobile, however, it became possible to separate these urban functions widely. Thus the development of residential suburbs, extending often in uniform patterns for many miles beyond the former city boundaries, occurred.

Cities, by their very nature, present problems of transportation. They are areas in which agricultural produce is processed or consumed and areas in which the various products of industry are manufactured. There must be a constant flow of goods into and out of the city. The modern industrial city consequently grew up around the railroad junction. The central railway station was the focus around which hotels, entertainment centers, stores, and offices were grouped. The railway line was the axis along which the city expanded into the countryside, the means by which city people travelled to seek recreation, the basis for the existence of satellite towns, resorts, and other urban-oriented developments. Within the city, public transportation systems, horsecars or, later, electric trolleys served to move people from the industrial or commercial centers to the residential districts. With the rise of the private automobile and the gasoline or diesel-powered truck, however, this old framework of the city was disrupted. New urban centers, more readily accessible by automobile, arose, and the area around the railway station disintegrated into a "skid row" or slum district. Highways, rather than rails, provided the new avenues for urban expansion into the countryside. Public transportation facilities disintegrated.

With ever-growing numbers of automobiles the traffic jam became a permanent part of the urban scene. The difficulties of reaching the city center and of parking when there, along with other factors, led to a breakdown of the central city. Business and industry followed the people to the suburbs. New centers of work and commerce, dispersed widely around the periphery of the urbanized area, began to replace the old centralized urban core. The central city became a place where the poor concentrated, where ethnic minority groups were forced to live, and where housing, schools, and all other urban facilities deteriorated. Cities, in the old sense of vital, thriving centers of human activity and interest, appeared to be dying.[10,11,15]

The suburbs have been the subject of many sociological studies since the end of World War II and have been blamed for many of the ills of modern society. Yet there is little doubt that most people who have moved there from the central city have gained a marked improvement in living conditions. The suburbs have become the established center of the American middle-class family, since they offer security and space for the raising of children in congenial surroundings. They have been consistently rejected by the adolescent and young adult who find them restrictive and dull. They have little appeal to the intellectual. In one form or another, however, they are likely to remain as part of urbanized America.[1,18]

There have been many different approaches to urban renewal. Some center on the belief that the automobile is here to stay and seek, through the construction of freeways and adequate parking facilities, to develop new patterns of automobile-oriented urban centers and residential areas. Others believe that the automobile is by its nature inimical to healthy cities and seek the development of clean, attractive, high-speed public transportation systems that will replace the private car, combined with pedestrian-oriented centers of shopping, business, and entertainment. Some seek to retain and rejuvenate the old urban residential areas, now frequently deteriorated into slums.[15] This approach has been followed with marked success in Georgetown in the nation's capital, in the North Beach area of San Francisco, Greenwich Village in New York, the French quarter in New Orleans, and elsewhere.

A more common approach to urban renewal is demolition and redevelopment. The old congested centers of Philadelphia, Pittsburgh, southwest Washington, D.C., and other cities have been replaced by gleaming new towers of office buildings and high-rise apartments. Such an approach is frequently disastrous for those people who lived in the old areas, but cannot afford to live in the new.[15]

Fig. 141. One approach to halting the deterioration of the central city has been to tear down and rebuild in a new pattern. Here in southwest Washington, D.C., new apartment buildings have replaced an old slum.

Fig. 142A and 142B. Many believe that the answer to the problems of the old cities lies in part in the building of new towns and new cities. Here is the start of the new town of Reston, Virginia, which features village clusters built around man-made lakes (photos courtesy of Reston).

The garden city concept, for which Ebenezer Howard was the best known early advocate, has its many followers today.[13,18] The new towns of Reston, Virginia, and Columbia, Maryland, essentially follow this pattern, with major emphasis on clustered development of housing around recreation lakes surrounded by green areas of open space. In both of these towns and in many other developments, emphasis has been upon formation of what is essentially an urban village within an urban town in an urban city. It is hoped that such small, unified communities will give the individual greater opportunity and scope for activity in the affairs of his society, and a greater feeling of personal identity.[22]

No one approach to urban development or renewal provides the answer for the cities of the future. Indeed, it is to be hoped that no single urban pattern will be allowed to prevail to the same extent in the future as, for example, the uniform detached-house suburban pattern was allowed to prevail after World War II. The preservation and creation of urban diversity, to provide different ways of living in different kinds of cities for people of differing tastes is a worthy goal for future development of urban environments.

## THE POLLUTION ISSUE

It is a characteristic of cities that they take in food and other raw materials from the environment that supports them and give off great quantities of waste materials. The waste, unless disposed of in some adequate way, pollutes the environment. The problems of water pollution have already been discussed. Other problems of urban areas are pollution caused by garbage and solid wastes and, perhaps most urgent, pollution of the air.

## SOLID WASTES

The problem of disposal of solid waste is difficult, since vast quantities of it are produced by an industrial society.[10] These may include radioactive wastes from uranium mines, old car bodies, shattered concrete and bricks from demolished houses, vast quantities of tin cans and bottles, and so on. Littered about the countryside or accumulated in junkyards, such debris renders areas of land useless and creates an ugly and repellent landscape. Cities have tried many ways of disposal, some successful, others less so. Southern California cities have had success with disposing of old car bodies to create underwater artificial reefs in the ocean, where fishes that prefer shelter might hide or breed. They have also had some success using solid wastes in filling in undesirable gullies or unwanted canyons, creating level land that is of greater use than that which was filled in. In England, solid wastes have been used to create artificial hills, subsequently covered with soil and planted to vegetation. Cities located on the ocean shore or on bays have used such wastes for land fill, adding to it soil removed in various types of urban-industrial construction. But, as San Francisco has found, there are limits to how far one can go in this direction. San Francisco Bay is now threatened with destruction as the fill proceeds outward and new residential communities are created on filled land where once were only the waters of the Bay. Not only would the value of the Bay as a scenic asset be lost by continued fill; its value as a climate regulator, keeping the Bay Cities cool, would also go. Lost also would be the enormous biotic resource, since the Bay produces fish and shellfish, water- and marsh-birds, and serves as wintering ground for the ducks and geese of the Pacific flyway. The loss of recreation space alone would be enormous.

Waste foods and other organic materials that go under the name of garbage present much of the same problem as that presented by sewage. Dumped into water they become a health menace, their decomposition depletes the oxygen supplies of water bodies, their released nutrients encourage blooms of undesirable algae, and so on. Frequently, these have been burned along with waste wood and paper, but this adds to air pollutants and increases the menace from this form of pollution.

The ultimate answer to garbage and solid wastes would seem to involve reprocessing and reclaiming that would reduce them to their constituent compounds, and the separation of these to make them available for future use. This is expensive but, in the long run, alternative methods that are now available represent only temporary solutions to the problem.

## AIR POLLUTION

Air pollution during the past decade has become one of the major environmental problems of urban-industrial society. Some would give it first rank among conservation problems, since it directly threatens the life and health of many millions of people. However, it is not a particularly new problem except in its present dimensions. People have been affected seriously and have been killed by polluted air during the entire period since the Industrial Revolution.

Particulate matter in the air, in the form of dust or smoke, has caused various problems to human health and comfort in some places at some times probably throughout history. To this was added, starting with the Middle Ages and increasing ever since, the by-products of the combustion of coal and later of petroleum. More recently, but in ever-growing quantities the by-products of the gasoline-powered internal combustion engine have been added and, most recently, radioactive materials derived from nuclear explosions or nuclear power production. To these pollutants can be added a whole range of by-products from various industrial processes: the fine dust from cement factories, the chemicals used in the production of paper pulp, the output of smelting plants, refineries and processing plants of many kinds. It has been said that we are adding new chemical pollutants to the air faster than we can analyze the effects or dangers from existing ones. In many places we have reached a crisis stage and could be on the verge of catastrophe. A new word, smog, has been added to the language to describe the poisonous mixture that has taken the place of what was once harmless fog and haze.[5,17]

The recent history of air pollution disasters starts with the Meuse Valley in Belgium. In December 1930 a heavy concentration of smog in this area killed 60 people. In Donora, Pennsylvania, in October 1948 a high concentration of air pollutants caused widespread respiratory illness and resulted in 17 deaths. In London, England, a long chain of minor disasters caused by the well-known black fogs, reached a peak in December 1952, when 4000 people were believed to have died from breathing polluted air. In all of these disasters, the primary blame was placed upon high concentrations of sulfur dioxide, a by-product of coal combustion or of the burning of fuel oil with a high sulfur content. The polluters were both the ordinary citizens, burning coal or fuel oil to heat their houses, and factories and industrial plants that burned large quantities of these fuels.[5,10]

Air pollution crises usually occur as a result of weather conditions. Normally, in day time, air temperatures will decrease from the ground upward. Warmed air, near the ground, tends to rise and, as it does so, cools. This upward movement of air carries many pollutants up and away from the zone where people live. Wind carries them away from the area of origin and disperses and mixes them. Under certain weather conditions, however, the normal air temperature gradient changes. A mass of warm air may move in with a weather front and may overlay the cooler air below. A temperature inversion is the result. The effect of this is to block the upward movement of warmer air from the ground and thus trap polluted air within the zone where human activities are concentrated. Inversions frequently persist for several or more days during times when there is little horizontal air movement to carry pollutants away from their source. The frequency at which inversions occur varies from one place to another. New York, which produces enormous quantities of air pollutants, escapes disaster because inversions are relatively rare and seldom long persistent. Los Angeles, with a lower total output of pollutants, has frequent inversions and frequent periods of heavy smog concentration.[5,16,17]

A region, such as the Los Angeles Basin, within which air masses tend to rest and to develop uniform characteristics differing from those in an adjoining area, is known as an *airshed*. Sources of pollution anywhere within an airshed can affect the entire region.

There are two major types of air pollution in the United States: that resulting primarily from the burning of coal and high-sulfur fuel oils, which characterizes the eastern and midwestern part of the country, and that resulting primarily from other causes, in particular the internal-combustion engine. However, the two intergrade in many places and, locally, a different source of pollution, such as that emanating from pulp mills, may be more important. Throughout the United States the automobile is rising rapidly to first place as the major cause of air pollution. In California it has long held this position.[5,16,17]

Pollution is not just a danger to human health. It also does many millions of dollars worth of architectural and industrial damage each year and affects all plant and animal life. Air pollution from San Francisco and the Central Valley does damage to pine trees in the Sierra Nevada. The cut-flower industry and many kinds of agricultural crops have been pushed out of the area of heavy air pollution in southern California.[16,17]

Control of pollution has barely started. Los Angeles and its environs, faced with the most urgent problem, have led the way in attempts to solve it. In 1947 the California legislature passed an enabling act assigning the authority to California counties to control stationary sources of air pollution. Los Angeles County moved to control the emissions from industrial plants and to stop the burning of refuse in municipal dumps. Next a more difficult step was taken and the burning of trash in home incinerators was forbidden. Space heating as a source of pollution was attacked with the burning of high-sulfur fuels forbidden. Despite all of these controls, which most communities have yet to emulate, smog problems continued to grow worse. In 1955 the California legislature passed an act creating multiple-county Air Pollution Control Districts, thus allowing for uniform regulations and controls in counties sharing a common airshed. However, in southern California it had become apparent that the major offender, the source of 80 per cent of pollution, was the automobile, and this could not be controlled by a local district. In 1960 a state Motor Vehicle Pollution Control Board was established. Through the action of this board it is now mandatory that all new motor vehicles registered in the state be equipped with devices that reduce the quantity of pollutants in automobile exhausts. However, such devices are as yet inefficient and the pollution problem grows.[16,17]

At the national level and in most communities, progress is far behind that made in California. Only in 1966 did New York City begin to move against some of the more obvious sources of pollution. The federal government started research on air pollution in 1955 when an Air Pollution Act was passed. In 1960 the Surgeon General was directed to study the effects of pollution from motor vehicle exhausts. A 1962 act was also directed at research only. In 1963 a Clean Air Act was a more positive step, providing 95 million dollars to help state and regional agencies develop control programs and permitting federal action to control interstate pollution problems, at the request of a state. In 1965, amendments to the Clean Air Act allowed the Secretary of the Department of Health, Education and Welfare to set standards for motor vehicle exhaust emissions and provided further money for developing demonstration control programs. In 1967 an air quality control act directed the government to establish criteria for air quality.

In the air pollution issue it has become apparent that not only are industries generally unwilling to police themselves, but the average citizen is also unwilling to regulate his own activities to the extent that he no longer contributes his share of automobile exhaust fumes and pollutants from space heating or outdoor incinerators to the already heavily-laden air. Air pollution will not go away if we ignore it; it will only grow worse. Stringent controls at all levels of government appear to be essential in order to force people to do what is necessary for their own health and survival. Writing in 1967, the author believes that we may have to face a truly major air-pollution disaster before we take the action that is needed.


# NUCLEAR ENERGY

The special problem of pollution of the environment with radioactive isotopes is one that originates with advanced urban-industrial societies, but which affects the entire world. The entire issue has been so confused by secrecy and muddled by fear and misinformation that it is difficult to be certain of the precise situation in which the human race exists. Because the military strength and national defense of nations is involved, it is impossible for the average citizen to be fully informed. He must therefore place his faith in government officials who have not always been either truthful or accurate in their statements.

Radioactive elements are those elements that undergo spontaneous disintegration. In this process they give off ionizing radiation and change ultimately into other stable elements. Ionizing radiation that is of primary concern to ecology is of two kinds: that consisting of particles of atomic or subatomic size and that consisting of electromagnetic radiation. In the former category are *alpha* particles, relatively large in size and with little ability to penetrate far through air or more solid media, and *beta* particles, which are high-speed electrons with greater penetrating power. Both of these are capable of doing biological damage through causing ionization of the elements that make up living protoplasm. In the second category are *gamma* rays, which are related to x rays, radiation similar to visible light but with extremely short wavelengths. These readily pass through organic material and can do damage throughout the body. Shields of lead or other heavy metals are used to screen against them.[20]

Measurement of radioactivity is based commonly upon the amount of radiation energy given off by the emitting materials, the rate at which atomic disintegrations take place, or upon the dose of radiation energy received by an organism. Thus the *curie* is the quantity of a radioactive substance in which $3.7 \times 10^{10}$ atoms will disintegrate per second and consequently give off that number of alpha, beta, or gamma particles or rays. Since 37 billion particles per second is a high rate of radioactivity, the more common measurements are millicuries (one-thousandth of a curie) or microcuries (one-millionth of a curie).[20]

The *roentgen* or *rad* is a measure of the dosage of radioactivity received by an organism and amounts to 100 ergs of energy per gram of tissue. One-thousandth of a rad, the millirad, is a convenient measure for dosages commonly encountered in the human environment.[20]

Radioactivity is not a human invention but a normal component of the biosphere. Uranium, thorium, and radium are the more common naturally occurring radioactive elements that are present in many of the rocks of the earth's surface. Cosmic rays, a mixture of particulate and electromagnetic radiation, continually enter the earth's atmosphere from outer space. These ionize atmospheric nitrogen to form radioactive carbon,[14] a normal component of the atmosphere. The radiation received from these natural sources, known as background radiation, amounts to an estimated one-tenth of a roentgen or rad per year, or perhaps 7 roentgens in a lifetime.[20]

Since World War II, man has made use of the energy contained within atoms for both destructive and constructive purposes. The dangers to the human environment are naturally greatest from the destructive uses of nuclear energy, but constructive uses also hold some threats. Large-scale atomic warfare would of course have disruptive effects that are for this writer incalculable. The testing of atomic weapons has already had effects that are only in part measurable. The increasing substitution of nuclear power for fossil-fuel power will bring growing dangers from pollution unless satisfactory means for waste control and disposal are available.

Atomic explosions and the generation of nuclear power from reactors can release in the environment radioactive elements of biological importance that do not occur naturally. The most well-known and infamous of these is strontium-90. This is picked up from the environment by plants and animals and is accepted physiologically as the equivalent of calcium. Among animals it is stored in the bony tissues from which it gives off ionizing radiation, almost all of which is absorbed close to its source. This does damage particularly to the growing cells of the bone marrow and can give rise to leukemia or other forms of cancer. Cesium-137 is accepted by organisms as a substitute for normal potassium and can be accumulated in the muscles and other soft tissues of the body. Iodine-131 is accepted in place of stable iodine and is stored particularly in the thyroid gland.[23]

Biological danger from radioisotopes depends in part on their concentration in the external environment, in part on the degree to which living organisms may concentrate the elements in their organs and tissues in excess of the concentration in the external environment, and in part on the length of time that they persist. The length of time that a radioactive element persists is measured in terms of its *half-life,* the time required for half the atoms in any given quantity of radioactive material to disintegrate.[20]

Naturally occurring carbon-14 has a half-life of 5568 years, meaning that for any quantity present in the environment now, one half will still be present in 5568 years. Iodine-131, however, has a half-life of only 8 days. Dangerous concentrations of this element are therefore short-lived. Strontium-90 and cesium-137 have half-lives of 28 and 33 years, respectively. Consequently, even though rates at which these are added to the environment from nuclear wastes or atomic weapons tests are low, they can potentially accumulate over the years in dangerous quantities.[20,23]

The ability of organisms to concentrate elements to a degree far exceeding that which exists in the external environment is well known. Thus in studies carried out at the Hanford atomic plant in Washington it was found that in the eggs of ducks and geese, breeding on the Columbia River below the plant, the concentration of phosphorus-32 was on the average 200,000 times greater than that which occurred in the river water. Jackrabbits feeding on vegetation in this area, which was contaminated with iodine-131 from the aerial discharge of the plant, concentrated the iodine in their thyroids to a level 500 times that which was found on the vegetation. Coots feeding on the ponds in which atomic wastes were held concentrated radiostrontium in their bones at a level 500 times that which existed in the pond.[20,23]

It has been pointed out that all of the atomic weapons testing up to 1958 increased the average dosage of radiation received as a result of fallout by only 0.005 roentgens per year, or an increase of 5 per cent above the normal background radiation dosage. This was the result of the explosion of about 100 megatons of nuclear weapons. Starting in 1961, however, the Russian atmospheric tests were of a much greater magnitude, with one bomb alone being the equivalent of 100 megatons. Since fallout is not evenly distributed over the world, average levels of radioactivity mean very little. Some dangerous situations have resulted from fallout locally, and continued testing of nuclear bombs can only be regarded as hazardous to humanity.

The use of nuclear energy for power production has as yet produced only localized problems. Up to 1957 the Atomic Energy Commission reported that about 9 billion gallons of low-level atomic wastes with 2 million curies of radioactivity were being discharged annually into rivers, the soil, and the oceans. Because of the extreme dilution of these wastes in the waters or soil, it was believed that they caused no measurable biological effects. In 1966, 15 nuclear power plants were in operation and these contributed only 1 per cent of the electrical power production in the United States. By 1980, however, it is estimated that nuclear plants will produce 25 per cent of the electrical power in this nation.

Current disposal methods for those wastes containing high levels of radioactivity include imprisoning them in concrete lined barrels, which are sunk in the depths of the ocean, and pumping them into underground storage deep within the earth. However, faced with the massive increase in production of radioactive wastes, the Atomic Energy Commission is seeking new methods for disposal. Work is in progress on techniques for evaporating and drying nuclear wastes and combining them with nonradioactive materials into insoluble, rock-like materials.

In a rational world the ability to make use of the power of the atom could be regarded as a blessing. The development of nuclear energy as a power source could proceed at a reasonable pace in balance with our ability to dispose of any unwelcome by-products. However, the world is not a place where reason prevails, and we are consequently in danger of using our own knowledge for our own destruction. Even in the peacetime development of atomic power we seek immediate economic gains at the possible cost of environmental deterioration. On the positive side, however, the Atomic Energy Commission, Public Health Service, and other agencies concerned with radioisotopes in the environment have exercised far more care than those agencies concerned with the prevention of other forms of environmental pollution. Apart from the threat of war, we are in far more hazard in the 1960's from pesticides and other nonradioactive pollutants of our air, soils, and waters than we are from any of the by-products of nuclear reactions.

# | 14 |

# The Problem of Population

Throughout most of the world today there is an unprecedented growth in human populations. This continuing increase intensifies all conservation problems. Any type of rational management of the environment becomes more difficult as each new increment of population is added to the world's total. With continued population growth up to the limits of the global environment, we would be faced not only with complete loss of those values that today contribute to the quality of living but ultimately with the destruction of life itself. Any planning for environmental conservation must be based on the assumption that human population growth will be controlled before many more decades have passed, just as it must be based on the assumption that mankind will not destroy itself with nuclear warfare. In the following pages the question of human populations will be examined, and some answers to the population dilemma will be explored.

## THE DISTRIBUTION OF THE WORLD'S PEOPLE

According to the estimates of the United Nations the world population in 1970 will stand between 3.5 and 3.7 billion people. It is not possible to state an exact figure even for existing populations since in some parts of the world population estimates are inaccurate. The United Nations estimates are broken down by region in Table 10. From these it is obvious that the continent of Asia holds almost two-thirds of the world's people. The technologically advanced areas of the world, confined with a few exceptions to Northern America, Europe, the Soviet Union, and Oceania, contain less than one-third of the world's population. The nations that have not achieved a high level of technological development contain more than two-thirds of the world's people. Three nations, China, India, and the USSR, contain nearly half of the world's people.

315

**Table 10. People and Land**

| Region | Area of Land and Inland Water in Square Miles | Population 1970 Estimates | People per Square Mile |
|---|---|---|---|
| United States | 3,676,000 | 206,000,000 | 56 |
| Northern America | 7,528,000 | 227,000,000 | 30 |
| Latin America | 8,767,000 | 282,000,000 | 32 |
| Africa | 11,635,000 | 346,000,000 | 30 |
| Europe (excluding Soviet Union) | 1,915,000 | 454,000,000 | 240 |
| U.S.S.R. | 8,599,000 | 246,000,000 | 29 |
| Asia (excluding Soviet Union) | 10,300,000 | 2,000,000,000 | 194 |
| Oceania | 3,295,000 | 91,000,000 | 6 |
| World (excluding Antarctica) | 52,125,000 | 3,574,000,000 | 69 |

If we relate population to area and resources the figures may appear more meaningful (Table 11). A total of 3.6 billion people represents approximately 70 people per square mile of the earth's land and inland water surface, meaning that each person has approximately 9 acres available for his support and living space. Looked at in this way the vast deserts, tundras, and tropical forest areas of the earth seem less extensive, since each person's share of the earth includes his share of desert, tundra, high mountains, and similar nonproductive land.

**Table 11. People and Resources. 1970 Estimates**

| | Nations of World where Diets Are Adequate | Nations of World where Diets Are Deficient |
|---|---|---|
| Population | 1,200,000,000 | 2,400,000,000 |
| Annual population growth in per cent | 1.3 | 2.1 |
| Density per 100 acres of agricultural land | 17 | 53 |
| Income in dollars per capita | 1,302 | 115 |
| Food consumption in daily calories per capita | 3,023 | 2,203 |
| Food consumption in grams protein per day | 86.4 | 57.4 |

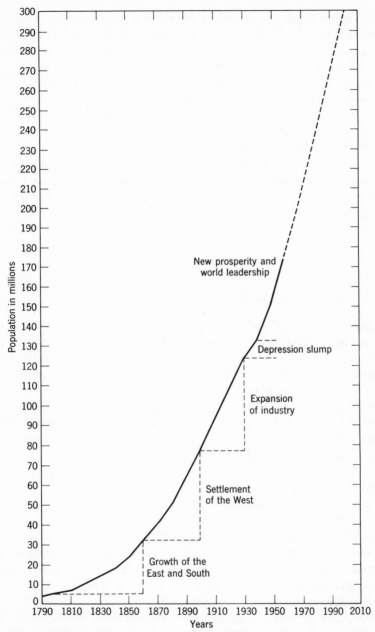

Fig. 143. Population growth in the United States (source U.S. Bureau of the Census).

317

The United States population in 1968 was approximately 200 million, an increase of nearly 21 million in the eight years since the 1960 census. These people were distributed over approximately 3.5 million square miles of land surface for an average of 57 per square mile or 11 land acres per individual. An estimated 80 million of these people lived in 30 large metropolitan areas. Approximately 70 per cent, or 140 million people lived in urban areas, towns or cities and suburbs.

In the United States we feel population pressure in terms of pollution, physical disorganization of the city and countryside, crowding of people in cities and in recreation areas, and so on. In most of the world population pressure is felt in terms of hunger and other forms of acute human suffering, although the relationship between cause and effect is seldom recognized, and the possibility of doing something about it is often not considered.

## THE INCREASE IN PEOPLE

It may not be realized that the population problem that faces us today is essentially a new problem, one that has arisen in the past century and that has no precedents in previous human experience. Our historical training, which emphasizes the events that took place in past centers of population, does not prepare us for this realization. To grasp the significance of what has occurred, we would need a history that cannot be written, for no one was there to record it. It would be a history of the vast open spaces of a little while ago, told by generations of buffalo and antelope and prairie wolf. It would be a story of a world that suddenly disappeared, of a changeless land that in a brief period was completely transformed.

If we do not know for sure how many people we have on earth today, much less can we know the past numbers of man. However, by careful detective work in the files of history, by piecing together the scraps of information left by tax collectors, military commanders, and others concerned with the number of heads in their domains, demographers have reached some estimates of the growth of populations. All of these estimates point to a past time when the world was big, people were few, and growth of populations was negligible. In Table 12 are some widely accepted estimates showing changes since 1650. It should be recognized that it took at least a million years for the human population of the earth to increase to the level of 1650. It took only 200 years after that for it to double again. Now the world's population is doubling

Table 12. Growth of the World's Population
(Estimated Population in Millions)

| Region | 1650 | 1750 | 1800 | 1850 | 1900 | 1950 | 1970[a] | 2000[a] |
|---|---|---|---|---|---|---|---|---|
| Anglo-America | 1 | 1.3 | 5.7 | 26 | 81 | 166 | 227 | 354 |
| Latin-America | 12 | 11.1 | 18.9 | 33 | 63 | 162 | 282 | 624 |
| Europe | 100 | 140 | 187 | 266 | 401 | 559 | 700 | 880 |
| Asia | 330 | 479 | 602 | 749 | 937 | 1,302 | 2,000 | 3,307 |
| Africa | 100 | 95 | 90 | 95 | 120 | 198 | 346 | 768 |
| Oceania | 2 | 2 | 2 | 2 | 6 | 13 | 19 | 32 |
| World | 545 | 728 | 906 | 1,171 | 1,608 | 2,400 | 3,574 | 5,965 |

[a] United Nations medium estimates (USSR included in Europe).

in less than 40 years. If population increase were to follow recent trends, there would be 22 billion people on earth in the year 2040, according to the United Nations estimates and, before a century had passed, we would long since have passed a point of world catastrophe.

To account for the great growth in population in relatively recent times, it is only necessary to look at the record of the most glowing accomplishments of modern times, told in our histories and recounted by our orators: the voyages of discovery, the settlement of the new worlds, the industrial revolution, the development of agricultural techniques, the miracle of modern medicine. In a short time, in historical terms, vast new continents were suddenly opened to exploitation by a new kind of man, armed with the tools provided by the new technology and science. Populations, held in check for generations by the limited food supplies provided by their limited lands, found new lands with vast productivity. Acres that had yielded a bare livelihood when farmed by the old methods, provided a surplus when handled with the new techniques. Diseases that once took their toll from all crowded populations fell back as food, medicine, and sanitation became available. Humanity, freed from the environmental resistance of the past, began to express more nearly its biotic potential.

The behavior of human populations today, in relation to their means of subsistence, has been such that there has been a widespread revival of the Malthusian outlook on populations. Thomas Malthus of England was one of the first to become concerned with the world population problem. In 1798 he published a book entitled *An essay on the principle of population as it affects the future improvement of society*.[8] The book stirred a controversy in its day, and today it can do the same. Some basic propositions of Malthus were: (1) Population is necessarily limited by the means of subsistence. (2) Population increases where the means of subsistence increase, unless prevented by very powerful checks. Furthermore populations tend to increase at a geometric rate (1, 2, 4, 8, 16, etc.), whereas food supplies can usually only be increased at an arithmetic rate (1, 2, 3, 4, 5, etc.). Therefore populations tend to outstrip their means of subsistence. (3) The powerful and obvious checks to population increase, the checks which repress the superior power of population and keep its effect on a level with the means of subsistence are all resolvable into vice, misery, and potentially, perhaps, moral restraint.

When Malthus lived, the population of western Europe was pressing on the limits of the then existing food supply. The overseas colonial empires were yet to be fully exploited. Vice and misery were widespread, and moral restraint was at a minimum. Fortunately for mankind, but unfortunately for the reputation of Malthus, this situation soon changed, as the full impact of the industrial revolution on the new lands of the world was felt. For a time the means of subsistence increased much faster than population. Malthus was forgotten until populations too suddenly began to catch up.

The problem of overpopulation is not new; many lands have known it in the thousands of years that man has been on earth. The problem of world overpopulation is new. Once, population problems were local problems, and states whose peoples outran their means of subsistence suffered alone or affected but a few neighbors. The rise and fall of the great Mayan empire of Central America created no concern in the courts of Europe. Only after it was gone, did European man find out that it had existed. Today, however, our means of transportation and communication have changed the relative size of the world. Populations no longer starve in silence. Empires no longer die quietly.

Not before in human history was there a time when all of the world was on the map. All pieces of land are staked out and claimed, even the barren polar ice caps are the subject of international dispute, and nations are casting a speculative glance toward the resources of the moon. The grave fact that must be faced today is that there are no more land frontiers.

## DYNAMICS OF POPULATION GROWTH

To understand the principles of human-population growth, we need at first only to review the principles governing the growth of animal populations in general. Population growth results when natality exceeds mortality, when there is an excess of births over deaths. The rate of population growth is dependent on two things: the biotic potential of the population and the amount of environmental resistance. The biotic potential for man is relatively low, by comparison with other species, but still high enough to cause serious concern where resources are limited. Fortunately this maximum potential rate of increase is seldom realized. The environmental resistance, the sum of those factors which tend to prevent a population from achieving its biotic potential, for man includes all of the various mortality factors and all of the factors which inhibit the birth rate. In the latter group of factors, perhaps the most important is the social behavior of man—the blocks that he himself puts in the way to prevent a maximum rate of population growth from being achieved.

Demographers have postulated various patterns of population growth characteristic of different types of human societies. In the first type (Fig. 144) is the primitive agricultural society. In such a society large numbers of children are considered a blessing, partly because they represent extra hands to do the labor of the farm. Hence birth rates tend to be high. However, control of mortality factors is at a minimum. Medical knowledge and the application of sanitary techniques have not yet appeared. Disease takes an annual toll. With little individual care for children possible, accidents can be an important factor. If the population is in close balance with its food supply, as is usually true, starvation is a threat in years of crop failure. Such a society has limited ability to store food for use in emergency periods. Transportation is inadequate to ship food from areas of plenty to areas of scarcity. Consequently death rates are high. Birth and death rates achieve a rough balance, and the over-all growth of population is slow.

At the other extreme, theoretically, is the industrialized society. In this society, large numbers of children are not considered a blessing because of the difficulty of providing them with the goods and services considered necessary in such a culture. Marriages tend to be delayed because of educational or employment needs. Family size is limited in a variety of ways; the over-all birth rate is low. At the same time the death rate has been lowered. Medical facilities, adequate sanitation, and a relatively high material standard of living keeps mortality at a minimum. Again a rough balance is achieved between births and deaths, and the rate of population growth is kept low.

Obviously neither of these basic types of societies are the ones contributing to past and present rapid rates of population growth. Societies in which population growth is rapid can be described as those which

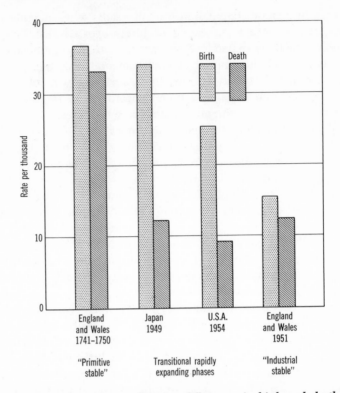

Fig. 144. Demographic patterns. Showing differences in birth and death rates in agricultural, industrial, and transitional societies [data from Political and Economic Planning (1955) and U.S. Public Health Service].

have not yet reached either of these two stable states or which are in the process of change from one to another. Examples from other animal species are illustrative.

Rapid population growth in wild animals is characteristic of a species introduced into a new and relatively unlimited environment. Thus, the starling or English sparrow, when introduced into the United States exhibited a remarkable rate of population increase. In such a new environment food supplies are plentiful. Disease and parasites are at a minimum because of the initial low population density. Predation losses, or accidental deaths, may be considerable at times, but the over-all effect is slight. At the same time, because of the available space and the plentiful resources, birth rates are high. A similar pattern is exhibited by man when a new land is colonized. Birth rates are high because large families can not only be provided for, but help to bring in greater

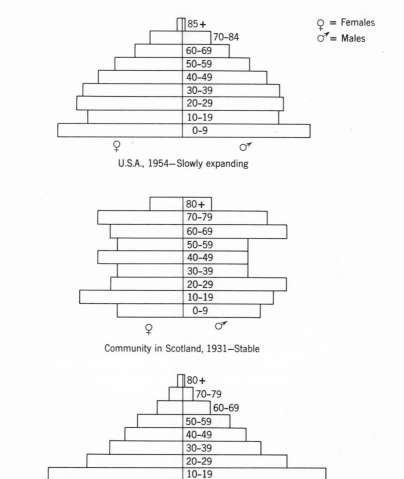

85+
70-84
60-69
50-59
40-49
30-39
20-29
10-19
0-9

♀ ♂

U.S.A., 1954—Slowly expanding

80+
70-79
60-69
50-59
40-49
30-39
20-29
10-19
0-9

♀ ♂

Community in Scotland, 1931—Stable

80+
70-79
60-69
50-59
40-49
30-39
20-29
10-19
0-9

♀ ♂

Korea, 1940—Rapidly expanding

Fig. 145. Age pyramids for rapidly expanding, slowly expanding, and static populations, showing relative proportions of the different age groups [data from political and Economic Planning (1955), U.S. Bureau of the Census, and F. F. Darling (1951), American Scientist, 39:250].

returns from the large amount of available land. Death rates, although not as low as in technologically advanced societies are nevertheless well below the birth rates, for epidemic disease and starvation losses are minimized. The balance is in favor of natality, and population growth is rapid. Such was the situation in the United States in the frontier days.

Rapid population growth in animals is also exhibited when some previously limiting factor has been removed from a stable population. Such a population increase is of the irruptive type exemplified by the Kaibab deer (Chapter 9). As previously described, the removal of the limiting factor of predation permitted a spectacular increase in the deer population. This resulted in the carrying capacity of the habitat being surpassed, the food supply being destroyed, and finally in a die-off of the deer to a new low level. A similar pattern of population growth is exhibited when the introduction of medical supplies or sanitary techniques takes place in a society of the primitive agricultural variety. Thus the population of India is believed to have been relatively stable over a period of centuries. The British, however, introduced western technology, medicine, and transportation. The result was a marked lowering in the mortality rate, not accompanied by a decrease in natality. The population began to grow rapidly. If India should proceed to become an industrialized society, an eventual lowering of the birthrate can be expected, and a new balance between births and deaths can be achieved. How large the population would grow before that time, however, is disturbing to contemplate. It has been sufficiently disturbing to the Indian leaders so that they are now attempting to encourage a reduction in birthrate well before the process of industrialization can have much effect.

The concept that rapid growth of human populations is largely restricted to those nations in a state of demographic transition, from agricultural to industrial society, is a useful one. Events since World War II, however, have revealed that industrialization does not necessarily bring population stability. Table 13 reveals that some highly industrialized nations have high population growth rates. This has been true of the United States, particularly in the 1950's, and is true of the other industrialized countries that still have a relative abundance of space and natural resources. There is no good reason to assume that full industrialization of nations such as Venezuela or Costa Rica will necessarily bring marked decreases in the growth rates.

Growth rates can also be misleading in the extent to which they conceal the size of the annual increment to the population. Costa Rica, with one of the highest growth rates of any nation, is still adding only

Table 13. Comparison of Population Growth in Various Nations[18]

| Country | Population | Annual Rate of Increase in Per cent | Number of Years to Double Population | Birth Rate per 1000 | Death Rate per 1000 |
|---|---|---|---|---|---|
| East Germany | 17,000,000 | −0.2 | | 16.5 | 13.4 |
| Ireland | 2,900,000 | 0.0 | | 22.2 | 11.5 |
| Hungary | 10,200,000 | 0.4 | 175 | 13.1 | 10.7 |
| Austria | 7,300,000 | 0.5 | 140 | 17.9 | 13.0 |
| Sweden | 7,800,000 | 0.6 | 117 | 15.9 | 10.1 |
| South Africa | 18,300,000 | 2.4 | 29 | | |
| Australia | 11,600,000 | 2.1 | 33 | 19.6 | 8.8 |
| Canada | 20,000,000 | 2.0 | 35 | 21.4 | 7.5 |
| United States | 197,000,000 | 1.6 | 44 | 19.4 | 9.4 |
| Libya | 1,700,000 | 3.7 | 19 | 35–43 | |
| Niger | 3,400,000 | 3.3 | 21 | 49–57 | 24–30 |
| Pakistan | 121,100,000 | 3.2 | 22 | 49–53 | 17–21 |
| Taiwan | 12,900,000 | 3.4 | 21 | 32.7 | 5.5 |
| Costa Rica | 1,500,000 | 4.3 | 17 | 40.8 | 8.8 |
| Venezuela | 9,000,000 | 3.4 | 21 | 47–51 | 8–12 |
| World | 3,346,000,000 | 1.7 | 41 | 34 | 16 |

around 65,000 people per year to the world population. The United States, with a much lower rate of growth, is adding over 3 million people each year. A growth rate of only 1 per cent on the island of Barbados, where over 1500 people are found on each square mile, can be an intolerably high rate of increase. A rate of 2 per cent in Canada, by contrast, may represent no immediate problem.

The disturbing fact about today's world is that areas that are already overpopulated have benefitted from those factors that control mortality, but have yet to gain the incentive or knowledge needed to control birthrates. Consequently, population increase defeats all efforts to raise living standards or to improve the quality of the environment.

## CONTROL OF POPULATION SIZE

The question of how to control population size is a familiar one to all who work with animal populations. The answers are simply stated but often incredibly difficult to put into practice. For either animal or human populations, control of population growth must involve either a decrease in natality, an increase in mortality, or movement to a new area.

In the far north of America or Europe, populations of lemmings follow a pattern of cyclic increase and decline, with population peaks being reached every 3 to 4 years. At the peaks the numbers of lemmings are far greater than the area can support. At such times a mass emigration sometimes takes place. Vast numbers of lemmings drift out of the overpopulated area into new, and usually unfavorable, terrain. The end result of this movement is usually death for the emigrants. Such an emigration temporarily alleviates the problem of overpopulation. The alleviation, however, is never final. In another 2 or 3 years the remnant population has built up to another peak, and another overpopulation problem exists.

Men are not lemmings, and their problems are more complex. Nevertheless, with human populations also, emigration alone provides no permanent solution to a population problem. Over the past three centuries, for example, many millions of people have left Europe and moved to new lands. This movement has not solved the problem of the homeland. Some countries which have contributed most to the emigrant stream are those which today have the most unfavorable balance between people and resources. The emigrants in turn have built the populations of the new lands to which they have moved until in some of these lands too the balance with resources is under threat. Emigration, with people or mice, can temporarily alleviate, but not permanently solve a population problem.

With animal populations control of numbers is usually exercised by the device of increasing mortality. This may involve encouraging a greater amount of hunting, a higher level of predation, or with pest species even wholesale poisoning. Increasing mortality is also an answer, although an unpleasant one, to human-population problems. Various peoples and cultures have tried many ways of doing this. Some eliminate the older members of the population. Thus, with some Eskimo tribes, a threat of food shortage and starvation for the tribe, may result in the older people removing themselves and going out alone into the tundra, thus in effect to their death. This is an emergency measure taken when the other consequence would be death for all. Other cultures attack the problem by eliminating the very young. Infanticide has been a common practice in primitive cultures, when the means for providing for another child are out of reach of a family. Some of the South Sea islanders, recognizing that the limited resources of the islands would support only a limited number of people, have solved the problem through a general acceptance of infanticide. The alternative was starvation. Still other cultures, particularly the more technologically advanced ones, have met the same problem by legalizing abortion, thus killing the new individual before he could endear himself to his relatives. Japan today has been forced to this solution in what it is hoped will be a temporary measure to alleviate a critical population problem.

The third way to control population size is not practical with wild-animal populations but is commonly used with domestic forms. This involves decreasing natality. This is perhaps the only acceptable way of limiting population size for those peoples with high respect for the individual and a "reverence for life." Decreasing the birth rate can be approached in a number of ways which vary both in effectiveness and in acceptability to various groups in the population. One approach is that of celibacy, encouraged by many religious groups but rarely effective on a mass basis. This means delaying either temporarily or permanently the sexual relationship. In a modified form, and a more common one, it means delaying those relationships that would be likely to lead to the production of offspring, or more frequently, delaying marriage. This is undoubtedly part of the reason for the relative stability of the population of Ireland in recent years. For economic and other reasons there has been a trend in this country toward delaying or permanently postponing marriage. In other technologically advanced countries this practice has had a depressing effect upon birth rates during times of economic stress or of war. How long the practice would remain effective in the face of long-continued, or permanent, economic stress is certainly questionable.

In general the sociological consequences and the effects on the individual of delaying marriage are undesirable. The reasons, in terms of personal well-being, are obvious. The practicality of this method for slowing down population growth over the world is most dubious.

Undoubtedly the means of controlling population growth most likely to be effective are those generally described as birth control. These involve little restriction on the sexual activities of the individual and thus are useful to those large segments of the population among whom "moral restraint" is usually short lived. Two general types of birth-control methods can be recognized: one involving so-called natural methods, the other involving mechanical or chemical, devices. Of these, the first is the less effective but the only acceptable form for members of many religious groups. In this method, sexual intercourse is restricted to the relatively infertile period of the menstrual cycle between menstruation and ovulation. For the individual this method is not always reliable.

For the population, it can lead to a marked reduction in birthrates. This method of population control has been attempted in India since, for much of the Indian population, the materials needed for any of the mechanical or chemical methods of birth control have not been available.

Mechanical and chemical methods of birth control are widely used in technologically advanced countries and are in part responsible for the reduced natality rates in the industrialized nations. Of these the most acceptable and effective have been birth control pills and intrauterine devices, both of which have only become widely available during the 1960's, and have been credited with the decrease in birthrates that have also occurred during that period. More effective methods of birth control are still needed if population growth is to be slowed down without unnecessary and undesirable side effects upon human relationships. The existing techniques, however, are adequate and could accomplish the objective if the materials could be made generally available and people educated to their use.

Not many years ago it seemed that there was little or no hope of selling the people of the world on the idea of restricting family size. Now the situation is both more desperate and more hopeful. Not only is the population problem recognized at both international and national levels but many of the more overcrowded countries are taking steps to alleviate it. Japan has shown that within the space of ten years a high population growth rate can be reduced to a tolerable level. Other nations are following suit. Yet it would be sanguine to think that the problem of population growth would be solved in a decade or two. Resistance from some groups of people and some nations is still too strong.

In the United States we have traditionally espoused the philosophy that growth is good and change is progress. We have been a dynamic, expanding nation to whom the future has always been better than the past. In outlook we have shared that of young, pioneer nations which recognize no past golden age and believe that the greatest accomplishments are yet to come. As we expanded westward into the wilderness we welcomed population growth, for growth meant settlement, development, and thus a higher measure of security and prosperity for all. With the frontier gone, however, we retained the frontier outlook. We believed that more people meant more hands to work and more customers to buy. We looked forward to an ever-expanding business and industrial economy, often without examining the environment in which it would be located. Those who espoused the virtues of growth called those who questioned it "prophets of doom." In this they were supported by many physical scientists and technologists who pointed out that food and other necessities could, in theory at least, be provided for much greater numbers of people.

In the latter half of the twentieth century, however, it has become increasingly apparent that we are losing more by growth than we are gaining. As problems of pollution, crowding, decay of the cities, urban sprawl, destruction of nature, and increasing ugliness of our environment became more apparent, most people have become aware that population growth cannot go unchecked epen in this wealthiest of nations. Perhaps the recent downward trend in our birthrates is a reflection of this knowledge. If so, it will continue, and the gloomy forecasts for the American future will be proved false. But as yet there is no room for complacency—only a growing need to make people aware of the inevitable consequences of continuing population growth.

# | 15 |

# Action for Conservation

Unlike most human enterprises, the conservation movement has an ultimate goal of self-elimination. Conservation will be a success when the word no longer need be used, when the activities that it comprises become an accepted and normal part of human behavior toward the environment and toward populations. In some limited areas inhabited by "backward" peoples, this success was once achieved. In the technological world, however, the struggle has scarcely begun.

## POPULATION POLICY

The major problem of conservation, the major threat to the human environment, is the continued increase in human populations. As one step toward a solution of this problem, there is the need for the development by the various nations of the world of rational policies toward the growth and distribution of human populations. With reference to population growth there are essentially only three possible choices:

(1) The existing population policy (even though it usually is not stated or accepted as a policy) in most of the underdeveloped nations is that populations will be allowed to increase to the limits of the environment, and every effort will be made to raise these limits to permit continuing growth. Thus most economic development efforts are aimed not at improving the standards of living but at increasing the supplies of bare necessities to provide a marginal existence for ever-growing numbers of people. Lauchlin Currie has illustrated this point with reference to the country of Colombia:[6]

In Colombia between 1951 and 1964 a major technical revolution occurred in agriculture. Large areas of new land were brought into production, agricultural mechanization occurred, and new means of transport were developed. The increase in food production for domestic use was estimated at approximately 60 per cent. In the same period of time, however, the population of Colombia increased 50 per cent. Currie asks "Did the nation gain greatly from this technical revolution coupled with the opening of rich new lands? Very little. Rural people today appear to be, if anything, poorer than they were in 1951, with more tiny farms and squatters evident. It is questionable whether urban people are consuming much more food per capita." Looking ahead it is apparent that such major increases in agricultural productivity cannot be expected indefinitely. Further gains will require greater capital input, the use of more marginal land, and the employment of more people in agriculture. "If we arrive at the point where 50 per cent of the working force in underdeveloped countries is actually needed to grow food efficiently for the other 50 per cent, we will already have lost the battle for development and will be where India is today." Colombia is tending toward this point.

(2) The apparent population policy in most technologically advanced nations, most markedly in the New World nations, is the belief that as long as economic growth keeps even with or exceeds population growth, all is well. In other words, there is no need to limit populations as long as a high material standard of living (measured in production and consumption of food, clothing, shelter, and various manufactured necessities and luxuries) can be maintained. Pressures on the individual caused by crowding or urban disorganization, increasing pollution of the environment, loss of outdoor space and natural environments are not considered in this calculation. Furthermore, it is widely believed that population growth stimulates economic growth. Any evidence of a downturn in the rate of population growth is considered likely to cause alarm in the business community.

(3) A rational population policy would be one that recognized the existence of some optimum population level within which a healthy, self-sustaining, diversified, and challenging environment could be maintained and within which the individual would have a maximum opportunity for material, psychological, and spiritual growth. This optimum level would be expected to change from time to time and place to place, depending upon the skills we develop in environmental management. Based on this recognition, national policy should seek to discourage growth beyond this optimum level.

In the world today, considering the level of environmental management, populations are now far in excess of any optimum level. Unless environmental management can be improved, national population policies should seek not just a stabilization of populations, but a decline in birth-rate to a point where population decrease to some lower level would be achieved.

A national population policy, however, must be concerned not only with the growth of human populations but with the distribution of peo-ple. The movement of people to areas where environmental problems already exist and will be intensified by further population increase should be discouraged. The settlement of people in areas where their presence will not cause environmental disruption should be encouraged.

Among the evidences of environmental deterioration, the level of pollution of air, water, and land must certainly be among the first consid-ered. The existence within the region of adequate space for outdoor recreation would be a major factor. The continuing existence within the region of representative wild areas of natural biota need also be taken into account. The availability of essential material resources is of course a recognized determinant of the level of population that can be supported.

What is the outlook for the development of rational population poli-cies, and ultimately for achieving some near optimum level of human population? Unfortunately, it is bleak. It seems most probable that popu-lations will continue to increase in many underdeveloped nations to a point where catastrophe, in the form of famine, disease, warfare, or other calamities, will occur. Continued increases and continued calami-ties may follow for some decades. In the developed nations it appears likely that population growth will continue at the expense of the human environment for the near and foreseeable future. Under these circum-stances, those who favor conservation will necessarily fight a rear-guard and apparently losing battle. The recuperative powers of nature, how-ever, are such that a battle of this kind is not hopeless. If conservationists can save the pieces, in some rational world beyond tomorrow, the whole may once more be put together.

In Arabia, the Arabian oryx was once a common and widespread antelope. But the Arabians have no particular concern for oryxes. While they are around they shoot them; when they are gone they don't miss them. Conservationists around the world, however, have been concerned with the oryx of Arabia. Consequently they have captured enough indi-viduals of this species to make up a breeding population. Outside of Arabia in reserves and zoos, the Arabian oryx has been preserved. If the people of Arabia ever develop a more rational attitude toward their environment, they can once more have oryxes, obtained from abroad.

In Costa Rica populations are increasing at a world-beating rate. There may be very little that the developed nations of the world can do toward instituting a sane population policy in Costa Rica. But the natural biota of Costa Rica, from its lowland rain forests to its high paramo, are of interest to informed people the world over. Perhaps the most that can be done is through land purchase and protection to save some remnants of that biota until the day when the people of Costa Rica, facing disaster, draw back and attempt to institute a rational policy toward their population and their environment.

The International Union for the Conservation of Nature and the World Wildlife Fund are attempting to save the pieces, save natural areas, and save wild species around the world against the day when people are willing to behave more sanely. It would seem worthwhile for all who pretend to an interest in conservation to offer such organizations their support.

## ECONOMICS AND CONSERVATION

In many institutions, conservation is considered to be most closely related to the field of economics. There is no doubt that a close relationship exists; yet the areas of conservation that interest economists most have been traditionally those areas readily subject to economic analysis. An economist can feel at home in the area of timber production, harvesting, and marketing, but quite at sea when asked to consider the value of wilderness. Even those economists most at home in the conservation area appear bored and disinterested when asked to give attention to the preservation of vanishing species.[7]

It should not be surprising that those areas of conservation that produce a profit to the landowner or enterpreneur receive ready acceptance, whereas those that cost money and produce no income lag far behind. It was relatively easy to sell farmers on the idea of using fertilizers, on stopping soil erosion, and on practicing water conservation since all of these practices result in higher yields and greater profits in the long run. It has been much more difficult to get farmers to leave edges alone, to plant hedgerows, or carry out other measures for wildlife conservation, since the returns from such practices are often not measurable in monetary profit. In the 1960's real-estate developers have accepted the idea of cluster-development which groups housing in a relatively small area and leaves the remainder of the tract in outdoor recreation space. Cluster developments often bring in a much higher net profit than would the construction of a standard, gridiron suburb of evenly spaced housing. It is the cash return, rather than the benefit in terms of ecology or sociology, that leads to increasing use of the cluster pattern.

At the public level, the use of common economic measures for determining the value of a proposed activity or development often causes difficulties. The Forest Service usually has little difficulty in having its budget for fire protection approved, since the lumber interests want it, and the economic benefits from fire protection are obvious. The budget for range research or wildlife-habitat improvement usually has much more difficult sledding.

The National Park Service has relatively little difficulty in getting budgetary approval for those activities directly related to increased visitor-days use in the national parks. However, if their goal of maintaining the natural values of the parks in an "unimpaired condition" is to be respected, they should be rewarded more realistically for maintaining a maximum number of days of nonuse for those areas to be kept in a primitive condition.

Water developments in the western United States are justified after a careful "cost-benefit analysis" of the project. The opponents of such developments maintain, with some justification, that the costs, in terms of wild-land values that are sacrificed, are always minimized; and the benefits in terms of power, irrigation, flood control, etc., are always overestimated in such calculations. In fact we have no way of measuring, in economic terms, the value of ten acres of lost wilderness compared to ten acres of increased irrigated cropland. It would seem, at face value, that the wilderness would always lose out in such a calculation; but what if it were the last wilderness, or if there were no obvious need for the additional cropland?

In an analysis of one major irrigation project, that of the Columbia Basin, George Macinko has shown how a careful study of the economic feasibility of a water-development project can lead in the long run to quite false conclusions.[13] The Columbia Basin project had its beginning with the construction of the Grand Coulee Dam. It was expected that the project would bring one million acres of dry land in the Columbian plateau into irrigation agriculture. It was expected also that surplus power revenues from the dam would pay back 50 per cent of the cost of irrigation development, and that the farmers who received irrigation water would repay most of the remaining costs.

In practice, before the project was completed, dry-land wheat farming underwent a minor revolution and began to pay off in an unexpected way. First, some 300,000 acres of the best lands in the project were withdrawn from the irrigation area to continue in dry-land agriculture. Second, because of inflation and other factors, the construction costs of the project far exceeded the original estimates. Third, it became necessary to expend far more money in draining the irrigated lands than had been anticipated, and some mistakes were made in the construction and location of drainage ditches and canals. Fourth, the small farm pattern anticipated for the project, based on the farming standards of the 1930's, proved uneconomical, and it was necessary to shift to a large farm pattern, with a 320 acre maximum size. Fifth, the farmers were unable, or unwilling, to plant the crops that were best suited to the lands, and concentrated on those that brought high immediate returns.

As a result of these factors, Macinko estimates that the farmers of the region are receiving a major subsidy from the federal government. The water users are not likely to repay more than 11 per cent of the cost of water development and, consequently, the owner of a 320-acre farm receives the equivalent of $220,000 dollars worth of water that he does not pay for. Although the region has benefitted from the development of the Columbia Basin Project it can be seriously questioned whether the region and the nation might not have benefitted more if the water had been used for purposes other than irrigation agriculture. Among the costs that some feel were not properly accounted was the value of the salmon fishery, cut off by the construction of Grand Coulee and other dams.

In an analysis of American society entitled "Can we stay prosperous?" Stuart Chase has pointed out some of the characteristics of our present affluence.[5] It is an affluence in which 2 out of 5 American families still receive less than, or no more than $3000 a year. It is an affluence that allows us to spend 70 billion dollars in 1967, or perhaps more, for efforts related to war and what is termed "national defense," and additional billions for landing a man on the moon, but does not permit us to buy a decent-sized Redwood National Park or afford the cost of pollution control. It is an affluence marked by 80 million automobiles that require highways and parking space and produce pollution before they turn into 80 million pieces of junk, further to pollute the landscape. We produce great quantities of what Chase calls "illth," the opposite of wealth: junk, sleazy products, materials harmful to our physical and mental health, noise, billboards, and rural uglification. We cannot, apparently, afford decent cities, education, adequate health facilities, clean water, or clean air. Chase summarizes his article: "Prosperity is more a myth than fact. . . . In dollars, we are rich beyond the dreams of avarice, but in things that make life worth living we are poor . . . ."

In his book, *The Affluent Society*, economist John Kenneth Galbraith has pointed out that we are still gearing our activities to fit the economics of scarcity when we need to substitute new standards based on our existing affluence.[10] We continue to encourage the private sector of our economy to produce goods that are not needed or are positively harmful, whereas we resent money spent by the public sector of the economy to produce needed services. In essence we are pleased when we can spend our money to buy a new automobile, but we do not wish to pay taxes to provide a road for it to run on. We are willing to buy a house, but unwilling to pay for a suitable environment in which to place that house. Even in the public sector we are much more willing to pay for something useful and substantial, such as a highway, than we are to pay for a highway beautification program. Yet there is reason to suspect that in the late 1960's the public may be more willing than their representatives in government to pay the cost of high quality in the environment.

# POLITICS AND CONSERVATION

Although economic information is commonly given greater weight in the decision-making process than in ecological information, neither category of data necessarily is used in determining the decisions we make about the environment. The major decisions of the twentieth century, namely, to make war, to exploit the power of the atom, and to conquer space, have had only the most tenuous economic justifications.

In a democratic society, the decisions about the environment are made by legislative, administrative, and judicial bodies elected by the people or appointed by their elected representatives. It is imperative, therefore, that those who would influence decisions about the environment be fully informed about the structure and functioning of government, about the ways in which it operates on the surface, and about the pressures below the surface that influence its operations.

In a small city political authority may rest with a city council or board of supervisors. The members of this body who pass legislation for the city, are elected presumably by all the people and represent, in theory, the interests of all the people. In fact, however, most people are indifferent to local election and take small interest in local politics. The local legislators therefore are more commonly elected by a minority within the city who are willing to devote time and money to local politics. Usually those who have their money invested in local property or business are most vulnerable to local political decisions and consequently take the most active interest in local elections. It is not strange therefore that a city council may reflect the interests of the local business community to a greater degree than it reflects the interest of the passive public. The average citizen may not be obviously affected by a local rezoning decision. The man with major investments in land and property will be affected. There is nothing sinister or underhand in his taking greater effort to see that a councilman sympathetic to his interests is elected. In cities where a single industry dominates the local economy in the way that mining, lumbering, or livestock dominate in many western communities, it is unlikely that local government will make many decisions adverse to the interest of the local industry. How then does a citizen who lives for example in the redwood region of California influence local politics in a way to control the activities of the lumber industry? The answer is fairly simple. He doesn't. His only hope for success is to operate at a higher political level, state or national, at which a single industry or interest group cannot exercise a major control. At the local level he will always be in a minority, since even those people who may at heart oppose the activities of the local industry will not act in a way likely to jeopardize their own source of livelihood.

This somewhat cynical appraisal of local political processes does not rule out the possibility that a local community will sometimes transcend its immediate interests and act in a way that benefits the broader society. The likelihood that this will occur, however, depends upon the degree to which local citizens are willing to take an active part in the politics of their community. Usually such activity is sporadic and centers around a particular issue of immediate concern: saving a popular local landmark, forcing an industry to cease poisoning the local air and water, or protecting a local recreational resource. To arouse such local action, those who are interested in conservation must be prepared to work with many disparate groups, from the local sportsmen to the League of Women Voters, from the Rotarians to the Students for a Democratic Society.

Above the city or town, the county or its equivalent (town in New England, parish in Louisiana) occupies the next political level. Here too the legislative authority rests commonly in a county council or board of supervisors, although there is wide variety, particularly in the eastern United States. At the city or county level rests the responsibility for most decisions over the use of private lands, the authority to carry out land-use zoning, to enact restrictions or codes to govern building and deveopment. Here too is the authority to tax land, a power that can be a major influence on the uses to be made of land. Most cities and many counties now include a planning commission as one of the local administrative agencies. This is a body of major interest to those interested in the quality of the environment. Although it is true that the best judgment of a planning commission may be set aside when it conflicts with powerful local interests, it is also true that proper land use is unlikely to occur unless it first appears in the plan for local or regional development.

Planners have not traditionally been educated in ecology nor have they necessarily been exposed to conservation philosophy in the course of their training. It is not surprising, therefore, that plans are made with due regard to engineering, architectural, and economic factors, but with a great disregard for ecological principles and conservation values. Since many planners are only too willing to give consideration to ecology and conservation, it becomes an important duty of those with such training or interest to work with their local planning agencies. Carrying a good plan into realization, however, requires the continuing cooperation of the local legislative authority. This, in turn, necessitates the continued alertness of those with an interest in local conservation and their willingness to work through all local organizations to accomplish conservation action.[7]

As Lynton Caldwell has pointed out, no government body has had responsibility in the past for the environment as a whole.[2,3] The highway commission may build roads, the park commission may manage parks, but no agency manages the environment. Consequently, decisions that influence the environment are usually made without due consideration for the many factors that are involved. It has been suggested by some that it would be beneficial at all levels of government to establish a Conservation and Development Board, or Environmental Quality Commission that would have responsibility for maintaining an overview on the activities of public and private agencies with concern for their effects on the total quality of the environment. Such a board, if endowed through its membership with adequate prestige, could recommend, to the public and to the highest level of government, against any development that might have a deleterious effect on the environment, and for any measures that were needed to improve the quality of the environment.[1,17]

A start in this direction has been made in New England, where the Town Meeting takes the place of the County Council or Board of Supervisors in other areas. Many New England towns have Town Conservation Commissions, appointed by the Town Meeting with the responsibility of maintaining just such a watchdog role on developments within the county and of recommending to the Town Meeting those measures needed to assure proper attention to conservation values. Where the membership of such commissions is dynamic and well-informed, the work of the commissions has been effective.[17]

Above the county level are to be found a great number of regional agencies. These may include such bodies as Soil Conservation Districts, Irrigation Districts, Air Pollution Control Districts, and the like, and may be constituted in various ways with representation from the state or federal government as well as locally elected representatives. These regional agencies are in a position to affect action that would be impossible at a local level. Flood control or air-pollution control, for example, seldom can be accomplished within a county and often cannot be accomplished within a single state.

The proliferation of local political authorities has been one of the more difficult hurdles to be overcome in accomplishing planning or conservation at a local level. In the New York metropolitan region, for example, there are 550 separate municipal governments, along with a variety of regional and state agencies with varying degrees of jurisdiction and authority. Planning at the local level becomes hopelessly complicated under such circumstances, and to be successful must be transferred to some regional organization. In Washington, D.C., a similarly complicated picture of local government has been brought to some semblance of order by the formation of the Metropolitan Council of Governments which now has planning authority for the entire metropolitan region. Similarly in southern California, the utter confusion of the local political scene has resulted in the development of a Regional Planning Agency charged with the preparation of a general plan for the many communities of the region.

Not surprisingly, considering the complexities of local government, the best way of achieving conservation action is often an indirect way. Gilbert White has pointed out that there is little point in haranguing the local populace against the dangers and ecological stupidity of building high-value structures on a flood plain where they can be readily damaged by floods.[7] Instead, far better results could be achieved by bringing the appropriate facts to the attention of the local bankers who make loans for flood plain construction. Similarly one could plead with slum landlords, or threaten them, without achieving one iota of environmental improvement. However, if the local tax laws were modified so that depreciation of slum property could not be deducted in calculating taxable income, or if local assessment practices were changed so that improvement of slum property did not result in higher tax assessments, the entire slum picture might be changed in a short period of time. Unquestionably one of the greatest skills to be developed is that of knowing at what point to apply pressure, or where to place the lever, to start motion toward a better environment.

At the state and national level the complexities of government exceed those of any single local community, and the opportunity for the individual citizen to influence decisions becomes correspondingly less. Nevertheless, the somewhat deplorable fact remains that at all levels of government the number of citizens who are willing and able to participate actively is small in proportion to the total electorate. Those who are active wield far more influence than those who are passive. Furthermore, at the state and national level the influence of any single private industry or of any special interest group becomes correspondingly less. The Supreme Court decision of 1964, calling for reapportionment of state legislatures on the basis of population was a decision of major interest to conservation. This decision removed control of the upper house of the state legislature from rural counties and effectively placed it with the urban majority of the people. Thus local special interest groups lost further authority.

Although the individual, acting as an individual, still can influence political decisions by his vote, his greatest effectiveness can be achieved as a member of an organization. It is virtually impossible for an individual to keep abreast of all activities at the local, state, and national level that are likely to have an effect upon the environment. It is relatively easy, however, for an organization to keep abreast of developments at various levels of government. There are numerous private organizations active in conservation, and it is profitable for those with an interest in environmental conservation to join those organizations that seem best to represent the philosophy they wish to espouse.

Among the citizen organizations in conservation, the Sierra Club has become one of the most influential. Although it had its beginnings as a society of California mountaineers, it soon was mixed up in most of the major conservation struggles in the nation that had reference to the preservation of wild country, the establishment or protection of national parks, or related issues. The National Audubon Society, starting as an organization of people who were interested in wild birds, has since become of major influence in all national conservation issues. The National Wildlife Federation and the Izaak Walton League are primarily organizations of sportsmen but now wield political influence in a wide range of conservation fields. The Wilderness Society and Nature Conservancy have also helped achieve major gains in conservation.

Professional organizations, although they rarely participate in political action, have an important function in keeping their membership informed of political issues of importance to the profession. The Society of American Foresters has been outstanding in this respect, as well as in taking a lead in influencing the education of foresters in colleges and universities.

It is most unfortunate that political scientists have taken relatively

little interest in problems of the environment, since our political organizations for environmental conservation would benefit from study and
could stand improvement. Lynton Caldwell has been an exception to
this general rule and has pointed out the need for a high-level public
agency that would focus on major issues of environmental policy.[2,3]
One of the shortcomings of environmental administration at the state
and national level has been the subdivision of responsibility among a
number of agencies whose interests often conflict.[15] Thus, in 1967, a
conservation issue of national interest was the effort to create a national
park in the North Cascades. Although presented to the public as another
case in which efforts were being made to preserve an invaluable wild-
land resource from exploitation, the issue was more truthfully a struggle
between the National Park Service and United States Forest Service
for administrative control over a large area of public land. No public
agency can be expected to give a frank evaluation of its own activities
and shortcomings. Each has its own agency interests to protect in addition to the public interest.

Caldwell's suggestion for a new high-level-public agency corresponds
generally to earlier suggestions by the geographer, Gilbert White, and
to recommendations of the Committee on Renewable Resources of the
National Academy of Sciences—National Research Council.[1,7,17] This
agency would not only be responsible for research on matters of public
policy, but would have the responsibility for defining the issues, the
consequences, and the alternatives in major matters relating to the human environment. Since it would not have administrative or management
responsibility, it would presumably have no special interests of its own
to protect.

No single piece of legislation nor act of governmental reorganization,
however, will guarantee that environmental conservation will become
a reality. The struggles to keep the world a fit place for people are
going to continue at least for decades to come. They will be fought at
the city, county, state, and national level. Their results will be determined by the efforts that those who have a concern for the human
environment are willing to expend in the interest of making conservation
not an issue but a way of life.

# | 16 |

# The Outlook

The outlook for conservation depends upon the response of people to the information now available about their environment and about the consequences of continuing population growth. We should not pretend that the problems of the world will automatically be resolved on the day that population stability is achieved. However, there will then be an opportunity to achieve some better balance between humanity and its environment, to create the kind of world that will offer the widest opportunity and challenge to people, and the best prospect for that development of the individual psyche upon which all hopes for the future must ultimately depend. The problems associated with the cessation of human population growth may well prove to be perplexing, but at least there will be a time available in which to seek solutions.

There is little doubt that the food potential of the world is adequate, if managed rationally, to meet the needs of the present world populations. If population stability were to be achieved, there would be time to develop the means for supporting some further growth, should this be considered advisable. We have hardly begun to apply the knowledge on food production that is now available. Three major obstacles stand in our way today in our efforts to increase food supplies in food-deficient areas. The first and most easily overcome is economic. Many nations do not have the capital to afford the necessary changes. This could be met, assuming population stability, if the industrialized nations were prepared to meet these expenses. A second, and more difficult, problem is that the crops and agricultural technology developed in the temperate zone do not transfer well to the tropics. New knowledge must be gained and new techniques developed. Great progress has been made, however, and assuming a lower rate of population growth, this new knowledge could be applied to meet human needs. The third problem is that food is produced by farmers, as in much of the world farmers are resistant to change. Many of the world's people prefer to live in old traditional ways and to farm by tried-and-true methods rather than accept foreign methods which might increase food yields at the expense of other values of life. Change, to be acceptable, must take shape within the basic patterns of living in these areas; it cannot be forced from the outside without irreparable damage. Such change from within comes slowly indeed. If the only purpose of change is to allow populations to increase, one may question if it is desirable at all.

With a lowered rate of population increase or with conditions approaching population stability, the many differing ways of life, the many methods of living with the land, that now exist throughout the world might well be preserved. It would not be essential to bring the supposed benefits of Western technology to people everywhere. We might better preserve the human diversity that in the long run may hold the best hope for the survival of the human species.[3,4]

## INDUSTRY, ENERGY, AND MATERIALS

At one time conservation was concerned to a major extent with energy resources and supplies of those industrial raw materials needed to keep the world's economy turning over. Dire predictions were made of the day ahead when our coal supplies would give out or we would finally exhaust the last reserve of iron ore. Today, because of the advances in physical science and technology, it is possible for a conservationist to pay relatively little attention to our reserves of metal, minerals, fuels, and ores. We not only have the prospect of transmuting metals of which the old alchemists once dreamed but the realistic capability of concentrating minerals from sources that were once considered far too low-grade or dispersed to be economically useful.

One of the prerequisites for improving material standards of living for world populations is a spread of industrialization. Agricultural machinery, fertilizers, efficient transportation, and the equipment needed to bring new areas of land into production are all products of industry. Industries require energy which must be obtained from coal, petroleum, water power, or other sources. In much of the world, industries and industrial-power sources are lacking.

The energy needs of modern industrial nations are exceedingly high. It has been estimated that people living at a primitive agricultural level, using hand labor and domestic animals to produce food and materials, can get by with a per capita consumption of about 10,000 calories of energy per day. This includes the calories in the food eaten by man and his domestic animals and that contained in the wood burned for cooking or heating. By contrast, in the United States in the 1950's the per capita consumption of energy was 162,000 calories per day to run industries, cities, transportation, and households. Ninety-two per cent of the energy consumed in the United States at that time came from coal, petroleum, and natural gas, in order of importance. About 8 per cent came from waterpower and wood fuel. The United States was using 60 per cent of the world's output of petroleum and 25 per cent of the world's coal output, and possessed 30 per cent of the world's harnessed waterpower. This supplied the wants of 7 per cent of the world's people.[1]

At present rates of world energy consumption, the available reserves of coal, petroleum, and natural gas are more than adequate to meet all needs for more than a century into the future. However, if most regions of the world industrialize, rates of energy consumption will step up markedly. Under such conditions the fossil-fuel supplies, coal, petroleum, and natural gas, will not for long be able to meet the world's requirements. At best, waterpower can contribute only a small portion of the energy required by an industrialized world. Only the new power sources (nuclear energy and energy obtained directly from the sunlight through solar engines) show promise of sustaining such a high level of energy consumption. However, the contributions of nuclear energy to the world's energy supplies are steadily increasing. Assuming continued technological advance, energy needs could be supplied.[1,2]

To maintain a high material standard of living, man requires not just food and energy but materials in great variety and quantity. We have long since left the age when stone and wood provided for most material needs. However, through exhaustion of our more concentrated mineral sources, we may be returning full circle to a period when stone and wood must once more supply most of our material needs.[1]

Agriculture and industry today are constructed from many kinds of metals and other minerals. The needs are growing. The United States, once relatively self-sufficient in metallic ores and nonmetallic minerals, has with two world wars and great industrial expansion become dependent upon imports from distant areas. Our industry depends on supplies from the far corners of the earth. Chile, Bolivia, Venezuela, and the Congo are as important to our industrial machines today as Montana and Arizona were a few decades ago. The United States is the world's greatest consumer of metals and other minerals but, with continued industrialization of other nations, we cannot forever obtain the lion's share of the world supplies. Present trends suggest that in the future we must seek our needed supplies in what are now considered extremely low-grade sources, the seawaters of the earth and the minerals tied up in such common rocks as granite and basalt. Extraction of minerals from these sources will require a far greater expenditure of fuel for energy than we now consider economically feasible. However, further development of nuclear energy sources could provide the supplies that we will need.[1,2]

In 1956 a war developed between Israel and Egypt in which Britain and France became involved. Despite the quick Israeli victory, the economy of Europe was threatened with disaster by Egypt's closure of the Suez canal. The oil supplies from the Middle Eastern fields upon which western Europe depended were no longer available. In 1967 a rerun of the Arab-Israeli war brought an even faster Israeli victory. Once more the Arabs retaliated by closing off the Suez Canal and by cutting off oil shipments. But technology had advanced during the period between wars. Oil output was simply stepped up in those fields that were not closed. New, fast supertankers carried oil around the Cape at speeds equal to those with which it once was carried through the canal route. The economy of Europe scarcely faltered. Threats to raw material sources and even major boycotts no longer offer the same danger to technologically advanced nations that they did in the periods preceding World War I and II.

Advancing science and technology now offer many answers to the problems of man's future. If population growth can be slowed and stability is in prospect, we can look forward to a time when throughout the world the material needs of all people can be supplied. Given time, we could provide the energy, materials, and food needed to maintain some reasonable level of world population at a high material standard of living and have space left for a great enrichment of life beyond material needs. Time, however, has become a scarce commodity as world problems intensify.

Since biblical times it has been pointed out that man "does not live by bread alone." In our emphasis upon the production of quantifiable material things we lose sight of those qualitative values that make life worthwhile. Lewis Mumford has pointed out that it has taken man a million years to develop those qualities that we call "human," to develop his humanity, his ability for social cooperation, his artistic talents, and appreciation of beauty. Only in the past few millennia has he been led astray by the "myth of the machine" and tempted to sell his soul for material riches.[5]

Many writers have pointed out that one inevitable consequence of our continued pursuit of population growth and material enrichment will be the restriction and regimentation of the individual, with the consequent loss of liberty and opportunity for becoming psychologically whole human beings. If our society and technology is developing to the point where the individual is stifled, where he becomes only a unit in some world anthill, then obviously it is time we changed our direction.

Part of the answer, which environmental conservation can supply, is in the value of diversity. If we can maintain human diversity, many different ways of life in many different kinds of environments, there will always be room for change and room for society to experiment with new directions. If we can maintain a diversity in environment, the whole rich fabric of life on earth, the entire spectrum of animal and plant variety, then we have space in which human diversity can thrive and develop in its separate ways.

Lewis Mumford has stated our position well.

"One of the best reasons for the conservation movement . . . . is that it demonstrates the irrationality of allowing any single factor to dominate the rest of the environment. Our technology has overemphasized, in every sphere of life, the factor of power, of mass production and standardization; it seeks to decrease variety in order to promote quantity. Our aim rather should be to promote variety in order to curb this monotonous quantification."

Further he says:

"When we rally to preserve the remaining redwood forests or to protect the whooping crane, we are rallying to preserve ourselves, we are trying to keep in existence the organic variety, the whole span of natural resources, upon which our own further development will be based. If we surrender this variety too easily in one place, we shall lose it everywhere, and we shall find ourselves enclosed in a technological prison, without even the hope that sustains a prisoner in jail—that someday we may get out. Should organic variety disappear, there will be no 'out.' "[2]

Building on these ideas and those discussed earlier, the goal of environmental conservation can be stated as the preservation and creation of diversity among human societies and in their organic environments. If this is done there will always be a door open for future change, a way out.

## References

GENERAL REFERENCES

1. Bresler, Jack. 1966. *Human ecology.* Addison-Wesley, Reading, Mass.
2. Bureau of the Census, 1964. *Statistical abstract of the United States, 1964.* 85th annual edition. Dept. of Commerce, Washington.
3. Bureau of Land Management, 1965. *Public land statistics.* Dept. of Interior, Washington.
4. Burton, Ian, and R. W. Kates, 1965. *Readings in resource management and conservation.* Univ. Chicago, Chicago.

5. Darling, F. Fraser, and John Milton, 1966. *The future environments of North America*. Natural History Press, New York.
6. Espensshade, Edward B., Jr., 1960. *Goode's world atlas*. 12th Ed., Rand McNally, Chicago.
7. Haden-Guest, S., J. K. Wright, and E. M. Teclaff, editors, 1956. *World geography of forest resources*. Ronald Press, New York.
8. Rand McNally, 1962. *Cosmopolitan world atlas*. Rand McNally, Chicago.
9. Stamp, L. Dudley, editor, 1961. *A history of land use in arid regions*. Unesco. Paris.
10. Thomas, William L., Jr., editor, 1956. *Man's role in changing the face of the earth*. Univ. Chicago, Chicago.

## Introduction

1. Ehrlich, Paul R., 1967. The food-from-the-sea myth. *The Commonwealth*, 61:115–117.

## Chapter 1

1. Daubenmire, R. F., 1959. *Plants and environment*. 2nd Ed., John Wiley, New York.
2. Elton, Charles, 1927. *Animal ecology*. Sidgwick and Jackson, London.
3. Graham, Edward H., 1944. *Natural principles of land use*. Oxford, New York.
4. Odum, Eugene P., 1959. *Fundamentals of ecology*. 2nd Ed., W. B. Saunders, Philadelphia.
5. Oosting, Henry J., 1956. *The study of plant communities*. W. H. Freeman, San Francisco.
6. Weaver, John E., and F. E. Clements, 1938. *Plant ecology*. 2nd Ed., McGraw-Hill, New York.

## Chapter 2

1. Clements, F. E., 1916. *Plant succession*. Carnegie Inst. of Washington. Publ. 242.
2. Dansereau, Pierre, 1957. *Biogeography, an ecological perspective*. Ronald Press, New York.
3. Daubenmire, R. F., 1959. *Plants and environment*. 2nd Ed., John Wiley, New York.
4. Darling, F. Fraser, 1960. Wildlife husbandry in Africa. *Scientific American*, 203:123–133.
5. Elton, Charles, 1927. *Animal ecology*. Sidgwick and Jackson, London.
6. Finch, V. C., and G. T. Trewartha, 1942. *Elemnts of geography, physical and cultural*. McGraw-Hill, New York.
7. Graham, Edward H., 1944. *Natural principles of land use*. Oxford. New York.
8. Holdridge, L. R., 1947. Determination of world plant formations from simple climatic data. *Science*, 105:367–368.
9. Kuchler, A. W., 1964. *Potential natural vegetation of the conterminous United States*. American Geographic Society, Spec. Publ. 36.
10. Merriam, C. Hart, 1898. *Life zones and crop zones of the United States*. U.S. Dept. of Agric., Biol. Surv. Bulletin 10.
11. Odum, Eugene P., 1959. *Fundamentals of ecology*. W. B. Saunders, Philadelphia.
12. Oosting, Henry J., 1956. *The study of plant communities*. W. H. Freeman, San Francisco.

13. Richards, P. W., 1952. *The tropical rain forest.* Cambridge Univ., Cambridge.
14. Rudd, Robert, 1964. *Pesticides and the living landscape.* Univ. Wisconsin, Madison.
15. Shantz, H. L., and R. Zon, 1924. *Atlas of American agriculture.* U.S. Dept. Agric., Washington.
16. Shelford, Victor E., 1963. *The ecology of North America.* Univ. Illinois, Urbana.
17. Warming, E., 1909. *Oecology of plants.* Oxford, London.
18. Weaver, John E. and F. E. Clements, 1938. *Plant ecology.* 2nd Ed., McGraw-Hill, New York.

*Chapter 3*

1. Bartlett, H. H., 1956. Fire, primitive agriculture and grazing in the tropics. (See Thomas, 1956.)
2. Brooks, C. E. P., 1949. *Climate through the ages.* Ernest Benn, London.
3. Clark, J. Desmond, 1959. *Prehistory of southern Africa.* Penguin, Harmondsworth.
4. Cole, Sonia, 1963. *The prehistory of east Africa.* New American Library, Mentor, New York.
5. Coon, Carlton S., 1954. *The story of man.* Alfred Knopf, New York.
6. Coon, Carlton S., 1962. *The origin of races.* Alfred Knopf, New York.
7. Dale, Tom, and V. G. Carter, 1955. *Topsoil and civilization.* Univ. Oklahoma, Norman.
8. Darby, H. C., 1956. The clearing of the woodland in Europe. (See Thomas, 1956.)
9. Davis, John H., 1956. Influences of man upon coast lines. (See Thomas, 1956.)
10. DeChardin, Pierre Teilhard, 1956. The antiquity and world expansion of human culture. (See Thomas, 1956.)
11. Evans, E. Estyn, 1956. The ecology of peasant life in western Europe. (See Thomas, 1956.)
12. Flint, Richard Foster, 1947. *Glacial geology and the Pleistocene epoch.* John Wiley, New York.
13. Glacken, Clarence J., 1956. Changing ideas of the habitable world. (See Thomas, 1956.)
14. Gourou, Pierre, 1956. The quality of land use of tropical cultivators. (See Thomas, 1956.)
15. Hamdan, G., 1961. Evolution of irrigation agriculture in Egypt. (See Stamp, 1961.)
16. Harris, David R., 1967. New light on plant domestication and the origins of agriculture. A review. *Geogr. Review,* 57:90–107.
17. Heichelheim, F. M., 1956. Effects of classical antiquity on the land. (See Thomas, 1956.)
18. Huntington, Ellsworth. 1907. *The pulse of Asia.* Houghton Mifflin, Boston.
19. Huzayyin, Soliman, 1956. Change in climate, vegetation and human adjustment in the Saharo-Arabian belt with special reference to Africa. (See Thomas, 1956.)
20. Johnson, Frederick, 1955. Reflections upon the significance of radiocarbon dates. (See Libby, 1955.)
21. Libby, W. F., 1955. *Radiocarbon dating.* Univ. Chicago, Chicago.
22. Linton, Ralph, 1955. *The tree of culture.* Alfred Knopf, New York.
23. Lowdermilk, W. C., 1953. *Conquest of the land through 7,000 years.* U.S. Dept. Agric., Washington.

24. Muller-Beck, Hansjurgen, 1956. Paleohunters in America: origins and diffusion. *Science,* 27 May.
25. Mumford, Lewis, 1956. *The transformations of man.* Collier, New York.
26. Mumford, Lewis, 1961. *The city in history.* Harcourt, Brace, World, New York.
27. Osborn, Fairfield, 1948. *Our plundered planet.* Little, Brown, Boston.
28. Osborn, Fairfield, 1953. *The limits of the earth.* Little, Brown, Boston.
29. Pfeifer, Gottfried, 1956. The quality of peasant living in central Europe. (See Thomas, 1956.)
30. Sauer, Carl O., 1950. Grassland climax, fire, and man. *Jour. Range Management,* 3:16–21.
31. Sauer, Carl O., 1952. *Agricultural origins and dispersal.* Amer. Geographic Society, New York.
32. Shapley, Harlow, editor, 1953. *Climatic change, evidence, causes and effects.* Harvard, Cambridge.
33. Stewart, Omer C., 1956. Fire as the first great force employed by man. (See Thomas, 1956.)
34. Vogt, William, 1948. *Road to survival.* Wm. Sloane, New York.
35. Wissman, Hermann von, H. Poech, G. Smolla, and F. Kussmaul, 1956. On the role of nature and man in changing the face of the dry belt of Asia. (See Thomas, 1956.)
36. Wittfogel, Karl, 1956. The hydraulic civilizations. (See Thomas, 1956.)
37. Zeuner, F. E., 1945. *The Pleistocene period, its climate, chronology and faunal successions.* Royal Society, London.
38. Zeuner, F. E., 1950. *Dating the past, an introduction to geochronology.* Methuen, London.

## Chapter 4

1. Dasmann, R. F., 1966. *Conservation planning on a national scale.* Proc. XIth Pacific Science Congress, Tokyo. The Conservation Foundation, Washington, mimeo.
2. Dasmann, R. F., 1967. Toward a world conservation program. *The Land,* 1:18–26, Harvard Conservation Club, Cambridge.
3. Graham, Edward, 1947. *The land and wildlife.* Oxford, New York.
4. Hart, William J., 1966. *A systems approach to park planning.* IUCN Publ., New Series. Supplementary paper 4, Morges.
5. Leopold, Aldo, 1949. *A sand county almanac.* Oxford, New York.
6. Lilienthal, David E., 1953. *TVA; democracy on the march.* Harper, New York.
7. McHarg, Ian, 1966. Ecological determinism. (See Darling and Milton, 1966.)
8. Mumford, Lewis, 1956. The natural history of urbanization. (See Thomas, 1956.)
9. Straight, Michael, 1965. The water picture in Everglades National Park. *National Park Magazine,* 39:4–9.

## Chapter 5

1. Albrecht, William A., 1956. Physical, chemical and biochemical changes in the soil community. (See Thomas, 1956.)
2. Bamesberger, John G., 1939. *Erosion losses from a 3-day California storm.* U.S. Dept. of Agric., Washington.
3. Bartelli, Lindo, 1966. General soil maps—a study of landscapes. *Jour. Soil and Water Conservation,* 21:3–6.

4. Bennett, Hugh H., 1955. *Elements of soil conservation*. McGraw-Hill, New York.
5. Borgstrom, Georg, 1965. *The hungry planet*. Macmillan, New York.
6. Brown, Harrison, 1954. *The challenge of man's future*. Viking Press, New York.
7. Carson, Rachel, 1962. *Silent spring*. Houghton Mifflin, Boston.
8. Cole, Lamont C., 1964. Pesticides: a hazard to nature's equilibrium. *Jour. Public Health*, 54:24–31.
9. Conway, R. G., 1965. *Crop pest control and resource conservation in tropical Southeast Asia*. Proc. Conference on Conservation of Nature and Natural Resources in Tropical Southeast Asia, Bangkok, mimeo.
10. Dale, Tom, and V. G. Carter, 1955. *Topsoil and civilization*. Univ. Oklahoma. Norman.
11. Darling, F. Fraser, 1955. West highland survey: an essay in human ecology. Oxford, Univ., Oxford.
12. Economic Research Service, 1965. *Changes in agriculture in 26 developing nations. 1948–1963*. U.S. Dept. of Agric., Washington.
13. Finch, V. C., and G. T. Trewartha, 1942. *Elements of geography, physical and cultural* McGraw-Hill, New York.
14. Fitter, M. S., 1967. Harmless chemical for elm disease. *Oryx*, 9:18.
15. Food and Agricultural Organization of the United Nations, 1956. *The agriculture division of FAO. A summary of its organization, development and accomplishments from 2 December 1946 to 31 December 1955*. FAO, Rome.
16. Food and Agricultural Organization of the United Nations, 1965. *The state of food and agriculture*. FAO, Rome.
17. Food and Agricultural Organization of the United Nations, 1966. *FAO/Industry Cooperative Program*, FAO, Rome.
18. Food and Agricultural Organization of the United Nations, 1966. *Indicative world plan for agricultural development*. FAO, Rome.
19. Graham, Edward H., 1944. *Natural principles of land use*. Oxford, New York.
20. Hockensmith, R. D., and J. G. Steele, 1943. *Classifying land for conservation farming*. U.S. Dept. Agric., Farmer's Bulletin 1853, Washington.
21. Hutchison, Claude E., editor, 1946. *California agriculture*. Univ. Calif., Berkeley.
22. Jacks, G. V., 1954. *Soil*. Philosophical Library, New York.
23. Jacks, G. V., and R. O. Whyte, 1939. *Vanishing lands*. Doubleday, Doran, New York.
24. Jain, S. P., 1966. *Mortality trends and social and economic development in India*. Proc. XIth Pacific Science Congress, Tokyo, mimeo.
25. Klimm, L. E., O. P. Starkey, and N. F. Hall, 1943. *Introductory economic geography*. Harcourt, Brace, New York.
26. Leopold, Luna B., 1956. Land use and sediment yield. (See Thomas, 1956.)
27. Nagel, W. O., editor, 1952. *Wildlife and the soil*. Missouri Conservation Commission, Jefferson City.
28. Oosting, Henry J., 1956. *The study of plant communities*. W. H. Freeman, San Francisco.
29. President's Science Advisory Committee, 1963. *Use of pesticides*. White House, Washington.
30. President's Science Advisory Committee. 1967. *The world food problem*. 2 volumes. White House, Washington.
31. Richards, P. W., 1952. *The tropical rain forest*. Cambridge Univ., Cambridge.

32. Rudd, Robert, 1964. *Pesticides and the living landscape.* Univ. Wisconsin, Madison.
33. Shantz, H. L. and R. Zon, 1924. *Atlas of American agriculture.* U.S. Dept. of Agric., Washington.
34. Smith, Guy-Harold, editor, 1965. *Conservation of natural resources.* John Wiley, New York.
35. Snyder, J. H., 1966. New program for agricultural land use stabilization: The California land conservation act of 1965. *Land Economics,* 42:29–41.
36. Soil Conservation Service, 1955. *Facts about wind erosion and dust storms on the Great Plains.* U.S. Dept. of Agric. Leaflet 394.
37. Tatton, J. O'G., and J. H. A. Ruzicka, 1967. Organochlorine pesticides in Antarctica. *Nature,* 215:346–348.
38. Thornthwaite, C. W., 1956. The modification of rural microclimates. (See Thomas, 1956.)
39. Waksman, Selman A., 1952. *Soil microbiology.* John Wiley, New York.
40. West, Quentin M., 1966. *World food needs.* U.S. Dept. of Agric., Washington.
41. Wohletz, L. R., and E. F. Dolder, 1952. *Know California's land* Calif. Dept. Natural Resources. Sacramento.
42. Woodwell, George M., 1967. Toxic substances and ecological cycles. *Scientific American,* 216:24–31.
43. Yamshima, Y., 1966. *Recent progress of nature conservation and preservation of natural resources in Japan.* Proc. 11th Pacific Science Congress, Tokyo, mimeo.
44. Yates, P. L., 1955. *So bold an aim.* FAO, Rome.
45. Zimmerman, G. K., 1966. Meeting urbanization and resource pressures in rural America. *Transactions of North American Wildlife Conference* (in press).

*Chapter 6*

1. Allen, Shirley W., 1955. *Conserving natural resources.* McGraw-Hill, New York.
2. Bamesberger, John G., 1939. *Erosion losses from a 3-day California storm.* U.S. Dept. Agric., Washington.
3. Banks, A. L., and J. A. Hislop, 1956. Sanitation practices and disease control in extending and improving areas for human habitation. (See Thomas, 1956.)
4. Black, John D., 1954. *Biological conservation.* Blakiston, New York.
5. Brown, Harrison, 1954. *The challenge of man's future.* Viking Press, New York.
6. Burton, Ian, and R. W. Kates, 1964. The perception of natural hazards in resource management. *Natural Resources Journal,* 3:412–441.
7. Burton, Ian, and R. W. Kates, 1965. *Readings in resource management and conservation.* Univ. Chicago, Chicago.
8. California Dept. of Fish and Game, 1957. *Forty-fourth biennial report.* Sacramento.
9. Clapp, Gordon R., 1955. *The TVA, an approach to the development of a region.* Univ. Chicago, Chicago.
10. Colman, E. A., 1953. *Vegetation and watershed management.* Ronald Press, New York.
11. Dale, Tom, and V. G. Carter, 1955. *Topsoil and civilization.* Univ. Oklahoma, Norman.
12. Davis, John H., 1943. *The natural features of Southern Florida.* Florida Geol. Surv. Bull. 25.
13. Davis, John H., 1956. Influences of man upon coast lines. (See Thomas, 1956.)
14. de Roos, Robert, 1948. *The thirsty land.* Stanford Univ., Stanford,

15. Dolder, Edward F., 1954. *Water—California's lifeblood*. In Conservation—concern for tomorrow. Calif. State Dept. Educ. Bull., pp. 45–63.
16. Downey, Sheridan, 1947. *They would rule the valley*. Privately printed, San Francisco.
17. Eaton, F. M., 1949. Irrigation agriculture along the Nile and the Euphrates. *Scientific Monthly*, 48:33–42.
18. Ellis, Cecil B., 1954. *Fresh water from the ocean for cities, industry, and irrigation*. Ronald Press, New York.
19. Farb, Peter, 1965. Disaster threatens the Everglades. *Audubon*, 67:302–309.
20. Gordon, Mitchell, 1965. *Sick cities*. Penguin, Baltimore.
21. Graham, Edward H., 1944. *Natural principles of land use*. Oxford, New York.
22. Higbee, Edward, 1957. *The American oasis. The land and its uses*. Alfred Knopf, New York.
23. Hill, Gladwin, 1965. The great and dirty lakes. *Saturday Review*, Oct. 23. pp. 32–34.
24. Hutchinson, Wallace I., 1956. *Water for millions*. Forest Service, U.S. Dept. Agric., San Francisco.
25. Kates, Robert W., 1964. *Hazard and choice perception in flood plain management*. Univ. Chicago Dept. Geog. Research Paper 78, Chicago.
26. Kauffman, Erle, editor, 1954. *The conservation yearbook*. Conservation Yearbook, Washington.
27. Kittredge, Joseph, 1948. *Forest influences*. McGraw-Hill, New York.
28. Kuenen, P. H., 1956. *Realms of water*. John Wiley, New York.
29. Lear, John, 1965. The crisis in water. What brought it on? *Saturday Review*, Oct. 23, pp. 24–28, 78–80.
30. Leopold, Luna B., and T. Maddock, Jr., 1954. *The flood control controversy*. Ronald Press, New York.
31. Leopold, Luna B., 1960. Water and the southwest. *Landscape*, 10:27–31.
32. Leopold, Luna B., and W. B. Langbein, 1960. *A primer on water*. Geological Survey, Dept. of Interior, Washington.
33. Leopold, Luna B., 1962. *The vigil network*. Int. Assoc. Scientific Hydrology, 7:5–9.
34. Lowdermilk, W. C., 1953. *Conquest of the land through 7,000 years*. U.S. Dept. Agric., Washington.
35. Maxwell, John C., 1965. Will there be enough water? *American Scientist*, 53:97–103.
36. Nadeau, Remi A., 1950. *The water seekers*. Doubleday, New York.
37. Nash, Hugh, 1966. Storm over the Grand Canyon. *Parks and Recreation*, June, pp. 497–500.
38. National Academy of Sciences—National Research Council, 1966. *Alternatives in water management*, Publ. 1408, Washington.
39. National Academy of Sciences-National Research Council, 1966. *Waste Management and Control*, Publ. 1400, Washington.
40. National Wildlife Federation, 1966. The wild rivers. *National Wildlife*, 4:3–9.
41. Outdoor Recreation Resources Review Commission, 1962. *Outdoor recreation for America*. Washington.
42. Rienow, Robert, and Leona Train, 1965. Last chance for the nation's waterways. *Saturday Review*, May 22, pp. 35–36, 96–97.
43. Saturday Review, 1965. Nor any drop to drink. *Sat. Rev.*, Oct. 23, pp. 35–44, 76–78.

44. Smith, Guy-Harold, editor, 1965. *Conservation of natural resources.* 3rd Ed., John Wiley, New York.
45. Spurr, Stephen H., *et al.*, 1966. *Rampart Dam and the economic development of Alaska.* Univ. Michigan, Ann Arbor.
46. Stegner, Wallace, 1965. Myths of the western dam. *Saturday Review,* Oct. 23, pp. 29–31.
47. Thomas, Harold E., 1956. Changes in quantities and qualities of ground and surface water. (See Thomas, 1956, General references.)
48. Thornthwaite, C. W., 1956. The modification of rural microclimates. (See Thomas, 1956.)
49. Time, 1965. Hydrology. A question of birthright. Oct. 1, pp. 70–79.
50. Udall, Stewart L., 1963. *The quiet crisis.* Holt, Rinehart, Winston, New York.
51. White, Gilbert F., 1964. *Choice of adjustment to floods.* Univ. Chicago Dept. Geog. Research Paper 93.
52. Wiln, H. G., 1957. Water. *America's Natural Resources.* Ronald Press, New York. pp. 42–60.
53. Wilson, Andrew, 1965. Climate and the sprawl of cities. *Landscape,* 14:20–21.
54. Wittfogel, Karl, 1956. The hydraulic civilizations. (See Thomas, 1956.)
55. Wolman, Abel, 1956. Disposal of man's wastes. (See Thomas, 1956.)
56. Zon, Raphael, 1927. *Forests and water in the light of scientific investigation.* Appendix 5, Final report of national waterways commission. Senate Document 469, 62nd Congress, 2nd session, Washington.

*Chapter 7*

1. Allen, Shirley W., 1950. *An introduction to American forestry.* McGraw-Hill, New York.
2. Allen, Shirley W., 1955. *Conserving natural resources.* McGraw-Hill, New York.
3. Camp, Wendell H., 1956. The forests of the past and present. (See Haden-Guest, *et al.*, 1956.)
4. Clepper, Henry, and L. Besley, 1957. Forests. *America's Natural Resources.* Ronald Press, New York.
5. Curtis, John T., 1956. The modification of mid-latitude grasslands and forests by man. (See Thomas, 1956.)
6. Dana, Samuel T., 1956. *Forest and range policy.* McGraw-Hill, New York.
7. Department of Agriculture, 1949. *Trees.* Yearbook of agriculture, Washington.
8. Egler, Frank E., 1956. Discussion in Thomas, 1956.
9. Forest Service, 1956. Timber resource review fact sheets.
10. Forest Service, 1965. *Timber trends in the United States.* Forest research report 17, Dept. of Agriculture, Washington.
11. Graham, Edward H., 1944. *Natural principles of land use.* Oxford, New York.
12. Guthrie, John D., 1936. Great forest fires of America. Dept. of Agriculture, Washington.
13. Josephson, H. R., and Dwight Hair, 1956. The United States. (See Haden-Guest, *et al.*, 1956.)
14. Lowenthal, David, 1956. Western Europe. (See Haden-Guest, *et al.*, 1956.)
15. McArdle, Richard E., 1955. *Timber resources for America's future.* U.S. Dept. of Agriculture, Washington.
16. Peace, T. R., 1961. The dangerous concept of the natural forest. *Advancement of Science,* 17:448–455.

17. Political and Economic Planning, 1955. *World population and resources.* George Allen and Unwin, London.
18. Quinney, Dean N., 1964. Small private forest landownership in the United States—individual and social perception. *Natural Resources Journal,* 3:379–393.
19. Raup, Hugh M., 1964. Some problems in ecological theory and their relation to conservation. *Jour. Ecology,* 52:19–28.
20. Richards, P. W., 1952. *The tropical rain forest.* Cambridge Univ., Cambridge.
21. Rostlund, Erhard, 1956. The outlook for the world's forests and their chief products. (See Haden-Guest, *et al.,* 1956.)
22. Smith, Guy-Harold, editor, 1965. *Conservation of natural resources.* 3rd Ed., John Wiley, New York.
23. Spurr, Stephen H., 1954. The forests of Itasca in the nineteenth century as related to fire. *Ecology,* 35:21–25.
24. Streyffert, K. T., A. Langsaeter, and E. Saari, 1956. Northern Europe. (See Haden-Guest, *et al.,* 1956.)
25. Tunstell, George, 1956. Canada. (See Haden-Guest, *et al.,* 1956.)
26. Udall, Stewart L., 1963. *The quiet crisis.* Holt, Rinehart and Winston, New York.

*Chapter 8*

1. Bryan, H. M., and H. W. Springfield, 1955. Range management in Iraq—findings, plans, and accomplishment. *Jour. Range Management,* 8:249–256.
2. Bryant, E., 1936. *What I saw in California.* Fine Arts Press, Santa Ana.
3. Buechner, Helmut K., 1950. Life history, ecology, and range use of the pronghorn antelope in Trans-Pecos, Texas. *Amer. Midland Naturalist,* 43:257–354.
4. Burcham, Lee T., 1957. *California range land.* Calif. Division of Forestry, Sacramento.
5. Clark, A. H., 1956. The impact of exotic invasion on the remaining New World mid-latitude grasslands. (See Thomas, 1956.)
6. Colman, E. A., 1953. *Vegetation and watershed management.* Ronald Press, New York.
7. Cook, O. F., 1908. *Change of vegetation on the south Texas prairie.* Bureau of Plant Industry, Dept. of Agriculture, Washington.
8. Curtis, John T., 1965. The modification of mid-latitude grasslands and forests by man. (See Thomas, 1956.)
9. Dale, E. E., 1930. *The range cattle industry.* Univ. Oklahoma, Norman.
10. Darling, R. F., 1955. Pastoralism in relation to populations of men and animals. *The numbers of man and animals,* Oliver and Boyd, Edinburgh, pp. 121–129.
11. Darling, F. F., 1956. Man's ecological dominance through domesticated animals on wild lands. (See Thomas, 1956).
12. Dasmann, R. F., 1963. *The last horizon.* Macmillan, New York.
13. Dasmann, R. F., 1964. *African game ranching.* Pergamon, Oxford.
14. Dasmann, R. F., 1965. *The destruction of California.* Macmillan, New York.
15. Davy, Joseph Burtt, 1902. *Stock ranges of northwestern California: notes on the grasses and forage plants and range conditions.* Bureau Plant Industry, Dept. of Agriculture, Washington.
16. Dyksterhuis, E. J., 1949. Condition and management of range land based on quantitative ecology. *Jour. Range Management,* 2:104–115.
17. Ellison, Lincoln, 1954. Subalpine vegetation of the Wasatch Plateau, Utah. *Ecological Monographs,* 24:89–184.

18. Forest Service, 1936. *The western range, a great but neglected natural resource.* Senate Document 199, Washington.
19. Graham, Edward H., 1944. *Natural principles of land use.* Oxford, New York.
20. Grover, D. I., 1945. *Range condiiton, a classification of the annual forage type.* Soil Conservation Service, Dept. of Agric., Pacific Coast Region.
21. Larson, F. D., 1957. Problems of population pressure upon the desert range. *Jour. Range Management,* 10:160–161.
22. Leopold, Aldo, 1949. *A sand county almanac.* Oxford, New York.
23. Linsdale, Jean M., 1946. *The California ground squirrel.* Univ. California, Berkeley.
24. Longhurst, W. L., A. S. Leopold, and R. F. Dasmann, 1952. *A survey of California deer herds, their ranges and management problems.* Calif. Dept. of Fish and Game, Game Bull. 6.
25. Malin, James C., 1956. The grassland of North America: its occupance and the challenge of continuous reappraisals. (See Thomas, 1956.)
26. Miller, Robert F. 1942. *Sheep production in California.* Agric. Extension Service, Univ. Calif., Berkeley.
27. Naveh, Z., 1960. Mediterranean grasslands in California and Israel. *Jour. Range Management,* 13:302–306.
28. Pick, Jock H., 1944. *Australia's dying heart.* Melbourne Univ., Melbourne.
29. Ratcliffe, Francis, 1947. *Flying fox and drifting sand.* Angus and Robertson, Sydney.
30. Ratcliffe, Francis, 1959. The rabbit in Australia. Biogeography and ecology in Australia. *Monog. Biol.,* 8:545–564.
31. Sampson, Arthur W., 1952. *Range management, principles and practices.* John Wiley, New York, 570 pp.
32. Sauer, Carl O., 1950. Grassland climax, fire, and man. *Jour. Range Management,* 3:16–21.
33. Schaller, George, 1967. *The deer and the tiger. A study of wildlife in India.* Univ. Chicago, Chicago.
34. Talbot, Lee M., 1961. *A look at threatened species.* Fauna Preservation Society, London.
35. Towne, Charles W., and E. N. Wentworth, 1955. *Cattle and men.* Univ. Oklahoma, Norman.
36. Weaver, J. E., 1954. *North American prairie.* Johnson, Lincoln, Nebr.
37. Wentworth, E. N., 1948. *America's sheep trails.* Iowa State, Ames.
38. Wolfe, L. M., editor, 1938. *John of the mountains; the unpublished journals of John Muir.* Houghton Mifflin, Boston.
39. Wyman, Walker P., 1945. *The wild horse of the west.* Caxton, Caldwell, Idaho.

*Chapter 9*

1. Allen, Durward, 1954. *Our wildlife legacy.* Funk and Wagnalls, New York.
2. Ardrey, Robert, 1966. *The territorial imperative.* Atheneum, New York.
3. Banfield, A. W., 1951. *The barren-ground caribou.* Canada Dept. of Resources and Development, Ottawa.
4. Bannikov, A. G., 1962. *Exploitation of the saiga antelope in the USSR.* Proc. Institute of Biology, London.
5. Darling, F. F., 1947. *Wild life of Britain.* Collins, London.
6. Darling, F. F., 1955. *West highland survey. An essay in human ecology.* Oxford, London.

7. Darling, F. F., 1960. *Wild life in an African territory*. Oxford, London.
8. Dasmann, R. F., 1963. Biomass, yield and economic value of wild and domestic ungulates. *Transactions 6th Congress, International Union of Game Biologists*. Nature Conservancy, London, pp. 227–235.
9. Dasmann, R. F., 1964. *African game ranching*. Pergamon, Oxford.
10. Dasmann, R. F., 1964. *Wildlife biology*. John Wiley, New York.
11. Edwards, R. Y., 1954. Fire and the decline of a mountain caribou herd. *Jour. Wildlife Management*, 18:521–526.
12. Eggeling, W. J., 1964. A nature reserve management plan for the island of Rhum, Inner Hebrides. *Jour. Applied Ecology*, 1:405–419.
13. Elton, Charles, 1927. *Animal ecology*. Sidgwick and Jackson, London.
14. Gordon, Seth, 1950. *California's fish and game program*. Senate, State of Calif., Sacramento.
15. Graham, Edward S., 1947. *The land and wildlife*. Oxford, New York.
16. Grinnell, J., J. S. Dixon, and J. M. Linsdale, 1937. *Furbearing mammals of California*. Univ. Calif., Berkeley, 2 volumes.
17. Hornaday, W. T., 1913. *Our vanishing wildlife*. Scribners, New York.
18. International Union for Conservation of Nature, 1963. *Conservation of nature and natural resources in moder African states*. IUCN publication, new series, no. 1, Morges.
19. Leopold, Aldo, 1933. *Game management*. Scribners, New York.
20. Leopold, Aldo, 1949. *A sand county almanac*. Oxford, New York.
21. Leopold, A. S., and F. F. Darling, 1953. *Wildlife in Alaska*. Ronald Press, New York.
22. Leopold, A. S., 1956. Hunting for the masses—can game departments supply it? *Proc. 36th Annual Conference*. Western Association State Game and Fish Commissioners.
23. Leopold, A. S., 1959. *Wildlife of Mexico*. Univ. Calif., Berkeley.
24. Longhurst, W. L., A. S. Leopold, and R. F. Dasmann, 1952. *A survey of California deer herds, their ranges and management problems*. Calif. Dept. of Fish and Game, Game Bull. 6.
25. Lorenz, Konrad, 1963. *On aggression*. Harcourt, Brace, World, New York.
26. Marshall, A. J., editor, 1966. *The great extermination*. Heinemann, London.
27. Murie, Adolph, 1944. The wolves of Mount McKinley. *Fauna of the National Parks of the United States*. National Park Service, Washington.
28. Nagel, W. O., editor, 1952. *Wildlife and the soil*. Missouri Conservation Commission, Jefferson City.
29. Odum, Eugene P., 1959. *Fundamentals of ecology*. W. B. Saunders, Philadelphia.
30. Rasmussen, D. I., 1941. Biotic communities of the Kaibab Plateau. *Ecological Monographs*, 3:229–275.
31. Schaller, George, 1967. *The deer and the tiger. A study of Wildlife in India*. Univ. Chicago, Chicago.
32. Stoddard, Herbert L., 1931. *The bobwhite quail. Its habits, preservation, and increase*. Scribners, New York.
33. Talbot, Lee M., 1957. The lions of Gir: wildlife management problems of Asia. *Transactions, 22nd North American Wildlife Conference*, pp. 570–579.
34. Talbot, Lee M., 1966. *Wild animals as a source of food*. Bur. Sports Fisheries and Wildlife, Washington.
35. Wodzicki, K., 1961. Ecology and management of introduced ungulates in New Zealand. *La terre et la vie*, 1:130–157.

36. Yocom, C. F., and R. F. Dasmann, 1957. *The Pacific coastal wildlife region.* Naturegraph, Healdsburg, Calif.
37. Zabinski, J., 1961. A propos du bison d'Europe. *La terre et la vie,* 1:113–115.

Chapter 10

1. Allen, S. W., 1955. *Conserving natural resources.* McGraw-Hill, New York.
2. Black, John D., 1954. *Biological conservation.* Blakiston, New York.
3. Borgstrom, Georg, 1965. *The hungry planet.* Macmillan, New York.
4. Brown, Harrison, 1954. *The challenge of man's future.* Viking, New York.
5. California Department of Fish and Game, 1957. *Forty-fourth Biennial report.* Sacramento.
6. Carson, Rachel, 1951. *The sea around us.* Oxford, New York.
7. Christy, Francis T., Jr., and Anthony Scott, 1966. *The common wealth in ocean fisheries.* Johns Hopkins, Baltimore.
8. Cooley, R. A., 1963. *Politics and conservation. The decline of the Alaska salmon.* Harper & Row, New York.
9. Croker, Richard, 1954. *The sardine story—a tragedy.* Outdoor California, 15:6–8.
10. Fish and Wildlife Service, 1956. *National survey of hunting and fishing.* Dept. of Interior, Washington.
11. Gordon, Seth, 1950. *California's fish and game program.* Senate, State of Calif., Sacramento.
12. Graham, Michael, 1956. *Harvests of the seas.* (See Thomas, 1956.)
13. Hedgpeth, Joel, 1964. *Man and the sea.* Pacific Marine Station, Dillon Beach, Calif.
14. Klingbiel, John, 1953. Are fishing restrictions necessary? *Wisconsin Cons. Bull.* 18:3–5.
15. Le Cren, E. D., and M. W. Holdgate, editors, 1962. *The exploitation of natural animal populations.* John Wiley, New York.
16. Odum, E. P., 1959. *Fundamentals of ecology.* 2nd Ed., W. B. Saunders, Phila.
17. Osborn, Fairfield, 1953. *The limits of the earth.* Little, Brown, Boston.
18. Smith, Guy-Harold, editor, 1965. *Conservation of natural resources.* 3rd Ed., John Wiley, New York.
19. Sverdrup, H. V., M. W. Johnson, and R. H. Fleming, 1942. *The oceans.* Prentice-Hall, New York.
20. Walton Smith, F. G., and H. Chapin, 1954. *The sun, the sea, and tomorrow.* Scribners, New York.
21. Welch, P. S., 1935. *Limnology.* McGraw-Hill, New York.

Chapter 11

1. Adams, A. B., editor, 1962. *First world conference on national parks.* National Park Service, Washington.
2. Brandborg, S. M., 1963. On the carrying capacity of wilderness. *The Living Wilderness,* no. 84, pp. 28–33.
3. Boyd, J. Morton, 1966. The changing image of the national park. *New Scientist.* 30:254–256.
4. Dasmann, R. F., 1965. *The destruction of California.* Macmillan, New York.
5. Dasmann, R. F., 1966. Conservation planning on a national scale. Proc. XIth Pacific Science Congress, Tokyo, mimeo.
6. Dasmann, R. F., 1966. Wildlife and outdoor recreation. *Virginia Wildlife,* 27:4–5, 21–22.

7. Dasmann, R. F., 1967. Toward a world conservation program. *The Land.* Harvard Conservation Club, Cambridge.
8. Douglas, William O., 1965. *A wilderness bill of rights.* Little, Brown, Boston.
9. Draper, W. H., Jr., 1966. Parks or more people? *National Parks,* 40:10–13.
10. Edwards, R. Y., 1967. The preservation of wilderness. *Canadian Audubon,* 29:1–7.
11. Fish and Wildlife Service, 1965. *Survival or surrender for endangered wildlife.* Dept. of Interior, Washington.
12. Fischer, V. L., 1966. Formula for mediocrity. *American Forests,* 72:16–17, 52–54.
13. Fosberg, F. R., editor. 1963. *Man's place in the island ecosystem.* Bishop Museum, Honolulu.
14. Hudson, Lois P., 1966. The benevolent wreckers. *The Nation,* April 4, pp. 393–396.
15. Kolipinski, M. C., and A. L. Higer, 1966. Ecological research in Everglades National Park. *National Parks,* 40:14–17.
16. Leopold, Aldo, 1949. *A sand county almanac.* Oxford, New York.
17. Leopold, A. S., *et al.,* 1963. Wildlife management in the national parks. *Transactions North American Wildlife Conf.*
18. Leydet, Francois, editor, 1963. *Tomorrow's wilderness.* Sierra Club, San Francisco.
19. Lowdermilk, W. C., 1953. *Conquest of the land through 7,000 years.* Soil Conservation Service, Dept. of Agric., Washington.
20. Nadel, Michael, editor, 1964. A handbook on the wilderness act. *The Living Wilderness,* no. 86.
21. National Park Service, 1964. *The redwoods.* Dept. of Interior, Washington.
22. North Cascades Study Team, 1965. *The North Cascades.* Dept. of Interior, Washington.
23. Outdoor Recreation Resources Review Commission, 1962. *Outdoor recreation for America.* Washington.
24. Pan-American Union, 1965. *The Cutibireni National Park: a pilot project in the selva of Peru.* PAU, Washington.
25. Platt, Rutherford, 1961. *Wilderness.* Dodd, Mead, New York.
26. Robertson, W. B., Jr., 1959. *Everglades—the park story.* Miami Univ., Coral Gables.
27. Russell, Carl P., 1957. *One hundred years in Yosemite.* Yosemite Natural History Assoc., Yosemite.
28. Thoreau, Henry David, 1961. *Walden.* Holt, Rinehart, Winston, New York.
29. Udall, Stewart L., 1963. *The quiet crisis.* Holt, Rinehart, Winston, New York.
30. United States National Committee for the I.B.P., 1967. *U.S. participation in the IBP.* National Academy of Sciences, Washington.

*Chapter 12*

1. Burchard, John E., 1965. Comment on Point Reyes. *Ekistics,* 20:260–261.
2. Burrough, Roy J., 1966. Should urban land be publicly owned? *Land Economies,* 42:11–20.
3. Clawson, Marion, 1963. *Land and water for recreation.* Rand McNally, Chicago.
4. Dasmann, R. F., 1966. Wildlife and outdoor recreation. *Virginia Wildlife,* 27:4–5, 21–22.
5. Forest Services, 1966. *A national recreation area in Sawtooth country.* U.S. Dept. of Agriculture, Washington.
6. Gruen, Victor, 1964. *The heart of our cities.* Simon and Schuster, New York.

7. Glikson, Artur, 1956. Recreational land use. (See Thomas, 1956.)
8. Howard, Ebenezer, 1902. *Garden cities of tomorrow.* Faber and Faber, London (1946 edition).
9. Jackson, James P., 1965. Conservation and the population explosion. *American Forests,* 71:31, 46–47.
10. Klukas, R. W. and D. P. Duncan, 1967. Vegetational preferences among Itasca Park visitors. *Journal Forestry,* 65:18–21.
11. Lucas, R. C., 1964. *The recreational capacity of the Quetico-Superior area.* U.S. Forest Service, Research paper LS-15, Lake States Forest Experiment Station.
12. Lucas, R. C., 1964. Wilderness perception and use: the example of the Boundary waters canoe area. *Natural Resources Jour.* 3:394–411.
13. Lynch, Kevin, 1960. *The image of the city.* MIT Press, Cambridge.
14. National Park Service, 1959. *Pacific Coast Recreation Area Survey.* Dept. of Interior, Washington.
15. Outdoor Recreation Resources Review Commission, 1962. Outdoor recreation for America, Washington.
16. Tunnard, Christopher, and Brois Pushkarev, 1963. *Man-made America: chaos or control?* Yale Univ., New Haven.
17. Udall, Stewart L., 1963. *The quiet crisis.* Holt, Rinehart, Winston, New York.
18. Weismantel, W., 1966. How the landscape affects neighborhood status. *Landscape Architecture,* 56:190–194.
19. Zisman, S. B., 1966. Urban open space. *Transactions North American Wildlife Conference,* Pittsburg.

*Chapter 13*

1. Alonso, William, 1964. The historic and the structural theories of urban form: their implications for urban renewal. *Land Economics,* 40:227–231.
2. Ayres, Eugene, 1956. The age of fossil fuels. (See Thomas, 1956.)
3. Bresler, Jack, ed., 1966. *Human ecology.* Addison-Wesley, Reading, Mass.
4. Commoner, Barry, 1966. *Science and survival.* Viking, New York.
5. Cousins, Norman, *et al.,* 1966. *Freedom to breathe.* Mayor's Task Force on Air Pollution in the City of New York.
6. Darling, F. F., editor, 1963. *Implications of the rising carbon dioxide content of the atmosphere.* Conservation Foundation, Washington.
7. Dubos, Rene, 1965. Humanistic biology. *American Scientist,* 53:4–19.
8. Duhl, Leonard J., editor, 1963. *The urban condition.* Basic Books, New York.
9. Geddes, Patrick, 1915. *Cities in evolution.* Williams and Norgate, London.
10. Gordon, Mitchell, 1965. *Sick cities.* Penguin, Baltimore.
11. Gruen, Victor, 1964. *The heart of our cities.* Simon and Schuster, New York.
12. Hall, Peter, 1966. *The world cities.* World Univ. Library, McGraw-Hill, New York.
13. Howard, Ebenezer, 1902. *Garden cities of tomorrow.* Faber and Faber, London (1946 edition).
14. Hoyt, Homer, 1966. Growth and structure of twenty-one great world cities. *Land Economics,* 42:53–64.
15. Jacobs, Jane, 1965. *The death and life of great American cities.* Random House, New York.
16. Middleton, J. T., and D. C. Middleton, 1962. Air pollution and California's state control program. *Bull. Division of Refining,* 42:636–641.

17. Middleton, J. T., 1965. Man and his habitat: problems of pollution. *Bull. Atomic Scientists,* 21:5.
18. Mumford, Lewis, 1961. *The city in history.* Harcourt Brace and World, New York.
19. Nairn, Ian, 1965. *The American landscape.* Random House, New York.
20. Odum, Eugene P., 1959. *Fundamentals of ecology.* W. B. Saunders, Philadelphia (2nd ed.).
21. Roszak, Theodore, 1967. California's instant cities. *The Nation,* Mar. 13, pp. 336–340.
22. Whyte, W. H., 1964. *Cluster development.* Amer. Conservation Association, New York.
23. Woodwell, George M., 1967. Radiation and the patterns of nature. *Science,* 156:461–470.
24. Zisman, S. B., 1966. Urban open space. *Transactions North American Wildlife Conference,* Pittsburgh.

*Chapter 14*

1. Bates, Marston, 1955. *The prevalence of people.* Scribners, New York.
2. Brown, Harrison, 1954. *The challenge of man's future.* Viking, New York.
3. Carr-Saunders, A. M., 1936. *World population; past growth and present trends.* Clarendon, Oxford.
4. Cook, Robert C., 1951. *Human fertility; the modern dilemma.* Wm. Sloane, New York.
5. Cragg, J. B., and N. W. Pirie, editors, 1955. *The numbers of man and animals.* Oliver and Boyd, Edinburgh.
6. Darling, F. F., 1951. The ecological approach to the social sciences. *American Scientist,* 39:244–254.
7. Day, Lincoln H., and A. T., 1965. *Too many Americans.* Delta Books, New York.
8. Malthus, Thomas, 1926. *An essay on the principle of population as it affects the future improvement of society, with remarks on the speculations of Mr. Godwin, M. Condorcet, and other writers.* Macmillan, London. (Originally published, 1798, St. Paul's, London.)
9. Mumford, Lewis, 1956. *The transformations of man.* Collier, New York.
10. Odum, Eugene P., 1959. *Fundamentals of ecology.* 2nd Ed., W. B. Saunders, Philadelphia.
11. Ordway, Samuel H., 1953. *Resources and the American dream.* Ronald Press, New York.
12. Osborn, Fairfield, 1948. *Our plundered planet.* Little, Brown, Boston.
13. Osborn, Fairfield, 1953. *The limits of the earth.* Little, Brown, Boston.
14. Osborn, Fairfield, editor, 1962. *Our crowded planet.* Doubleday, New York.
15. Political and Economic Planning, 1955. *World population and resources.* George Allen and Unwin, London.
16. Population Reference Bureau, 1966. The senate looks at population. *Population bulletin,* 22, no. 5.
17. Population Reference Bureau, 1966. California; after 19 million, what? *Population bulletin,* 22:29–57.
18. Population Reference Bureau, 1967. *World population growth accelerates.* PRB Press Releases, Monday, Jan. 16.
19. Russell, Sir John, 1954. *World population and world food supplies.* George Allen and Unwin, London.

20. Stamp, Dudley L., 1952. *Land for tomorrow*. Indiana Univ., Bloomington.
21. Thompson, Warren S., 1956. The spiral of population. (See Thomas, 1956.)
22. Udea, Masao, 1966. Population growth in Japan. Proceedings 11th Pacific Science Congress, Tokyo, mimeo.
23. Vogt, William, 1948. *Road to survival*. Wm. Sloane, New York.

*Chapter 15*

1. Burton, Ian, and R. W. Kates, 1965. *Readings in resource management and conservation*. Univ. Chicago Press, Chicago.
2. Caldwell, Lynton K., 1963. Environment: a new focus for public policy? *Public Administration Review*, pp. 132–139.
3. Caldwell, Lynton K., 1966. The human environment. *Journal Higher Education*, 37:149–155.
4. California State Office of Planning, 1965. *California state development plan program*. Dept. of Finance, Sacramento.
5. Chase, Stuart, 1967. Can we stay prosperous? *Saturday Review*, Feb. 11, pp. 20–22.
6. Currie, Lauchlin, 1967. Economics and population. *Population Bulletin*, 23:25–38.
7. Darling, F. F., and John Milton, 1966. *The future environments of North America*. Natural History Press, New York.
8. Dasmann, R. F., 1965. *The destruction of California*. Macmillan, New York.
9. Day, Lincoln H., and A. T., 1965. *Too many Americans*. Delta Books, New York.
10. Galbraith, J. K., 1958. *The affluent society*. Houghton Mifflin, Boston.
11. General Electric Forum, 1965. *Keeping America Beautiful*. General Electric Forum, 8, no. 4.
12. Leopold, Aldo, 1949. *A sand county almanac*. Oxford, New York.
13. Macinko, George, 1965. The Columbia Basin Project: expectations, realizations, implications. (See Burton and Kates, 1965.)
14. Minnesota Division of Community Planning, 1966. *Minnesota planning legislation*. Dept. of Business Development, St. Paul.
15. Moss, Senator Frank, 1966. Why I'm for a Department of Natural Resources. *American Forests*, 72:16–17, 46.
16. Rockefeller, Laurence S., 1965. *Report to the President and the President's response*. White House Conference on Natural Beauty, Washington.
17. Scheffey, A. W., 1967. *The New England Town Conservation Commission*. Manuscript, Univ. Mass., Amherst.
18. Train, Russell E., 1966. *A new revolution*. Conservation Foundation, Washington.
19. Whyte, W. H., 1964. *Cluster development*. Amer. Conservation Association, New York.
20. Winthrop, Henry, 1967. Modern proposals for the physical decentralization of community. *Land Economics*, 43:1–9.

*Chapter 16*

1. Brown, Harrison, 1954. *The challenge of man's future*. Viking, New York.
2. Darling, F. F., and J. Milton, 1966. *The future environments of North America*. Natural History Press, New York.
3. Dasmann, R. F., 1968. *A different kind of country*. Macmillan, New York.
4. Levi-Strauss, Claude, 1965. "Man has never been so savage as he is today." *Realities*, no. 175, pp. 48–51.
5. Mumford, Lewis, 1966. *The myth of the machine*. Harcourt, Brace, and World, New York.

# Index